Advance Praise for **The Sage Guide to Mutual Funds**

"Individual investors have never had better resources or better investment options than they enjoy today. And no one knows the ins and outs of this new world of on-line investing better than the brothers Cohn. Read this book and you'll agree with me: Sage Rules!"

—Don Phillips, CEO of Morningstar

"The Sage Guide should help both novice and expert online investors understand the power of the Internet in selecting, transacting and tracking mutual fund investments. It's a great tool for the serious investor to keep right next to the mouse."

—Blake Darcy, CEO of DLJ Direct

"With the same verve, insight, and determination that made them an online success, Alan and Stephen Cohn have created an investor primer that should be of great interest to all who want to learn more about the world of mutual funds."

—Rob Shenk, America Online

"Sage has led the way in creating and maintaining an active online community of fund investors. This is a thorough and professional compilation of sage advice."

—William Miller, manager of Legg Mason Value Trust Fund

"Alan and Stephen Cohn have worked hard to bring sense and community to the world of mutual fund investing and the Internet. *The Sage Guide to Mutual Funds* brings that same practical, good-natured advice to the world of wood-based firmware—that is, to print. It's a solid guide for investors at all levels."

—John Waggoner, columnist, *USA Today*

"More than a guide to mutual funds, the Cohn brothers have written a thoroughly modern instruction kit for investors geared to the Internet age. This is a solid primer for beginning investors, but even fund experts will find out how much they don't know!"

—Shane Chalke, founder and CEO AnnuityNet.com

"[A] sound message and one that even the beginning investor can profit from."

—Jersey Gilbert, financial editor, *SmartMoney* magazine

"*The Sage Guide to Mutual Funds* is a great tool that all mutual fund investors can utilize. This book is especially helpful in assisting investors that are setting their goals and objectives."

—Louis Navellier, president of the Navellier Funds

"In *The Sage Guide to Mutual Funds* authors Alan and Stephen Cohn do an outstanding job explaining the basics to successful mutual fund investing. In addition, this book differentiates itself from the crowd by educating readers on the advantages and opportunities of online community investing. E-xcellent."

—David P. Brady, CFA, Senior Portfolio Manager, Stein Roe Young Investor Fund

"Sophisticated and starter mutual fund investors alike can benefit from *The Sage Guide to Mutual Funds*—its accessible guide to building a portfolio using a wealth of online tools show do-it-yourselfers how to create and monitor their investments."

—Brenda Buttner, TheStreet.com

The

Guide to
Mutual Funds

Superior Investment Wisdom
from the Number One
Online Mutual Fund Gurus

Alan and Stephen Cohn, CFPs

Founders of Sage Online

HarperBusiness
A Division of HarperCollins*Publishers*

This book is designed to provide readers with a general overview of investing in mutual funds and online investing methods. It is not designed to be a definitive investment guide or to take the place of advice from a qualified financial planner or other professional. Given the risk involved in investing of almost any kind, there is no guarantee that the investment methods suggested in this book will be profitable. Thus, neither the publisher nor the author assume liability of any kind for any losses that may be sustained as a result of applying the methods suggested in this book, and any such liability is hereby expressly disclaimed.

THE SAGE GUIDE TO MUTUAL FUNDS. Copyright © 1999 by Alan and Stephen Cohn. All rights reserved. Printed in the United States of America. No part of this book may be used or reproduced in any manner whatsoever without written permission except in the case of brief quotations embodied in critical articles and reviews. For information address HarperCollins Publishers Inc., 10 East 53rd Street, New York, NY 10022.

HarperCollins books may be purchased for educational, business, or sales promotional use. For information please write: Special Markets Department, HarperCollins Publishers Inc., 10 East 53rd Street, New York, NY 10022.

FIRST EDITION

Printed on acid-free paper.

Designed by Nancy Singer Olaguera

Library of Congress Cataloging-in-Publication Data
Cohn, Alan, 1964–
    The Sage guide to mutual funds : superior investment wisdom from the #1 online fund gurus / Alan Cohn and Stephen Cohn.
      p. cm.
    Includes index.
    ISBN 0-06-662007-4
    1. Mutual funds—United States. 2. Investments—United States. I. Cohn, Alan, 1964– . II. Title.
HG4930.C64   2000
332.63'27—dc21   99-38442

00 01 02 03 04 ❖/HC 10 9 8 7 6 5 4 3 2

*To our wives, Darlene and Ivy Cohn, and our parents,
David Cohn and Harriet Cohn, who provide us the support
that allows us to pursue our dreams.*

Contents

Acknowledgments

Thank you to all the people who made this book possible. A special thanks goes out to our parents, David and Harriet Cohn, who taught us to live life according to the golden rule. Thank you to our wives, Darlene and Ivy Cohn, who have stood by our side well beyond the call of duty. Thank you to our in-laws, Sy and Marge Listman and Stu and Flo Bednoff, for being understanding and supportive. An extra-special thanks goes out to our inspiration: our children, Ross, Alyssa, Eric, and Ian Cohn, and children on the way. They do not yet realize the profound impact they have on our work.

Thank you to our extended Sage family: the team, the community, the business partners, and the clients. They are Sage's foundation. A special thanks goes out to our friends at America Online, including but not limited to Rob Shenk, Allan Halprin, and Bill Youstra. They have been integral to our online accomplishments and provided much sound advice and guidance along the way.

Thank you to our editor, David Conti, at HarperCollins, who provided invaluable feedback as the book was developed. Thank you to Lisa Berkowitz, HarperBusiness Director of Marketing and Communications, who has marketing wisdom beyond her years. Thank you to our agent, Barbara Lowenstein, who represents us in a professional and supportive manner beyond what we ever expected.

Finally, we'd like to thank you, the investor, without whom this book would have no reason to exist.

SPECIAL ACKNOWLEDGMENT

We would like to give a special thanks to Wade Williams, whose contributions helped make this book possible. Wade's research, editorial, and writing skills were invaluable as the book developed and grew. His special brand of humor, charisma, and wisdom helped us shape our message. Thank you, Wade.

Foreword

We all want to make our lives easier and more convenient. That simple truth goes a long way to explain the extraordinary growth in both the Internet and mutual funds during the last several years.

The online medium makes it easier for people to get their news, shop, learn new things, communicate with friends, and manage their personal finances.

Mutual funds allow individuals to invest in a diverse selection of stocks or bonds with less effort and at less cost than separately buying each of the individual stocks or bonds contained in the fund.

Alan and Stephen Cohn have combined the two worlds—building an online community around mutual fund investing. And now they've taken what they've learned during the past four years as founders of Sage Online and pulled it together into a guide to online investing.

The Internet has sparked an investment revolution. The information and tools that used to be just in the hands of Wall Street professionals are now in everyone's hands. Individuals know more, for example, about a mutual fund's fees, track record and management than ever before.

Comparison-shopping for mutual funds, cars, stereo equipment, vacations, you name it—has reached a whole new level with the Internet. The well-informed consumer rules the marketplace, transforming the relationship between buyers and sellers.

Information is literally at people's fingertips—and they're using it to devise their investment strategies, research products and then, of course, to trade. A consumer with Internet access can scroll through the latest analyst reports; check up-to-the minute quotes, chat with leading mutual fund managers and share opinions with fellow investors. It used to be that you had to pay steep fees for company research reports; now you can chat live with some of the best minds in the mutual fund industry—for free.

Online, consumers are able to screen by specific criteria, such as rate of return, fund assets, and load, to find the mutual funds that are the best fit for them. And of course, information travels very quickly on the Web, so a well-informed consumer can educate thousands of his or her peers on message boards, in chat rooms and other interactive forums.

Communities have sprung up around shared financial interests—whether it's a common commitment to a particular fund or a debate over the merits of mid-cap vs. small-cap investments. People want not only to share the positive experience and satisfaction of watching their wealth grow, but also to get advice and perspective of experts, friends and others.

Our world is quickly changing. It doesn't require a lot of imagination to see a day where stock trading will be available to individuals around the clock—the same way that consumers can go into online stores 24 hours a day, seven days a week. In cyberspace, there are no closing hours, no holidays, no battles for a parking spot.

In this era of increasing personalization, where consumers can decide what news they want to get and routinely share online calendars with their neighbors, it may not be that long before mutual fund companies enable individuals to construct their own mutual funds, made up of stocks and sectors based on a person's individual preferences.

As individuals become more and more educated about sound investing practices, the balance of power will increasingly favor the consumer. The pace of this consumer empowerment will accelerate in the coming years, as millions of more people come online and see for themselves the magic of the new medium.

Steve Case
Chairman and CEO, America Online

Introduction

Welcome to a dramatic revolution. Never in the history of the market has information flowed so freely as it does today over the Internet. The us-versus-them attitude that has permeated Wall Street for over a hundred years is rapidly breaking down. The days of insider or premium information are vanishing. The computer and modem tandem has placed the J. P. Morgans and the John Smiths of the world on the same plane. Information is everywhere and it is all free!

In the mad rush for investment knowledge, the online investment world has inadvertently crushed itself. A search for the term *mutual fund* on AltaVista (www.altavista.com) yields over 75,000 results. The word *investment* on GO Network (www.go.com) results in some 6.5 million matches. Look up *stock* on Infoseek (www.infoseek.com) and you end up with more than 9.6 million sites from which to choose.

As the popularity of the Internet grows, the number of sites dedicated to investment-related subjects explodes exponentially. This unprecedented growth presents challenges and opportunities. For every John Bogle answering your questions online, there is a Joe Shark lurking in the background, plotting to take advantage of an unsuspecting soul. Without proper guidance, you too may be a victim.

That is why we have written this book. We are the brothers Cohn, certified financial planners and the founders of Sage Online, the most popular mutual fund investment forum in all of cyberspace. Every day, Sage users engage in mutual fund investment chats with industry experts and top fund managers, learn about funds, and gain up-to-the-minute knowledge on how to become a superior mutual fund investor. We are also the principals, along with our dad, of the family business, Sage Financial Group, a Bala Cynwyd, Pennsylvania–based financial planning firm we founded in 1989. We have spent years managing peoples' mutual funds,

401(k) plans, pensions, and nonretirement portfolios. Online mutual fund investing has empowered us, and it can empower you.

The purpose of this book is to invite you into our world. We will share our financial planning and investment tips. We will reveal success and horror stories from our years online. Whether you are an investment expert or a beginner, our goal is to make you a savvier online investor.

We speak from personal experience. Until a few years ago, we were what you would call technologically stunted. Intel sold millions of Pentium chips before we ever touched a computer. When compiling clients' reports, we would hand-write them out and type them up on an old IBM typewriter.

We would take a weekly jaunt down to the Bala Cynwyd public library to research potential investments for clients. One week we entered the library in search of the trusty Value Line manual. An old local was using it, researching stocks. The next week the same thing occurred. We grew frustrated, but saw no other option than waiting the guy out.

The following day in the office a client spoke glowingly of the cool computer he just bought a few months back. His daughter in high school used it regularly to do research for English class.

A few days later we called up Gateway and ordered our first computer. It was a huge, ugly, beige monstrosity with wires popping out all over. A Sage coworker hooked it up for us, and we were flying.

We loved the research the Internet provided, but we saw the need for something more: a community of like-minded people working together with the goal of becoming better investors. America Online (AOL) gave us the opportunity to implement our dream with our Sage Online mutual fund site.

A few years later here we are. Our staff has grown from two to more than fifty. Each day our site is populated with numerous Sage community leaders who patrol the message boards, answering investment questions within forty-eight hours, and staff the chat rooms, helping investors in real time. Each week hundreds of financial professionals, including Don Phillips of Morningstar and Steve Harmon of e-harmon.com, share their wisdom with our audience. Each month hundreds of thousands of investors gravitate to the Sage site for interaction with financial industry leaders, helpful conversation with Sage friends, and insightful information.

The Sage Online site transforms investment data from an abundant feast into digestible bites. Our task here is much the same: We will mold the Web from its amoebic form into a useful investment tool. We will tell you how we pick funds, and help develop a fund investment strategy just for you. We will give you insight into the investment techniques of the fund manager gurus we speak with on a daily basis.

We will teach you to be a more astute online investor. We have a lot to do in a short amount of time, so without further delay, let's go!

Getting Started

KNOWLEDGE IS LIKE MONEY: TO BE OF VALUE IT MUST CIRCULATE
AND IN CIRCULATING IT CAN INCREASE IN QUANTITY AND,
HOPEFULLY, IN VALUE.

Louis L'Amour, author of *Education of a Wandering Man*

The book you hold in your hands will make a big difference in your life, but only if you take full advantage of the wealth it contains.

The combination of online investment wisdom and plain, old-fashioned, financial planning know-how and experience is what separates this from the rest of the books that crowd the bookstores. You will not find highbrowed hyperbole here. You will learn about funds from the firsthand experiences of the Sage Online user community, people no different from you. You will hear from a wide spectrum of Sage Online community participants, seasoned online staffers, and industry experts.

The combined knowledge and expertise from various investment sources has resulted in a superior investment tool. For years we have leveraged our unique position to enhance Sage Financial Group's clients' portfolios and make the Sage Online site a powerful investment force in the online world. This book is our opportunity to share our experience and expertise with you via a more traditional medium.

● WHAT WE WILL COVER IN THIS BOOK

The core of Sage is community. A community where people learn from each other, talk with industry experts, and share experiences—not unlike the type of community you will see at your local YMCA, Weight

Watchers, or at various other support groups. Communities that have existed for decades in the offline world are rapidly taking hold across the online medium. As evidenced by the range of interests, from those with mass appeal, like the NFL or country music, to those that occupy an obscure niche, like Prader-Willie Syndrome or welding—no matter what the subject, there is surely an area in cyberspace dedicated to it, and at least a handful of active participants. The Sage community brings together folks from across the world to talk about investing. We offer opinions, help, expert commentary, solutions, and what is most important, support.

This book will teach you how to become a better, or a beginner, online mutual fund investor. It will simplify the investment process and it will enhance the returns of your portfolio. The lessons you will learn are lessons we have all learned together. The misfortunes you will read about are ones we have all suffered. The triumphs you will witness are the kind we see every day on the Sage site.

This book is not about glossy covers and foolproof investment schemes. It is about the reality of online fund investing. It is about learning how to use the available tools as moneymaking resources.

The convergence of mutual funds and the Internet is one of the greatest achievements ever presented to the public since the microwave and the VCR. The knowledge gleaned from this book will allow you to harness the moneymaking power of mutual funds with the vast resources of the Web. This marriage has created an opportunity for those who know how to exploit both the fund industry and the Web. We are not going to turn you into an expert in academic mutual fund studies or a cyber-surfing, vending-machine junkie. But we will teach you how to make money.

Our goals are modest:

To give you the tools you need to develop a long-term personal investment portfolio.

To launch you into a life of financial freedom free of monetary fears.

Our pledge is honest:

We will share with you our follies and our triumphs so that you may reduce your own mistakes and increase your successes.

We will bring the Sage Online community to your fingertips so that you can understand, firsthand, the power of collective wisdom.

We will always be there for you. Check us out online for up-to-date links to Internet tools and to talk to us via our chat rooms and message boards.

The benefits you will reap will be plentiful:

You will be a better investor once you read and implement this book.

You will possess the tools to make informed financial decisions.

You will enhance your future standard of living.

Welcome to Sage Online. Your goals are our goals.

Online investing is attractive to everyone. The Web gives prospective investors the ability to download fund prospectuses (legal documents that outline how specific funds operate and invest); track model and real-money portfolios; paper trade (trade stocks and funds with fake money to test out investment strategies); research stocks, funds, and mutual fund managers; interview managers via chat; and much more. The Internet has abolished the need to wait for the following day's *Wall Street Journal* to see how your investments fared. The Web is real-time, and once you taste its power, going back to the olden days of snail-mailing checks to your fund company, waiting on quarterly fund reports, and reading the financial history section in offline press will become an impossibility.

To master the online investing world, you need a plan of action that will ensure you will reach your financial goals. Welcome to the ten pillars upon which Sage is built.

TEN STEPS TO BECOMING A SAGE MUTUAL FUND INVESTOR

1: Establish sturdy footing with the basics.

2: Determine your investment profile.

3: Adopt the Sage investment philosophy.

4: Select winning funds.

5: Use the power of allocation to your advantage.

6: Design your portfolio.

7: Use online tools to track and monitor your portfolio.

8: Develop selling strategies.

9: Select the best e-account.

10: Profit from online communities.

We will sharpen these ten Sage points throughout the book.

● ONLINE INVESTING—THE BASICS

We have come a long way from the time when you had to physically walk into a fund company's office to buy shares in a mutual fund. Today, through technological marvels like routers, hubs, switches, and other tech breakthroughs that we take pride in not fully understanding, you can buy, sell, or exchange shares in a mutual fund in less than ninety seconds. And that includes the amount of time it takes for your modem to log on to the Internet. Best of all, you do it from the comfort of your own home or office (depending how Dilbertesque your boss may be).

You will become an expert online mutual fund investor by the time you complete this book. We intend to do for you what we have successfully accomplished for Sage Financial clients and Sage Online community members. Let's get rolling.

● IMPEDIMENTS TO ONLINE INVESTING

The biggest obstacle to online investing is fear—fear of monetary losses and fear of technology.

We remember what it was like to deal with computers during our early years. We even used to have a coworker boot up our computer every morning. When she could not make it in due to a cold, blustery West Philly squall, the office would virtually shut down. It was back to the local library to do research, and on to the old IBM typewriter to type up clients' reports.

Eventually our technological confidence grew. First we were able to start up our computers on our own, then we moved on to more advanced tasks like printing.

In retrospect, it was not the technology that held us back; it was our fear of technology. We are not what you would call digitally inclined. Our VCRs still blink 12:00 . . . 12:00 . . . 12:00, twenty-four hours a day, seven days a week; but we can surf the Web and invest online with the best of them. Do not let your fear of computers or all things digital deter you from launching yourself onto a successful online investment path.

But even after you become comfortable with your computer and the Internet in general, security is still an issue. How secure are the transactions you make over the Internet? Will the personal information you give over the Internet remain personal?

When Sage Online community members ask us about the security of online transactions, we put things in perspective. One of our favorite anecdotes involves clients and cheese steaks.

One day we had some clients down from northern New Jersey. They were more interested in talking about famous Philly cheese steaks than finances. It was nearing lunchtime so we decided to take them to a local restaurant to talk funds and indulge in some of Philly's finest. When the check arrived, we laid down the corporate Visa card. The young waiter picked up the card, took it to the back room, and returned a few minutes later. We signed and thought nothing of it.

A month later we noticed some odd charges on our account statement. Seems that our waiter friend had made a copy of our card number and used it to make some purchases.

We have bought thousands of dollars of computer equipment over the Internet from Dell, ordered countless books from Amazon.com, and bought and sold hundreds of funds online for clients. Not once have we ever had a problem. Sure, occasionally a book is back-ordered or a computer takes a couple of extra days to reach our office. But we have never had a billing discrepancy or any hint of impropriety. And we are confident we never will.

When you make an online transaction, your personal information is bundled up and encrypted. Only the server—the computer where the information is sent—has the ability to decode this information. Once the server receives your information, it communicates with various other computers (your bank, your credit card company, and your online account) to grant confirmation of your purchase. Once the transaction is approved, the order heads to the people who make computers, sell books, or trade stocks.

There is no human contact with your personal information. There is little risk of wrongdoing because the opportunity for impropriety rarely presents itself.

● MUTUAL FUND BASICS

Think of a mutual fund as a flatbed truck. The mutual fund manager is the driver. He can fill the truck with anything he likes, such as big heavy aggressive growth stocks or wimpy little Treasury bonds. How the bed is filled determines how the truck rides. Too many aggressive stocks and the truck may crash when the market weather gets grim. Too light a load and the truck may not transport enough. So that you can fully appreciate the cargo you may be carrying, we will take a moment to introduce some mutual fund basics. Even if you are a fund guru, read this section carefully, as we will continually refer to it throughout the book. It is essential that you have a sound education before you venture into the world of online fund investing.

Throughout this book, we have taken quotes or excerpts from Sage Live Event guests and put them into sidebars that help illustrate or explain the text. Each weekday at Sage Online we host chats with industry experts, where community members fire off questions to the pundits.

Jim O'Shaughnessy, famous stock fund manager, discusses investing in a Sage chat: "The stock market is not a game. It is one of the best compounding machines ever created, but you must learn patience, discipline and the ability to price securities rationally. If you want to play for the short term, go to Vegas."

● TYPES OF FUNDS

Stock Funds

Stock funds are mutual funds that own equities of varying types and styles. Stocks are wild to watch and fun to invest in. They can go to the moon (eBay gained over 1,000 percent during its first year of existence) or come crashing down to earth in a very short time span (Centennial Technologies fell from $52 to $0 in two months; the year before, it was the top performing stock on the New York Stock Exchange). Stock funds help buffer the wild swings of individual stocks.

Stocks exist to provide capital to companies. When in 1986 Microsoft needed some money to finance its attempt at world domination, the company went public. Microsoft essentially sold a piece of the company to the public via an IPO (initial public offering). Since that time its stock price has risen as the company's earnings and market share have grown.

Microsoft's stock price, like the stock prices of all publicly traded companies, is tied to its ability to generate earnings.

Each corporation must report earnings on a quarterly basis. Earnings, simply stated, are the revenue a corporation brings in minus any expenses (such as wages, taxes, rent). To assure that earnings are uniform from company to company, all U.S. corporations must follow Generally Accepted Accounting Principles (GAAP), and have their balance sheets audited by an outside accountant agency. A company's reported earnings compared to analysts' estimates dictate how a stock will perform. For example, if analysts were expecting Microsoft to earn $400 million and the corporation reported earnings of $800 million, the market would react favorably.

As earnings of a company rise, its stock price should follow. But what makes the market so interesting is that in the short term, stock prices do not follow earnings. Rather, they are driven by emotions. Political, economic, and military events cause massive moves in stock prices on a daily basis. But long term, stocks follow earnings.

Sage investors can profit from this market madness by viewing market movements in perspective. In 1990 the U.S. and Iraq entered into what would soon be dubbed "Desert Storm." The war caused an immediate market drop of over 10 percent. Calls poured into our office.

Client: "Alan, Stephen, what should I do? I am concerned, I want out!"

Sage: "The invasion into Kuwait is not going to have a material affect on how Coca-Cola does business. It is not going to hurt how many washing machines General Electric sells. In fact, it may even help certain corporations, such as Exxon and Raytheon."

Because of many conversations such as these, the Sage team had an important meeting. We, along with our dad and a few coworkers, huddled together to discuss the situation in the Gulf and how we should position our clients' portfolios.

We decided to hold on to stock funds despite the negative short-term thinking that ran throughout the market. We felt that the reaction was unjustified and that earnings growth would continue (and stock prices would eventually follow). A few weeks after, the market kicked off what would later be called the longest bull market in history.

The Gulf War was a major event that had far-reaching effects on the stock market, but each month there are mini-crises to which the market overreacts. Understanding the nature of a crisis and its true implications allows the Sage investor to profit from the manic nature of the market.

> "The time to buy is when there's blood in the streets."
> *Anonymous*

Now, we do not want you to get the wrong idea. We do not advocate market timing.

Market timers advocate buying and selling stocks or funds based on the short-term outlook of the market. In theory, if an investor can time the ups and the downs of the market, there is unlimited upside potential and no risk of losing capital. Unfortunately, there has yet to be a consistently successful market timer or a successful mutual fund based on market timing.

In fact, we stress just the opposite, a buy-and-hold approach. More important than an investor's ability to base investment decisions on the overactive whims of the market is his ability to know his limits. The stock market is an unforgiving place, devoid of feelings or compassion. Wade into it without the right knowledge or a sound financial plan, and you run the risk of losing it all. We prefer to use the market as a wealth-building tool, not as a one-night stand at a Las Vegas casino. Hence, we approach the stock market with a long-term strategy, centered on stock mutual funds.

The following stock funds are the most common types you will encounter:

- Growth Funds: These funds invest in stocks with rapidly rising earnings and high investor expectations. When growth stocks are in favor, as they were for most of the 1990s, these funds fare extremely well. However, if the market gets a case of the jitters or if a few stocks fail to live up to expectations, these funds are the first and fastest to fall. Examples of growth stocks in the '90s include America Online and Intel.

By investing in highly visible stocks with strong growth—such as MCI WorldCom, Microsoft, General Electric, and Cisco Systems—Harbor Capital Appreciation has consistently posted above-average returns. Even during such difficult years as 1990 and 1994, the fund easily beat the market by sticking with its stated growth objective. This type of managerial fortitude has rewarded shareholders with ten-year annualized gains that rank it, as of midway through 1999, in the top 10 percent of all funds.

- Value Funds: These funds invest in stocks that are beaten down and unloved by the market. An earnings shortfall (failure of a company to meet stock market analysts' earnings predictions) or a negative editorial in the *Wall Street Journal* can knock a stock down. Funds pick up these stocks at a discount in hope that the companies will turn themselves around. Examples in the '90s include Philip Morris and Kmart. Because these stocks are already beaten down when fund managers buy them, if the market falls, they typically hold up better than growth stocks.

The Victory Diversified Stock Fund has avoided market pitfalls in 1990 and 1994 by sticking strictly with stocks that no one else wants. Since the fund's inception through the end of 1998, it has never posted an annual loss. Only twenty-four other funds, out of the thousands available, can match that feat.

- Blend Funds: These hold a combination of value and growth stocks. Since many fund managers own both growth and value stocks, many funds are blend funds. In addition, the S&P 500 Index Fund is a blend fund.

Growth, value, and *blend* refer to the type of stock a fund holds. In addition, the size of the stock a fund invests in defines whether a fund is a large cap, mid cap, or small cap fund.

- Large Cap: These funds buy stocks with high market capitalizations such as Dell Computer, Procter & Gamble, and Merck.

- Mid Cap: Funds in this category invest in medium-size companies like ServiceMaster, Ames Department Stores, and Burlington Coat Factory.

- Small Cap: These funds buy tiny stocks like Mauna Loa, Sovran Self Storage, and Au Bon Pain. Because small stocks are emerging companies, they possess significantly more risk than mid and especially large stocks. Sovran Self Storage is more likely to file for bankruptcy than McDonald's is. Likewise, McDonald's earnings will generally be more stable than Sovran Self Storage's because of the sheer size and diversification of the Big Mac king.

Classifying a fund as growth, value, or blend and large, mid, or small gives you a picture of the fund's portfolio. After a little research, you will understand how particular funds will behave in different market environments.

Morningstar, a popular mutual fund rating company, uses a "style box" like the one in Figure 1.1 to graphically represent where a fund falls in the large/medium/small, value/blend/growth spectrum.

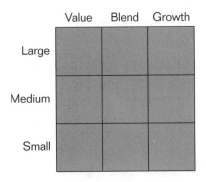

Figure 1.1. Morningstar equity style box.

This box also tells us a lot about the risk of specific funds. Since we know value stocks are more stable than growth stocks, and small caps are more volatile than large caps, the box can be modified, as in Figure 1.2, to interpret volatility.

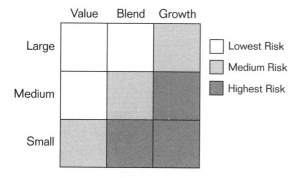

Figure 1.2. Morningstar risk equity style box.

Bond Funds

Bonds are simply IOUs from companies or governments. When a company needs money to fund, say, a new corporate wing, or a government needs to build a new bridge, they sell bonds. They repay these loans at a set interest rate, which is determined by the financial strength of the government or company. For example, when Coca-Cola issues bonds, they pay low interest rates because the company is a financial titan and investors can sleep well at night knowing that Coca-Cola is not going to fizzle out of existence. On the other hand, if Boston Market decides to issue bonds, the interest rate the bonds will pay must be quite high to compensate purchasers of the bonds for the risk they are taking. After all, Boston Market lacks the financial muscle of a Coca-Cola and could go belly up and default on its loans. (Boston Market in fact filed for Chapter 11.)

> Dr. Ed Yardeni, a leading economist, talks about the importance of bonds in a Sage Online chat: "I would suggest that individual investors become less aggressive in the stock market and buy more government bonds."

Likewise, different governments pay different rates on their bonds depending on financial strength. Russia, for example, must pay ultra-high rates because the country has a history of financial strife and has missed debt repayment on more than one occasion. The U.S., in contrast, pays low rates because it has serious financial power.

Outside agencies, such as Moody's and Standard & Poor's, rate companies and governments. The grade they assign determines the interest rate that must be paid.

Bonds are typically considered safe investments, but they range in quality from Government and AAA to BBB and Investment Grade (aka "junk" bonds). Although U.S. government bonds are guaranteed, government-bond funds are not. A bond's price will fluctuate over its lifetime in response to the state of the economy and the level of interest rates. So, while thirty-year Treasury bonds may be guaranteed at maturity (in this case maturity is thirty years from the date the bonds were issued), they will fluctuate in price and may at times be worth less than they were when issued by the government.

Some fund managers attempt to predict the price changes in bonds, and buy and sell accordingly. If a manager miscalculates the direction of interest rates, the fund will suffer. Such was the case in 1994, when the Fundamental U.S. Government Securities fund failed to anticipate the fall in bond prices, which resulted in a loss of almost 26 percent for the fund. Although the fund held bonds backed by the U.S. government, the fund suffered a dramatic loss due to poor management decisions. Investors who sold their fund holdings realized a huge loss.

Throughout this book you will read stories from Sage Online community members. The stories, often taken from the message boards and chats, are always proceeded by a screen name such as "SageABC" or "Mary5." Sage members, like those on America Online, Yahoo!, and other online services, are given a screen name, similar to a CB handle. The screen names have been changed for the purposes of this book. Following is one such story.

Mary5: "Not fully understanding what the term 'junk' meant with respect to bonds, I purchased an emerging market income fund right at the beginning of 1998 when the fund opened up, at the recommendation of my broker. The fund, so he told me, would be a good hedge against the U.S. market. I equated hedge with safety, and for a while the fund was stable. Over the first two months, the fund gained about 6 percent, which I considered to be pretty good. Then the fund started to slide a little, until August when it hit an air pocket. Down over 43 percent! The irony here, if there is any, is the fact that all the bonds held by this fund were government bonds, albeit third world countries. So much for the safety in bonds and so much for my broker."

Let us review the basics of some of the most popular types of bond funds.

- Government Bond: These funds hold the highest-rated bonds available, backed by the full faith and credit of the U.S. government. Examples of these funds are Vanguard Long-Term U.S. Treasury and Smith Barney Global Government Bond.

- Municipal Bond: Such funds hold bonds issued by a state, county, city, or other nonfederal agency. Interest on municipal bonds is exempt from federal taxes and in some cases state and local taxes. Thus, they are often considered triple-tax-free bonds and are appropriate for high-net-worth individuals looking to shelter their investments from taxes. Examples include the Franklin Washington Municipal Bond and Oppenheimer New Jersey Municipal funds.

- Corporate Bond: These funds hold bonds issued by corporations to finance company activities. Examples include Vanguard Short-Term Corporate and Strong High-Yield Bond.

- Money Market: These funds are spruced-up savings accounts, but without FDIC security. Fortunately, money market funds invest in short-term bonds and none has ever lost money. Money market returns fluctuated between 16 percent in the high inflation 1980s to about 4 percent in the calmer 1990s. Most provide check-writing capabilities. Money markets are used as a place to park cash that cannot lose value, such as money for a house down payment.

Although money market funds are not insured against financial loss, the fund industry has gone to great lengths to assure that none has ever "broken the buck." All money market funds are eternally pegged at a share price of $1. Interest is paid on each dollar and new shares are automatically bought with the proceeds, unless you elect to receive your interest in cash. For example, if you have $200 in a money market fund, you in essence have 200 shares. If, over the course of a year, you earn $10 in interest, you will then have 210 shares.

In 1997 subprime auto lender, Mercury Finance, issued short-term bonds. A corporate financial cover-up was later revealed, showing that Mercury Finance allegedly was cooking its books. The company defaulted on its repayments, and its bonds were rendered worthless. A fund family held Mercury Finance bonds in its money market fund. Rather than break the buck, the fund's management stepped in with personal funds to assure that its money market fund shareholders would not lose value.

The mutual fund industry has such a vested interest in the safety of the money market fund that investors can rest assured that money market accounts, though not technically insured, offer safety that rivals that of a bank or checking account.

Hybrid Funds—Balanced and Asset Allocation Funds

Hybrid funds, as their name implies, invest in both stocks and bonds. Balanced funds keep a near fifty-fifty split (hence their name) between stocks and bonds, though specific funds deviate slightly from this mix. Asset allocation funds invest in stocks and bonds and hold a percentage of their assets in cash. These mutt-like funds provide investors with instant exposure to all domestic investments—cash, stocks, and bonds.

Jane10AZ: "I was late into the investment game. I did not start until I was in my late sixties, but I was determined to grow my money, at least a little. I was worried about the volatility in the market, but I knew bonds would not offer enough growth. So I bought a market opportunity fund (an asset allocation fund). I figured it would give me some growth and some protection. Man, was I right! When the market falls the fund holds up better than most stock funds and when the market rises it does much better than bond funds. I was hoping to obtain a return of 8 percent a year, at least that was my goal. Over the past four years, I have averaged something like 23 percent! My original investment, though modest by almost any standard, has more than doubled!"

International Funds

International funds invest almost exclusively outside of the U.S. Because markets throughout the world vary in terms of economic development, funds in this category can range from the ultra-risky to the sedate. The more developed the country or region in which a particular fund invests, the less risky it is. Funds that invest in Western Europe are only slightly more risky than their U.S. counterparts. Funds that invest in Latin America, Eastern Europe, Asia, or Africa, however, can be quite risky because economies in these regions are still in their development stages.

Just how risky is risky? During 1998 the Russian market dropped more than 80 percent. If the Russian market averages 10 percent a year from then on, it will take investors over sixteen years just to break even!

Global Funds

Global funds invest all over the world, inside and outside of the U.S. Typically, these funds invest about 80 percent of their assets in foreign lands and the remaining 20 percent in the U.S. In general, these funds concentrate on Eastern Europe, Japan, and the U.S., forgoing investments in smaller emerging countries.

Other Fund Types

We have touched on growth, value, small, large, foreign, and domestic bonds and stocks. You probably do not realize it, but you have already developed a solid foundation. You are not quite ready to dive onto your computer and select funds, but you have enough upstairs to impress your coworkers around the water cooler.

Beyond the types of funds just discussed, there are popular breeds of funds that are always the rage on Wall Street. Index and sector are two kinds of fund offerings that have caught the attention of investors for the gains they can deliver.

Index Funds

"The value of broad diversification, discipline, and low cost together control index fund returns."

John Bogle, chairman of the Vanguard Group,
chatting on Sage about the success of indexing

Index funds simply hold all of the stocks in a specific index, such as the Dow Jones Industrial Average, the S&P 500 Index, or the Morgan Stanley Europe Africa Far East Index. Since computers do the fund management—buying and selling stocks—index funds can replicate a specific segment of the market with low costs. Low fees and the adherence to a strict investment plan have pushed index funds far past many of their people-managed competitors.

Sector Funds

> "What's great about sector funds is not what they invest in, but what they do not. With sector funds I can avoid slow growth areas, allowing me to create a portfolio that fits my aggressive profile."
>
> *SageMath, Sage community leader*

Sector funds invest in specific industries such as health care, utility, technology, financial services, retail, Internet, and many others. Imagine a fund that invested in Pfizer, Warner-Lambert, Eli Lilly, Merck, Johnson & Johnson, and Bristol-Myers Squibb. It would be a stellar performer during times when pharmaceutical stocks are all the rage; it would be an atrocious performer when the sector fell out of favor. Because of this concentration, these funds can make or break a portfolio. When you are right, you win big. When you are wrong, you are down for the count.

Sector funds are favorites among momentum investors and traders. These rogues of the market buy and sell based on what sector is hot, no matter what its long-term outlook may be. Sage prefers to take a long-term investment approach, favoring funds that invest in a variety of industries to narrower sector offerings.

The Internet Fund is one of the best examples of a pure sector fund. The fund invests, as the name implies, in high-growth online companies such as Yahoo!, Inktomi, and DoubleClick. A $10,000 investment in the fund in the beginning of 1998 would have been worth $67,000 by April of 1999. That same $10,000 invested in the broad stock market would have grown to only $14,000.

Now that you know the basics of mutual funds, you are ready to start to learn about Sage's investment philosophy. As financial planners, we advise our clients to diversify their mutual fund portfolios and stay invested for the long term. We preach the same thing on our online site. Those are our bedrock personal investment tenets. Investors must take a few initial steps to prepare for the financial future. Here is a quick list of what you need to do to get ready for the investment process:

- Organize your personal financial information.

- Prioritize your goals and objectives.

- Lay out a goals schedule, such as, "I am going to invest by such and such," or "I am going to set aside X dollars a month in a bank account." Use a free online calendar such as can be found at www.when.com to get your goals in order.

- Read the rest of this book, and make a lot of money.

CHAPTER WRAP

- Online investing is a relatively new phenomenon that has given the individual investor the tools that were formerly the stuff of only the pros. It is natural to be a little intimidated by the massive Internet and all it offers, but we are here to break down the confusion and fear.

- Mutual funds are baskets of stocks and/or bonds, managed by professional money managers. Types of funds include large cap, small cap, mid cap, growth, value, blend, stock, and bond. Different types of funds offer different levels of volatility. In general, the smaller the stocks a fund holds, the more volatile that fund is.

- Sector funds offer advanced investors the ability to tailor their portfolio exactly to their needs by investing in the areas they want to be in and avoiding the areas they do not want to be in. Index funds allow investors a low-cost, highly disciplined method to broadly invest over a range of stocks and/or bonds.

● IN THE TRENCHES WITH SAGE

Each day we take time out to host a chat with the Sage community. It provides us a chance to meet community members and stay in touch with the topics our members deem important. At the end of each chapter we will highlight a Q&A from the Sage chat room.

Mary5372: Alan, I am a little confused. I heard some investors talking about growth funds in Sage chat and I do not understand what they mean. Is the goal of all funds to grow? I mean, isn't this the point of investing?

Alan Cohn: Growth funds are merely mutual funds that invest in stocks with above-average earnings growth potential. For example, a growth fund might invest in General Electric since the company regularly grows corporate earnings by 12 to 14 percent a year, which is much better than the average company. Now, the logical question would be: 'Why wouldn't all funds invest in stocks with above-average earnings growth?' The market has high expectations of stocks like General Electric, so much so that the market often pushes these stocks up to very high prices. When a growth stock fails to live up to expectations, which does happen from time to time, the stock will suffer a massive sell-off—or fall. In effect, a sell-off occurs when investors attempt to sell a stock en masse. Because there are so many more sellers than buyers and because stocks move on supply and demand, the stock will fall to a level where there are equal numbers of buyers and sellers.

Value stocks tend to be stocks that have been perennial underperformers. They are so beaten down that even in the case when they do disappoint investors, they tend to hold up well. The negative news, as they say, is already 'priced into the stock.' The market essentially already expects more bad news. Now, when a value stock reports good news, these stocks often shoot higher since expectations were so low.

So there are really two different kinds of stock funds—growth and value. Interestingly, the market tends to favor only one type at a time. Some years value stocks are popular, other years growth stocks are popular. Because one type of fund is no better than the other over the long term, and it is impossible to tell which type will do well in the near future, you are best off holding both growth and value funds to smooth out your portfolio's returns.

● SELF-HELP TEST

Before one is eligible to become a Sage, that person has to pass several tests. Are you Sage material? Here are some questions from Sage School.

I.   Growth mutual funds may hold the following:

   A. Stocks only.

   B. Stocks and bonds.

   C. Stocks, bonds, and international securities.

II. Microsoft and Dell are examples of:

   A. Value stocks.

   B. Blend stocks.

   C. Growth stocks.

   If you are stumped on some of these questions, reread this chapter for the answers.

Developing an Investment Profile

After making the monumental decision to get started with mutual funds, the next step is to define your investment profile. After all, billionaire investor Warren Buffett did not get wealthy without a plan, and neither will you. When advising clients or talking with our online audience, we start the financial planning process by determining the investor's personality. The second step is applying the fundamental principles of mutual fund success to the investment personality to come up with an investment profile. Starting in Chapter Three we will put a Sage spin on your profile to allow you to profit from our tricks of the trade.

DETERMINE YOUR INVESTMENT PERSONALITY

Understanding your investment personality (i.e., your emotional makeup, risk tolerance, resources, time horizon and goals) is the foundation of a successful mutual fund investing strategy.

What Is Your Emotional Makeup?

Two individuals can view the same situation differently, depending upon their emotional makeup. For example, during the market drop of

August 1998, a Sage community member e-mailed us saying he wanted to be aggressive and get in and buy while the market was down. A minute later another Sage community member e-mailed us to say that she was pulling her money out of stock funds and into cash until things calmed down. While we always take the view that fund investing—or any type of investing, for that matter—is for the long haul and investors should minimize drastic strategies once they have settled on a portfolio strategy, we found the back-to-back messages ironic. Despite different investment philosophies, you see, both Sage community members were dealing with risk in their own way.

What Kind of Investor Are You?

- The Nervous Investor: This investor has trouble sleeping. He tortures himself by constantly second-guessing his investment choices and watching the market constantly.

- The WSJ/CNBC Investor: This type of investor reads the *Wall Street Journal* and watches CNBC each day, trading on the newest economic data or the latest upgrade or downgrade. As a result of this hyperactive, follow-the-experts type of strategy, this investor has a portfolio that is in a constant state of disarray with overall returns that are dismal.

- The Buy-It-All Investor: Some investors become excited by flavor of the month investments—stocks or funds that are the rage on Wall Street during any given time. Buy-it-all investors typically start with a good foundation, but add hot stocks and funds over time. Eventually they assemble a scattered portfolio that does not fit into a long-term strategy and is doomed to mediocrity.

- The Buzz Investor: This type of investor is always buzzing about the latest hot stock pick he has made or how much money he makes. He invests to impress. He takes far too much risk, picking up speculative stocks or funds in the hope of hitting it big.

- The Sage Investor: He or she trusts his or her ability to weather the ups and downs of the market and knows how to manage personal emotions.

At Sage we ask people to invest within themselves. Only if you know your investment risk level, time horizon, and goals will you be a content investor. Some investors like funds that plod along, others like offerings that are more volatile. Some like large caps, others like small caps. Once you find the most appropriate investment mix for you, you will become a Sage investor. You will easily weather the ups and downs of the market and manage personal emotions because you will have confidence in the investment choices you have made and you will be comfortable with the volatility associated with them.

What Is Your Risk Tolerance?

The next step in determining your investment personality is to understand how comfortable you feel about the ups and downs of a particular investment. To determine your risk tolerance, decide how much risk your financial condition will allow you to take, and how much risk you are willing to take. The answers are not always the same. Sometimes it is psychological—some people just do not like to lose money. Ask what kind of a person you are. How would you react if you were to lose 10 percent to 15 percent of your portfolio, even if you knew it would probably come back?

You might not be fully aware of your risk tolerance until a market event transpires that tests your investment resolve. You may think you have a high tolerance for risk, only to discover that you become tormented when a loss occurs. The key is knowing where you stand before any investment loss occurs. Some people simply do not take enough risk. Others take far too much risk. The buzz investor we mentioned above considers the financial markets just as much of an adrenaline rush as a Las Vegas casino. These investors relish the opportunity for large returns—and the fantasy to make the big killing. It drives them to take risks. The downside is that they fail to realize the opportunities for great losses as well. Most people's eyes light up with success. They do not look at the downside—they look at the positives, but not at the negatives.

The following piece, written by Sage community member Suz147, succinctly summarizes Sage's stance on risk: "Risk is a different animal to different people. In general, it is the probability that you will not have as much money as you want when you need it. Let us take a young, under fifty-five, investor who is saving for retirement. What is her biggest risk? Is it losing 30 percent of her portfolio due to a correction? No. The market bounces back. This is just a short-term swing.

"The biggest risk she and anyone under fifty-five faces is fear of volatility, not volatility itself. Fear leads the investor into conservative vehicles. Fear sells when it should buy. Fear asks, 'What did my portfolio do today?' instead of 'What has my portfolio done over the past ten years?' Fear invests in bonds at a young age. Fear holds cash. Fear will leave you short."

Let us take two investors, Brian and Bill. Each is twenty, each has $5,000 to invest. Brian has no fear. Brian thinks he will live forever. Brian wants money, big money, when he retires. Risk is not in Brian's vocabulary. He chooses an aggressive growth fund.

Bill is a bit more prudent. He is a thinker; he is a planner. His knees quiver at the thought of volatility. He chooses a nice balanced fund.

Forty-five years later Brian and Bill are ready to retire. It is time to tap their respective portfolios. Bill's balanced portfolio achieved 7 percent annually, with very low volatility. Bravo for Bill. He is left with $105,012! Brian's risky portfolio achieved 14 percent, but with heavy volatility. He has $1,818,395.

Let us now assume both place their money in T-bills (earning 6 percent) and live off the interest and principal for thirty-five more years.

YEARLY INCOME

Bill $6,833.10
Brian $118,332.38

Bill, who chose the path of less risk, is now sixty-five years old, earning $6,833 a year. Was it worth it? Did he achieve his goal of risk reduction? No, he is in deep water now. He does not have enough money to live on, let alone to take his honey on a vacation. But he can sleep well knowing he accumulated his money with less risk.

Risk is not volatility. As long as you do not touch your money for ten, twenty years, it does not matter if your portfolio drops 20 percent tomorrow. Volatility is nothing but a detail. It does not matter. It is not a measure of risk. Risk is not having enough income once retirement begins. Risk is not allowing your portfolio to grow to its full potential.

It may sound odd, but the best way for many investors to reduce risk is to invest aggressively. Remember that the greatest risk any of us will ever face is outliving our money.

What Are Your Resources?

Assets are to your investment personality as physical features are to your psychological personality. They can facilitate or constrain the attainment of your goals. Take a personal financial inventory. Record your current household assets, including investments, on paper or on your personal computer. Calculate your net worth (the value of all your assets minus all your debts).

Assets	Your Value	Example
House	_____	$ 200,000.00
Car	_____	$ 15,000.00
Checking account	_____	$ 1,000.00
Savings account	_____	$ 2,000.00
Investments	_____	$ 3,500.00

Liabilities	Your Value	Example
Mortgage	_____	($ 125,000.00)
Home equity loan	_____	($ 10,000.00)
Credit card	_____	($ 2,500.00)
Student loan	_____	($ 15,000.00)

Net Worth	_____	**$ 69,000.00**

Chart 2.1. Net worth worksheet.

Determine how much you can contribute to your savings plans in the future. These resources may determine the amount of risk you have to take to increase the probability of realizing a certain return to achieve your objectives.

Monthly Income	Your Value	Example
Net salary	_____	$ 3,750.00
Alimony	_____	$ 0.00
Investment income	_____	$ 0.00

Monthly Expenses	Your Value	Example
Utilities	_____	($ 500.00)
Insurance	_____	($ 450.00)
Mortgage	_____	($ 1,500.00)
Child support	_____	($ 400.00)
Other	_____	($ 500.00)

Net Monthly Income	_____	$ 400.00

Chart 2.2. Monthly income worksheet.

What Is Your Time Horizon?

Another component of your investment personality is your time horizon. The more time you have until you will need the money, the more risk you can afford to take, since over time, high short-term volatility tends to lead to strong long-term gains.

> Suzanne Oliver, contributing editor of SmartMoney.com, chats about time horizon on Sage: "If your asset allocation is based on your time horizon, you should not change your allocation with the volatility. Nobody has ever consistently timed the market properly. So keep your long-term investments in equities."

What Are Your Goals?

Your investment personality is shaped by your goals. Are they long-term or short-term? Are they necessities (like retirement) or luxuries (like a second home)? Do they affect only you (like a speedboat) or do they have an impact on others (like college for your kids)? Investments are no different from life itself, and trade-offs may be necessary. Prioritize your goals, compromise where necessary, and take a course of action.

Your tolerance for volatility, attitude towards investing, resources, goals, and time horizon all tie together to determine your investment personality. Once you have identified where you stand with respect to risk, attitude, and so on, you will have an investment profile—conservative, moderate, or aggressive—that will dictate how you go about setting up a personal portfolio.

Here is an investment test that will assess your risk tolerance, emotional makeup, and investment profile. Give yourself one point for each answer A, two points for each answer B, three points for each answer C, and four points for each answer D. Your score will determine which type of investor you are. We will then take this measure and choose a portfolio model that is most appropriate for you.

● INVESTMENT PROFILE TEST

I. If someone made you an offer to invest 15 percent of your net worth in a deal he said had an 80 percent chance of being profitable, how would you feel about that investment?

  A. No level of profit would be worth that kind of risk.

  B. The level of profit would have to be seven times the amount I invested.

  C. The level of profit would have to be three times the amount I invested.

  D. The level of profit would have to be at least as much as my original investment.

II. What role will your portfolio play in your life?

  A. My portfolio provides me with monthly income and an occasional splurge or two.

  B. My portfolio supplements my monthly income and provides me with a safety net for emergency needs.

  C. I enjoy the extra income my portfolio provides, but it is not necessary to sustain my daily financial needs.

  D. My portfolio is for long-term savings. I will not, under any circumstances, touch it.

III. How much time do you have to reach your primary investment goal?

    A. Less than one year.

    B. One to five years.

    C. Six to ten years.

    D. More than ten years.

IV. How old are you?

    A. Sixty-five or older and proud of it!

    B. Fifty to sixty-four.

    C. Thirty to forty-nine.

    D. Under thirty and holding.

V. How would you feel if your portfolio was worth $100,000 and then the market crashed 30 percent, making your $100,000 now worth $70,000?

    A. The thought makes me shudder.

    B. I could handle it, but I would like to avoid such a nasty occurrence.

    C. It is not the end of the world. The stock market crashes from time to time.

    D. The market always bounces back; it would be a great time to buy.

VI. How do you plan to make your investment decisions?

    A. Never on my own.

    B. Sometimes on my own.

    C. Often on my own.

    D. Totally on my own.

VII. If a stock or fund you bought doubled in a year, what would you do?

    A. Sell all my shares.

B. Sell half my shares.

C. Not sell any shares.

D. Buy more shares.

VIII. If you have a certificate of deposit (CD) that is about to mature, the most likely place you would invest the money is:

A. U.S. savings bond.

B. A short-term bond fund.

C. A long-term bond fund.

D. A stock fund.

IX. As an investor you think you will be:

A. Terrible.

B. Average.

C. Better than average.

D. Fantastic.

X. You think investment success is mainly due to:

A. Fate.

B. Being in the right place at the right time.

C. Taking advantage of an opportunity.

D. Carefully planned work and analysis.

Results

19 points or less: You are a conservative investor who feels uncomfortable taking risks. You probably realize that you will have to take some calculated risks to attain your financial goals, but this does not mean you will be comfortable doing so.

20 to 29 points: You are a moderate investor who feels comfortable taking moderate risks. You are probably willing to take reasonable risks without a great deal of discomfort.

30 or more points: You are an aggressive investor who is willing to take high risks in search of high returns. You are not greatly stressed by taking significant risks.

● KEYS TO MUTUAL FUND SUCCESS

The next step to developing your fund investment profile is to apply the fundamental principles of investment success to your investment personality. These timeless nuggets are regular investments, patience, diversification, asset allocation, tax efficiency, dollar cost averaging, and online investing.

Regular Investments

Investing is a beautiful thing for one simple reason: You make money by doing nothing. Add some money to a fund at regular intervals and you will be living comfortably a few years hence.

Consider a twenty-year-old with a midrange job. If she deducted $100 a month from her paycheck into a mutual fund, by the time she reached sixty-five she would have saved $54,000 (45 years × 12 months × $100). By age sixty-five, due to compound growth in her investments, she would have approximately $2.17 million, assuming a 12% annual rate of return. Invested money grows exponentially. This means that the longer your money is invested, the more rapidly it grows.

Patience: Time Is On Your Side

The amount of time an investment is allowed to grow is more important than the quantity of money you invest. As you will see from Chart 2.3, it is better to start early with a little money than late with a lot of money.

Time/Investment	$100/Month	$300/Month	$1,000/Month
10 Years	$ 23,200	$ 69,700	$ 232,000
20 Years	$ 99,900	$ 299,700	$ 999,100
30 Years	$ 353,000	$ 1,059,000	$ 3,530,000
40 Years	$ 1,188,200	$ 3,565,000	$ 11,900,000

Chart 2.3. The growth of different investment amounts over time, assuming a 12 percent annual return.

Let us take an example that nicely illustrates the benefits of an early, regular investment program.

Mary and Bill are about the same age, but in terms of lifestyles they are polar opposites. Mary likes stability. She reveres reason and cherishes sensibility. When Mary was thirty she started investing $500 a month on a regular basis.

Bill was a procrastinator. He did not start investing until he was fifty. Realizing that he was behind the game, he decided to invest $1,167 a month.

At age sixty-five, Bill and Mary decided it was time to give up the daily grind for something a little more peaceful. Mary looked at her portfolio and was delighted to see she had accumulated over $3.2 million. Bill's portfolio, however, was worth only $589,000.

Bill and Mary both invested the same $210,000, yet Mary has four times more money than Bill. Because Mary took the responsible path starting early, she let the exponential power of compound interest work for her.

Now, suppose both decide to live off their portfolios until they reach one hundred years old. Mary can draw an annual income of $349,000. Bill can draw about $64,000 a year. Both assume a 12 percent annual return.

Bill has two choices: he can live well for just a few more years, or live long and less extravagantly than Mary.

If you do not need the money that you invest within the next three years, then you should remain committed to the market, even during market downturns. Long-term investors generally do better than those who jump in and out of the market.

Drew Kupps, fund manager from Strong Capital Management, highlights the importance of diversification: "The markets do not go straight up and the world is not a euphoric place all the time. Keep a long-term horizon and stay diversified in your portfolio so that any one position or group does not ruin you."

As much as it sounds like a cliché, the only constant in the market is change. Because it is impossible to predict the long-term winners, the wisest move is to hold funds of various market caps and investment styles.

Our advice: invest early and often.

Diversification: Expose Your Portfolio

Diversification is the act of spreading your assets over a wide range of different investments. By investing in many different stocks and bonds, you reduce the risk that any one security will adversely affect your portfolio. If, for example, your portfolio held only Russian stocks and the Russian financial market fell hard, as it did in 1998, your portfolio would suffer a substantial loss. If, on the other hand, your portfolio held stocks in Russia, Latin America, Canada, and Australia, the impact on your portfolio of the Russian market would be lessened.

Bob862HW: "For many years I traded stocks on a regular basis. I thought I was doing very well. I was steadily making money and I felt like I was making real headway towards my retirement. One day I picked up a *Money* magazine and started flipping through the mutual fund scorecard. This fund achieved 30 percent, that fund did 20 percent, and on and on and on. I never kept track of my returns on an annualized basis, but seeing the nice layout in *Money* magazine gave me the push to do it. I transferred all of my old brokerage statements to a spreadsheet and calculated my annualized return. I am embarrassed to say exactly what it was, but it was substantially less than most of the funds had posted. I figured I surrendered over $20,000 in returns by jumping in and out of the market on my own."

Asset Allocation: Breaking Down Your Portfolio

Asset allocation, as you will see in the following chapter, is the major driving force behind the gains of your portfolio. Simply put, asset allocation is the practice of separating your portfolio into different asset classes and investment styles. Bonds, stocks, and cash compose the basic asset classes, but beyond these, there are specific types of bonds (Treasury, junk), stocks (large cap, growth), and cash equivalents (money market, CD). How you break down your portfolio among these asset classes will dictate the type of return you will achieve and the volatility you may be exposed to. A great portion of this book is dedicated to asset allocation—how it works and how to harness its power.

Tax Efficiency: Keep It All

In order to maximize the gain of your portfolio, you must consider the tax consequences associated with buying and selling investments. Each time you make an investment transaction, you will likely incur a tax hit. To minimize the tax bite you should maximize your tax-sheltered and -deferred contributions, such as into an IRA or 401(k), and invest in a tax-efficient manner. This subject is so important that we devote an entire chapter to it later in the book.

Dollar Cost Averaging: Consistent Investing

Dollar cost averaging is the practice of investing equal dollar amounts regardless of what the market conditions are or the outlook may be. When you dollar cost average, you buy more shares when prices are low and fewer shares when prices are high. This gives you a cost basis that reflects a fund's average share price. It also protects against investing a lump sum in a market that is at a peak. Dollar cost averaging is suitable for the long-term investor who seeks to accumulate wealth by systematically putting money into the market.

Online Investing: Simplify the Process

Diversifying and allocating your portfolio can require a great deal of work. Just how much should you invest in large caps? Should you consider investing in Europe? What should your portfolio look like if you are thirty years from retirement? What about three years? What if you are currently retired?

A great deal of research has been done on the topics of asset allocation and diversification. Esteemed academics have gone to great lengths to create "efficient frontier" models—mathematically created portfolios that maximize returns and reduce volatility.

Based on historic data, financial statisticians have created countless "efficient" portfolios. Previously this information was buried deep within trade journals and high-priced proprietary institutional money management literature.

Online investment tools such as the one from SmartMoney.com put the average investor on equal footing with the professional. Complex, highly expensive portfolio simulation software is no longer a luxury, it is a commodity. But you have to know where to find it and how to use it. When we cover asset allocation and diversification in a future chapter, we will reference the pertinent online tools and show you how to get the most out of them.

Once you learn how to use these tools, not only will you cut down the amount of time needed to create a portfolio; you will assemble an investment plan that will stand toe-to-toe with the portfolios of the pros.

You now possess the fundamentals needed to become a Sage fund investor. You have formulated a personal investment profile, understand the true meaning of risk, and know that diversification and asset allocation are the keys to investment success. You are now ready to internalize the Sage investment philosophy.

● CHAPTER WRAP

- The first step in becoming a successful investor is assessing your investment profile. Without a firm grasp of what you want and how much you are willing to risk to get it, developing an overall financial plan of action is impossible.

- You now have an investment profile score, which we will use throughout the book to determine the right investments for you. Based on that score, we will assign to you a model portfolio in a future chapter.

- More important than the amount you invest is how early you start. If you are behind in the game, you will have to play catch-up. Do not worry, the power of compound interest is on your side. Just make a commitment to yourself that you will invest a fixed amount at regular intervals.

- Online tools can enhance the returns of your portfolio and cut down the research burden. In the coming chapters we will expose you to the better online investing tools offered and teach you how to use them to increase profits and reduce volatility.

● IN THE TRENCHES WITH SAGE

Jill57656: I have three children, ages seven, five, and one and a half. How much money needs to be set aside now to pay for private four-year colleges for each? I know the numbers cannot exactly be predicted, so I am just looking for general guidance to see if we are on track. The oldest child has about $30,000; the middle, $20,000; and the youngest, $7,500, each in a mix of stocks and bonds. Are there any tables out there or general information?

Stephen Cohn: Yes, there are several good calculators available on the Web. Check out www.troweprice.com. They have an excellent college planning area. On a related note, we are assuming by the large amounts already saved that this money is in the children's names and that you are in a high tax bracket. You may wish to sit down with your financial advisor and determine both the most tax-efficient way and the safest way to save such large sums of money. Generally, we recommend parents maintain this money in their own names so the risk of junior buying a Maserati with it is minimal. Be sure you are funding your tax-advantaged retirement accounts first; you can pull from these if you need to for the kids schooling. You may also wish to establish some sort of trust that would belong equally to all your children, but that you could maintain control of well beyond their eighteenth birthdays.

Risks and Rewards

DON'T MISTAKE ACTIVITY FOR EFFECTIVENESS.

Bennett Goodspeed, author of *The Tao Jones Averages:
A Guide to Whole-Brained Investing*

We live funds. From six o'clock in the morning to eleven-thirty at night, we talk funds with clients and community members. We can recite great management follies and talk about the glory mutual days gone by. Nevertheless, we are not blinded by our commitment to mutual fund–based financial planning. We know there are both positive and negative aspects of funds.

🔘 ADVANTAGES OF MUTUAL FUNDS

Diversification

Funds hold between 10 and 3,000 positions—stocks and/or bonds. By spreading their assets over so many positions, funds reduce risk. If a company abruptly files for bankruptcy, in the worst-case scenario the diversified fund holding this stock will lose just a few percentage points. Boston Market, Sunbeam, and Mercury Finance are all stocks that were widely held by individual investors and mutual funds, and that dropped dramatically, some after the company filed for bankruptcy. Investors in funds that held these stocks—and there were many—probably did not even notice their negative effects thanks to diversification and the low percentage the stock represented of the funds' total holdings.

DarList90: "I was totally duped in one of the worst stock market scams that has ever taken place. Last month I bought shares in a Canadian gold stock called Bre-X. Bre-X shares ran up a tremendous amount, as investors like me thought Bre-X hit the mother lode in their Busang gold mine located in rain forests of Borneo, Indonesia. Then word broke out that the company had tampered with the mine, falsifying the existence of gold. Bre-X's geologist, Michael de Guzman, mixed locally obtained river gold with crushed rock, essentially "salting" the mine. Once it became apparent that there was foul play, the stock immediately dropped to zero. Not $1 a share, $0.00!

"But wait, it gets better. De Guzman is said to have committed suicide by jumping from a helicopter over a Borneo rain forest after he was discovered, although some doubts lingered about whether the badly decomposed body recovered from a jungle swamp was his. Bre-X vice chairman John Felderhof meanwhile remains incommunicado at his luxury retreat in the Cayman Islands.

"Thirteen percent of my portfolio is gone because I made the mistake of putting my faith behind a company. It will likely take a year or more of decent gains in the rest of my holdings to overcome this ridiculous occurrence."

Economy of Scale

The Internet has lowered commissions and made it possible for small investors to get in on the action. Not too many years ago commissions for buying and selling stocks were well over $100. Today you can buy and sell stocks for less than $10 through many e-brokers. But the task of developing a diversified portfolio in individual stocks is still a costly endeavor. Suppose you want to buy thirty stocks. Just to create this portfolio would cost $300. That is a huge sum when you are starting with modest means.

Additionally, each time you buy or sell a stock in your brokerage account, you must pay a commission. Therefore, if you buy thirty stocks and hold each for a year, you will spend a total of $600 in commission, which is equivalent to a 30 percent yearly fee in a relatively small portfolio of just $2,000.

With a fund, you essentially buy hundreds of stocks with no up-front fee or commission. Moreover, when you want to put additional money in a fund account, you can mail off a check and it costs you nothing. Even better, you can set up an automatic investment plan (AIP) and have a fixed amount deducted from your checking account or paycheck invested in a fund on a regular basis.

Because you are pooling your money with hundreds of other investors, when the fund invests your money it buys stocks in bulk. And when you buy in bulk, you get a volume discount. The discount is passed down the line to the fund holders.

Liquidity

Funds allow you the freedom to redeem shares whenever you want. With some thinly traded stocks (stocks that trade very few shares a day, if at all), there are times when stockholders cannot sell their shares. Sometimes there are simply no buyers. When you own individual stocks and are confronted with a situation like this when you need your money, there is nothing you can do.

Fund investors will never have this problem. When investors want out, they get out. If the fund is holding stocks they cannot get rid of, it is their problem, not yours.

Bill667SR: "About ten years ago at the behest of my brother, I bought a large block of stock in a small steel company. It was a considerable portion of my portfolio, but I was confident (or at least my brother was) that it was going to be a major industry force. It dropped a little, but I held. After time, activity dried up in the stock. There were days when it did not trade at all. I put in an order to sell and my broker just gulped. I knew there was some- thing wrong, but I just let it go. When he did not call by the end of the day with my trade confirmation, I grew a little worried. The next morning I called him up to see what was going on. 'Asking $1, bidding 50 cents,' he said.

"I bought this piece of junk for $8 and the best price some- one was going to give me was 50 cents! 'Sell!' I screamed in dis- gust. I unloaded all of my shares over the course of the day. I got an average price of 40-some cents a share. What a nightmare this investment turned out to be.

"Needless to say, my brother and I did not speak for a week."

Professional Management

> "I am concerned that investors in general are undereducated."
> *David Brady of Stein Roe Young Investor Fund*
> *appearing in a chat on Sage Online*

Most of us do not have the time, energy, or desire to track individual stocks. Most of us simply lack the skills it takes to be a successful direct stock investor. It is a full-time job. Yet many of us succumb to macho bravado, thinking we are the best keepers of our own nest eggs. Just as most men will never stop to ask directions, many skilled Net-jetters balk at the idea of letting a professional manage their money.

Karen12NFL: "I did not need a high-powered money manager to teach me how to invest. I had it all figured out. Early in 1999 I got caught up in the Internet craze. I bought Amazon.com, VerticalNet, Inktomi, and Safeguard Scientifics. I did well after my initial purchases, but then the bottom fell out. By the end of the second quarter, my portfolio was down over 60 percent. I sold all of my stocks and moved to cash—not so much because I thought there was more downside left in these stocks, but because I just could not handle seeing my portfolio dwindle away on a daily basis.

"I thought I could work a forty-hour week and successfully manage my portfolio, essentially taking on two jobs. It was a hard lesson to learn, but an important one. I am just glad that I made this mistake now, while my portfolio is relatively small, and not later on in life when I would not have the extra years needed to recoup my losses. I have since swallowed my pride and invested in mutual funds. I have not gained back all my losses, but at least with a real expert watching my portfolio, I know I will in time."

Mutual fund managers spend their entire days researching companies, talking with CEOs, reading annual reports, studying balance sheets, and trading stocks. This is what they do; this is all they do. If you do not have the time to do this research on your own, you owe it to yourself and to your family to let a professional money manager do it for you.

● DISADVANTAGES OF FUNDS

Like any industry, the mutual fund business is not above reproach. The following points need to be ironed out industry-wide before the mutual fund sector can be inducted into the Corporate America Hall of Fame.

High Fees

Many mutual funds levy reasonable year-over-year expenses, but a fair number of outlandish funds regularly overcharge. Some examples of fund families with historically high fees include Steadman, Waddell & Reed, and Dean Witter.

Fortunately, Internet mutual fund databases offer the ability to screen out funds with high fees. If you were in search of funds with expenses below 0.5 percent, for example, you could simply enter this information in a database such as the one located at Morningstar.com and click a button. The database would generate a list of low-fee funds.

Too Many Choices

Mutual funds have proliferated as investors have turned to them because of their many benefits. When we jumped into the fund business in 1989, there were about a thousand funds. When our dad started out there were fewer than one hundred. Today there are well over ten thousand. At the industry's current growth rate there will be over a hundred thousand funds by the year 2020. There are just too many funds out there, which is the result of a long bull market and investors' unquenchable thirst for new fund products.

At a point in the not-too-distant future, consolidation will occur in the industry, reducing the number of duplicate funds. Until then you will have to rely on online screening tools such as the one found at Morningstar.com that do most of the number crunching for you.

In Chapters Four, Five, and Six we will explain different methods that will help you reduce the large number of offerings to just a handful of funds. In fact, while there are thousands of funds, you will never look at more than twenty or so at a time. We accomplish this feat by performing a numerical screen on the entire pool of funds, which eliminates the vast majority of funds that do not meet our predetermined criteria. While this may sound like a daunting chore, in practice it is quite an easy task that we will walk through together.

Poor Performance

There are many outstanding funds available to individual investors. Unfortunately, there are a fair number of mutual funds that simply do not make the cut.

We eliminate poorly performing funds from our holdings by screening for those with the best performance compared to their peers over the past three years. By doing this we avoid wasting time scrutinizing funds that are unworthy of investment dollars.

Poor performance, high fees, and too many choices, however, are an online investor's best friend. With the free online fund screening tools, you can whittle down the list. What starts out as an incomprehensible mass of thousands of funds can easily be pared down into a digestible pool of five or ten offerings.

● FUND FEES

One of the greatest disadvantages of funds is that they all charge fees. There simply is no free lunch on Wall Street. Even no-load funds have a little way to part investors from their cash. It is called the expense ratio.

If you are a casual investor, you will never know that your fund is charging fees. Fees are deducted on a regular basis before daily share prices are updated each day. Moreover, posted returns are adjusted for fees. In addition, fees are so small that you will not feel them in one fell swoop. However, this does not mean fees should be neglected. All things being equal, ten times out of ten, the fund with the lowest cost structure will be the strongest performer.

Because fees have such a bearing on performance, and performance is the end-all name of the investment game, we place considerable emphasis on the fees that funds charge. In the numerical screens that we will employ in the coming chapters, we will use online mutual fund databases to eliminate all funds with expenses that fail to remain under our maximum expense ceiling.

Expense Ratio

The expense ratio is the total operating expenses for a fund on an annual basis divided by its assets. A fund with an expense ratio of 1 percent, for example, deducts that amount over the course of a year, and the effects are not immediately noticeable. Over time, however, such fees add up and hinder a fund's overall return.

Steadman American Industry, a fund with one of the worst track records in history, boasts the largest expense ratio in the entire industry. Former manager, Harvard doctoral graduate Charles Steadman, nearly ran the funds into the ground before passing away in early 1998. In 1976 the fund carried an expense ratio of 2.64 percent and had assets of $22 million. By the end of 1998 the fund's assets had plummeted to $800,000 (over a thousand times smaller than the average growth fund) and its expense ratio had ballooned to more than 22 percent.

Suppose you made a ten-year investment in a fund that returned 10 percent before expenses. The higher the expense ratio, the greater the fees you would have paid to your fund. Because expense ratios are expressed as a percentage of assets, the greater your investment, the more money you pay in absolute fees. The following table illustrates the amount of money the fund company would make off of your investment over those ten years.

| Investment | Expense Ratio | | |
	0.25%	0.50%	1.00%
$ 1,000	$ 58	$ 116	$ 226
$ 10,000	$ 583	$ 1,155	$ 2,264
$ 100,000	$ 5,835	$ 11,551	$ 22,638

Chart 3.1. The amount paid in expenses over ten years.

For example, if you were to invest $1,000 and leave it in a fund with an expense ratio of 0.25 percent for ten years and that fund returned 10 percent before expenses, you would pay the fund family a total of $58. Your actual annual return would be 9.75 percent after expenses. In a fund that has an expense ratio of 1 percent, you would pay a total of $226 and the fund's after-fee annual return would be just 9 percent.

On a $1,000 investment, a couple of hundred dollars over a decade does not feel like much. In fact, if you did not read your fund's litera- ture, you would never even notice. But over that decade your portfolio would feel the bite of the fund's fees.

The following table illustrates the effect fees have on your investment over ten years.

	Totals after 10 years with an expense ratio of:		
Investment	0.25%	0.50%	1.00%
$ 1,000	$ 2,535	$ 2,478	$ 2,367
$ 10,000	$ 25,354	$ 24,782	$ 23,673
$ 100,000	$ 253,439	$ 247,823	$ 236,136

Chart 3.2. How the growth of an investment is dependent on expenses.

If you invest $100,000, your portfolio would grow to $253,439 over ten years, assuming an annual return of 10 percent before an expense ratio of 0.25 percent. That same investment in a fund that returns 10 percent annually before an expense ratio of 1 percent would grow to $236,136. The difference of 0.75 percent annually (1.00% minus 0.25%) results in a final portfolio value disparity of over $17,000! You can see why Sage investors consider expense ratios a determining factor in fund selection.

The best way to keep overall portfolio expenses down is by carefully investing only in funds with low expense ratios. Unfortunately, many new investors fall prey to tricky marketing ploys or funds with short-term red-hot performance. To avoid this we screen strictly by the numbers, so the sleekness of the fund's full-spread advertisement in the *Wall Street Journal* cannot sway us. By using online databases to select funds, you are assured that each fund you will choose will have a low expense ratio. Consequently, you will assemble a portfolio that will carry an overall expense ratio that is quite low, and performance that will be correspondingly strong.

12b-1 Fee

The 12b-1 fee is a marketing fee that pays for a fund to sell itself. Some funds charge 12b-1 fees to cover TV commercials, glossy brochures, and Web advertisements. The 12b-1 is capped at 1 percent and is included in the expense ratio calculation.

Loads

Front-end loads are up-front sales charges, which range from 9 percent to less than 1 percent but typically fall in the neighborhood of 4.35 percent. These fees are levied by the fund on top of its expense ratio. Funds with front-end loads are usually considered "A" shares. A shares typically have lower expense ratios than "B" and "C" shares.

Back-end loads are deferred charges that are imposed when you sell shares of a fund before a certain time. Over the course of a few years, back-end loads on B shares typically decline. Once the deferred load has vanished, the fund usually converts into low-expense-ratio A shares. (During the conversion to A shares, no new front load is imposed.)

Level loads apply to C shares, which may have a low front-end load, a low back-end load, and a high expense ratio. Unlike B shares, most C shares do not convert into A shares over time. If you buy a C share, you are stuck with the high expenses for the life of your holding period.

Load funds are suitable for investors who need advice and hand-holding. It is how some financial advisors are paid for recommending these funds to clients. These funds have a place in the mutual fund and financial planning industries. Not everyone has the time, knowledge, and desire to do it all on their own. A load is a small price to pay when the alternative is potential financial disaster or a poorly developed personal financial plan.

Management Fee

The management fee is what the stock or bond picker takes home. In theory, as a fund's assets increase, the management fee—and in turn the expense ratio—should decrease. Since the management fee is included in a fund's operating expenses, we do not screen directly for management fees. The numeric screen we will employ will eliminate funds with high operating expenses, which will automatically include funds that charge excessive management fees.

Turnover Ratio

This is not a fee per se, but it is an important hidden cost. Turnover ratio refers to how often a manager buys and sells holdings. For example, a turnover ratio of 100 percent indicates that the manager sells and buys the average stock in his portfolio once a year. Since selling stock can result in taxable gains and the act of buying or selling a stock costs the fund money (commissions, traders, et cetera), lower-turnover funds generally result in lower taxes and have lower expenses.

To screen for fund turnover, you need to record each fund's turnover in a spreadsheet and sort the data. This is not much of a task when you are looking at just a few funds, but when dealing with thousands of funds the chore is almost impossible. But there is no need to screen for turnover. Because expenses and turnover are directly correlated, when you screen for expense ratios (an easy task) you are essentially screening for turnover and other high-expense features.

As you can see from Chart 3.3, expense ratios and fund turnover ratios are inextricably intertwined. The table summarizes a 1999 Sage study, which showed that as the turnover ratio of a fund declines, its expense ratio is likely to decline. A pool of 1,280 growth funds was assembled and ranked in descending order in terms of turnover ratios. We then broke the funds into 64 groups of 20 funds. Our findings: as a fund's turnover increases, its expense ratio will likely increase, and vice versa. Intuitively this relationship makes a lot of sense. A fund that buys a few stocks and sits on them for years at a time would operate in a much lower fee bracket than a fund that aggressively buys and sells stocks on a daily basis.

Fund Rank	Average Turnover	Average Expense Ratio
Highest 20 funds	510%	2.00%
Middle 20 funds	71%	1.57%
Lowest 20 funds	2%	1.05%

Chart 3.3. High-turnover funds often have high expenses.

Because so many different fees and expenses can be imposed, it might be confusing to keep track of which fees are included in the expense ratio. Chart 3.4 will provide you with an at-a-glance breakdown of some of the various fees that funds charge.

Fee	Included in the Expense Ratio	Range
Front load	No	0%–9%
Back load	No	0%–6%
Level load	No	N/A
12b-1	Yes	0%–1%
Management	Yes	0%–2.5%
Operating expenses	Yes	0%–1%

Chart 3.4. Selected fund fees and their relationship to the expense ratio. (Load figures as of 1999.)

● THE MATTER OF RISK

Aside from the advantages and disadvantages of mutual funds, it is of paramount importance that you have a handle on the matter of risk. Without an understanding of risk, you are likely to make investment decisions based more on emotion than reason. Only after you have a firm grasp of what risk is and what it is not, will you be able to prosper in the market without making untimely or ill-advised buy and sell decisions.

Types of Risk

- Interest Rate Risk: This is the risk that the value of your investment, especially a bond, will fall if interest rates increase. Some of the smartest people around fumble when talking interest rates and bonds. Just keep these two rules in mind: As inflation rises, bond yields (interest rates) rise. As bond yields rise, bond prices fall. If you can memorize those two sentences, you will, at the very least, sound intelligent.

  Overcoming interest rate risk entirely is impossible. The market as a whole—stocks and bonds, foreign and domestic—will react in a negative way to rising interest rates. Different segments of the market, however, will react in varying degrees. For example, financial and real estate stocks as well as high-yield bonds tend to suffer worse than the rest of the market during times of rising interest rates. The poor performance in these segments of your portfolio will be offset by relatively strong performance in other areas of your portfolio. The key, of course, is a well-diversified portfolio. Without diversification, there is no way to reduce interest rate risk.

- Market Risk: This is the risk that your investment will lose value if the market falls. Keep in mind, this risk is perceived. It becomes a reality only if you sell. Sage investors take advantage of market dips by buying. We look at market dips as an opportunity, not a risk.

  The only tried and true way to reduce market risk is by assembling a well-diversified portfolio. Different segments of the market flow in and out of favor, due to a variety of reasons, such as a sectorwide scare like health care reform, or a disaster like an oil spill. By holding different segments of the market within a portfolio, you shield yourself from extreme sector gyrations. You will not have to spend countless hours checking your portfolio for broad diversification. The method we employ to select funds ensures broad diversification.

- Company Risk: When investing in individual stocks or bonds, there is a risk that even if the market is stable or rising and interest rates are tame, the underlying stock or bond can fail. Sometimes even when the market flourishes, a company can falter.

  Most funds keep their holdings in any one stock or bond to below 5 percent of assets. In the worst-case scenario, if a fund's largest holding represented 5 percent of its assets and went bankrupt, the fund would lose only 5 percent. If you had four other funds in your portfolio, all other things being equal, your entire portfolio would lose only 1 percent. When you assemble your entire portfolio over the next few chapters, you will stock it with a number of funds, thereby almost eliminating the risk that any one company will bring down your portfolio.

As the financial industry blossomed over the late 1980s and 1990s, the old-line media companies struggled to keep pace. Dow Jones, the parent company of *Barron's* and the *Wall Street Journal*, lost over 14 percent from February of 1987 through March of 1999. The Dow Jones Industrial Average, a widely followed group of thirty large U.S. stocks, over this span gained more than 340 percent, excluding dividends.

- Currency Risk: Drops in foreign currencies can affect the U.S. dollar. When you invest in an international mutual fund, you are, in a sense, buying another nation's currency. Currencies fluctuate with the strength of economies. If Mozambique's economy weakens, for example, its currency, the metical, will fall. Likewise, if the Haitian economy strengthens, its gourde will rise. When foreign currencies are translated back into dollars, as they must each day for mutual fund share price reporting, the strength of international currencies relative to the U.S. dollar will affect fund share prices. Since many economies are unstable, especially those of emerging nations, funds that invest in overseas markets carry an added risk that domestic funds do not have.

Because only one of your mutual funds will invest exclusively in overseas markets, your exposure to currency risk will be limited.

Risk becomes a problem only when a portfolio is constructed in a haphazard manner. Using the Sage selection techniques, which we will review in the coming chapters, you will create a portfolio that will counteract the risk factors that we have outlined above. No portfolio is immune to all forms of risk, but a soundly constructed, well-diversified portfolio, such as the one you will soon create, will be in a position to handily overcome almost anything the market throws at it.

Measuring Risk

Some common measures of risk include:

- Standard Deviation: This is a mathematical measure that shows how much a fund moves around its average return. If a fund averages 30 percent and has a standard deviation of 10, it should (in academic theory) return between 40 percent (30 percent plus 10) and 20 percent (30 percent minus 10) most of the time.

- A word of caution: The market does not like math and does not like theories. It makes fools of those who try to predict results based on complex formulas. Standard deviation is, fortunately, a good indicator of how volatile a fund will be in the future, but it is not a good indicator of future returns.

- Beta: This is the relative volatility of a fund compared to the overall market. The market, by definition, carries a beta of one. A fund that has a beta of 1.2 should rise 20 percent more than the market when stocks move higher, and should drop 20 percent farther when stocks head lower.

- Alpha: This is the difference between the return you would expect from a fund, given its beta, and the actual return of the fund. If a fund acts exactly as its beta predicts it should, then its alpha is zero. If a fund rises higher and falls lower than its beta would predict, the fund has a positive alpha. If it does not rise as far and falls farther than its beta would predict, however, the fund has a negative alpha. Alpha is often considered a direct gauge of the value added by fund management.

To varying degrees, we will use these measures in the Sage fund selection process, which we will discuss in detail in the next chapter.

Risk and Time

"The market is guided by fear and greed, so sometimes it becomes an emotional decision to sell. In this environment, perhaps the greatest risk has been in selling too soon."

Eugene Peroni of John Nuveen & Co.

- Short-Term Risk: This risk is related to short-term price fluctuations. The shorter your investment time period, the more vulnerable you are to short-term swings in value. Expect the market to lose value on average once out of every three years. The market typically falls faster than it rises, but rises more often than it falls.

- Long-Term Risk: Inflation erodes the purchasing power of stocks less than it erodes other investments. Interest-bearing investments, like bonds and CDs, are the most vulnerable to the damaging effect of inflation because they have lower returns. From 1930 through 1997, stocks earned on average 6.7 percent more than inflation, which represented their real return. On the other hand, bonds experienced a real return of approximately 2 percent. Treasury bill and CD returns barely exceeded the inflation rate. Therefore, while conservative investments such as bonds and CDs are more stable investments over the short term, they are more risky investments over the long term since they will outpace inflation only by a narrow margin, if at all.

● ONLINE TOOLS

There is a wealth of information about mutual fund basics online. Not surprisingly, some of our favorite stuff is right on the Sage site in our own Sage School. If you are tired of reading a lot of mumbo jumbo that you just do not understand, Sage School or a comparable online resource is a great place to start. Some of our other favorite sites for mutual fund basics include Morningstar.com, MFEA.com, and Vanguard.com.

Now that you have a basic knowledge of mutual funds and their risks and rewards, it is time see what you are made of. In Chapter Four we will start to develop a fund investment strategy just for you by using the same tools and techniques that we use online and in our financial planning practice. Once you know what type of investor you are and establish the proper groundwork, you will be able to assemble a portfolio of funds to your liking and start investing online. If you still have some questions, feel free to venture into one of Sage's chat rooms or post on one of Sage's online message boards. We guarantee you a timely, accurate response.

● CHAPTER WRAP

- Funds offer diversification, liquidity, economy of scale, and professional management. However, not all funds live up to their billing. The fund industry is scarred with poor performance, high fees, and too many choices.

- Fund fees have a direct bearing on fund performance. Everything else being equal, the higher a fund's expenses are, the lower its returns will be.

- The greatest risk any investor will face is not market risk; rather, it is failing to plan adequately or invest aggressively enough. There is no better way to reduce risk than to hold a mutual fund for a long period of time.

- Online tools are an excellent way to learn more about funds. Some of our favorite educational sites are Morningstar, MFEA, Vanguard, and of course, Sage.

● IN THE TRENCHES WITH SAGE

Frank67a: On a daily basis, why do markets go up and down? What drives this madness?

Alan Cohn: Though we tend to talk about the market as an animate object—the market did this or that today—market activity really results from millions of individual human decisions based on greed, fear, information, and analysis.

A marketwide decline in stock prices is usually a sign that investors have temporarily lost confidence in stocks, often due to outside political or economic factors. Professional investors love predictability and hate anything—the path of a Korean missile, a wayward president—that creates the sense that the environment has become unpredictable. They also dislike anything that could threaten profits, such as a sudden increase in oil prices or interest rates.

So in a nutshell, on a daily basis the market goes up or down based on millions of decisions, some rational and, unfortunately, some not. That is why we recommend that you track the market only as frequently as your stress level can handle.

The Sage Investment Philosophy

MONEY IS LIKE MANURE. YOU HAVE TO SPREAD IT
AROUND OR IT STINKS.

J. Paul Getty, billionaire author of *How To Be Rich*

When our dad, David Cohn, started in the financial business, only a handful of stocks were trading on the venerable old New York Stock Exchange. Steel and automotive sectors were considered growth industries. The notion of investing overseas or spreading your assets over hundreds of stocks and bonds was inconceivable.

You bought American Cotton Oil, Distilling & Cattle Feeding, Tennessee Coal & Iron, and Chicago Gas (all original members of the Dow Jones Industrial Average). That was it. That was all you needed and that was about all that was offered. You were happy about it.

Efficiencies grew and new companies were born. As the nation moved away from a natural resource–driven economy to a service- and technology-based society, new industries were created. It became more important to spread your assets over many companies as emerging leaders grappled with the old stogies. The need for diversification was no longer a social issue. It was a financial one. "Diversify or die" became the mantra of financial gurus.

Now, decades since dear old dad used quill and ink to track the daily performance of Standard Oil of New Jersey and International Nickel, we are confronted with a very different market. Dynamic, entrepreneurial-driven corporations have literally become giants overnight. Intel and Microsoft were once dwarfed by the massive size of IBM. Today both companies outsize IBM by billions of dollars, despite Big Blue's nearly eighty years of solid performance. Young, high-growth Internet companies are challenging traditional retailers such as Sears, Roebuck and Ames. Automotive titans like Ford and General Motors are in a death match with overseas manufacturers.

The imperialistic America that once was lives no longer. Global leaders flip-flop daily. The only way to survive financially is through diversification.

The Sage investment philosophy is built around diversification. We reduce the risk of one stock, fund, industry, or nation having adverse affects on your portfolio by diversifying into many holdings.

Through consolidation, mergers, acquisitions, and financial mishaps, of the original Dow Jones Industrial Average list compiled in 1896, only one company remains a member today: General Electric. GE, founded in 1892 by the merger of the Edison General Electric Company and the Thomson-Houston Electric Company, was eclipsed in market value in 1997 by Microsoft, a company founded in 1975. The Dow Jones Industrial Average, though still often quoted, has become an old-world measure. The editors of the *Wall Street Journal* choose Dow components. Unfortunately, the keepers of the Dow failed to foresee the power that the technology sector would have on our economy. Instead of including leading representative stocks such as Microsoft and Intel in the Dow, editors of the *Wall Street Journal* have stuck with corporations of yesteryear, such as Aluminum Company of America (Alcoa), Union Carbide, and International Paper.

● HOW DIVERSIFICATION WORKS

Suppose you bought 100 shares of four stocks back in 1925—General Electric, Horn & Hardart, Johns-Manville, and Woolworth. By the close of 1998 you would have 153,600 shares (due to stock splits) of General Electric stock worth over $17 million, whereas your other investments would be almost worthless. Horn & Hardart went bankrupt in the

1960s; Johns-Manville, an asbestos company, filed for bankruptcy under the weight of heavy lawsuits; and Woolworth, though still alive under the Venator name, has been in a steady decline for decades.

1925	Original Purchase	100 Total Shares
1926	4-for-1 stock split	400 total shares
1930	4-for-1 stock split	1,600 total shares
1954	3-for-1 stock split	4,800 total shares
1971	2-for-1 stock split	9,600 total shares
1983	2-for-1 stock split	19,200 total shares
1987	2-for-1 stock split	38,400 total shares
1994	2-for-1 stock split	76,800 total shares
1997	2-for-1 stock split	153,600 total shares

Chart 4.1. How 100 shares of GE stock bought in 1925 multiplied due to stock splits over the years.

Had you bought shares in only one of these companies back in the roaring 1920s, you would have had only a 25 percent chance of making any solid gains. But since you bought four different stocks, you ended up making a lot of money. The strong performance in General Electric stock compensated for the fact that the other three stocks you purchased either went bankrupt or performed terribly.

This is how diversification works. When you spread your money over a range of investments, you lessen the likelihood that any one position will kill your portfolio. Because the average fund holds more than 120 stocks or bonds, it is impossible for a fund to lose all of its value and quite possible for it to reap the gains of a GE.

But simply buying a truckload of domestic stocks via a mutual fund does not fully diversify your portfolio. To slash risk you must buy stocks from regions across the globe. The economic strength of countries throughout the world will fluctuate over an investor's life span.

In the early 1970s the U.S. was in economic distress, marred with high inflation and sagging stock prices. In the late 1980s, as the Japanese economy and stock market collapsed, the U.S. regained economic dominance. In 1994, after years of stock market buoyancy, the Mexican peso crisis took hold, rocking Latin American countries.

Economies are impossible to predict with any certainty. With the strength of a nation's stock market tied to its economy, when economic disasters take place, global markets deteriorate. This high degree of uncertainty and year-by-year volatility within and among national stock markets makes global diversification a necessity.

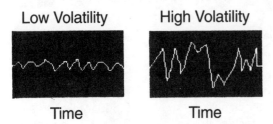

Figure 4.1. Standard deviation measures volatility over time.

From 1987 through 1998, the average domestic growth fund sported a standard deviation of 13 percent. The average European fund was slightly less volatile, with a standard deviation of 12 percent. However, a portfolio equally split between European and domestic growth funds would have had a standard deviation of just 11 percent.

Standard deviation is a popular financial statistical term used to measure how volatile a fund is—or how much a fund bounces around. The higher the standard deviation the more volatile the fund is. The graph on the right in Figure 4.1 has a higher standard deviation than the graph on the left.

Intuitively this sounds impossible. If you took two volatile funds and placed them side by side in a portfolio, the result would be one very volatile mass—or so you would think. The key lies in the correlation between the two groups of funds. Because domestic funds zig when European funds zag, they tend to cancel each other out.

For example, in 1992 European funds dropped a little over 5 percent. Domestic funds countered this with a gain of over 9 percent. In 1994 domestic funds slipped almost 2 percent, but European funds added about 3 percent.

Economies and markets throughout the world do not move in lockstep. The lack of strong intermarket correlations is a diversified investor's best friend. From a long-term perspective, diversification across different types of stocks and multiple regions of the world makes sense. It makes *a lot* of sense. But actually implementing and sticking with a diversified portfolio can be difficult.

When Japanese and Hong Kong stocks were hot in the 1980s, that is where investors wanted to be. In the 1990s, domestic large cap stocks stormed past their small cap and mid cap brothers and sisters. When a particular industry or region of the world or segment of the market is hot, investors instinctively gravitate towards those sectors and neglect the parts of the market or globe that lack appeal.

Eventually the lagging parts of the market become leaders and the leaders slip into the laggard column. Many investors again overload their portfolios with the current hot trends, and the cycle continues. To commit to diversification is to commit to a long-term, highly defined plan. The only constant in the market is change. Sage investors create a diversified financial plan and stick with it. The result is strong and smooth returns.

● ASSET ALLOCATION

Ask a real-estate agent who has just sold a crumbling old beachfront cabin for a million dollars how it was done and she will say, "Location, location, location." Ask a Sage investor how he made such handsome profits and he will say, "Allocation, allocation, allocation." Diversification is only one pillar in the Sage investment philosophy. Just as it is important to buy many stocks through mutual funds, it is imperative to spread your portfolio over different types and styles of asset classes.

Asset allocation is defined as how a portfolio is apportioned among different types of investments or asset classes, such as stocks, bonds, and cash. The types of investments you buy are even more important than the specific investments you make. For instance, buying Oracle is not as important to your portfolio as is the fact that you bought a technology stock. Stocks from the same industries, or sectors, tend to move in near lockstep. In the early 1990s, biotechnology was hot, and in the late 1990s, Internet stocks soared higher, with some rising over 1,000 percent in a year. In the beginning of the decade, it mattered little whether you bought Amgen or Biogen (both biotech stocks); or at the end of the decade, America Online or @Home (both Internet stocks). The mere fact that you bought biotechnology stocks or Internet stocks was enough to drive your portfolio to new heights.

An investor could buy Texas Instruments (a U.S. tech stock), SAP (a German tech stock), Creative Technology (a Singaporean tech stock), Galileo Technology (an Israeli tech stock), and Alcatel (a French tech stock), and technically achieve diversification. After all, this portfolio would hold stocks of various sizes from different regions from around the globe. But if the global tech sector had a serious prolonged downtrend, that portfolio would fall a substantial amount.

A Sage portfolio will hold stocks from various industries and a multitude of regions. Investing should never involve overloading a portfolio in a specific area or region. Allocation ensures that a portfolio will maximize growth by participating in sectors and regions on the rebound and minimize risk by avoiding an overconcentration in one type of stock or bond.

As your investment experiences grow, you will come to appreciate the importance of asset allocation. Some financial experts, overzealous financial journalists, and active investors lose sight of the power of allocation. It is not a difficult concept to understand or embrace; it has been proven by numerous financial academics. But in an information-driven market of buy-what's-hot-and-buy-it-now, it has become increasingly easy to stray from the axiom of asset allocation.

The following study provides the numbers and the justification for our investment rationale. Asset allocation is not a practice we developed, but it is a tangible concept that we have come to rely on for one very simple reason: In all our years as financial planners, asset allocation has never let us down. Not once. There have been periods of time when the portfolios we have developed have performed sluggishly. But in the end, asset allocation has protected us from the persistent cyclical and unpredictable motions of the market.

A study by Brinson, Singer, and Beebower found that 91.5 percent of a portfolio's return is due to asset allocation. In essence, most of the gains of a portfolio are due to the area of the market in which the money is placed, not what specific funds or stocks you choose.

Figure 4.2 illustrates the factors that influence the gains of a portfolio.

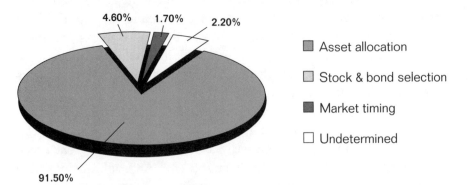

Figure 4.2. The effect asset allocation has on returns.

As you can see, fund-picking skills affect the gain of a portfolio very little over time. How you divide your assets among different asset classes (stocks, bonds, and cash), different size stocks (small and large), and different regions of the world, dictates how your portfolio will perform over time.

Accordingly, the majority of research and study we conduct in the office deals with asset allocation, not specific fund selection. After years of research and analytical study, we have developed a few powerful asset allocation models, which we implement in our clients' portfolios. These models are tweaked based on economic conditions; and the specific mix of growth, value, and blend (remember those terms from Chapter One?) funds in each class will vary based on economic conditions and forecasts. In addition, mid cap funds are included when appropriate. Until the writing of this book, these models were considered proprietary.

Class	Conservative	Moderate	Aggressive
Bonds	30%	20%	0%
Large cap	50%	40%	40%
Small cap	10%	20%	30%
International	10%	20%	30%
Total	100%	100%	100%

Chart 4.2. Portfolio asset allocation by investor type.

Not everyone has enough money to adequately diversify his or her portfolio. In those cases, we suggest that people stick with balanced funds, which provide diversification in one holding. Chart 4.3 lists Sage's Top Ten Balanced Funds as of February 1999. Check out our online site for frequent updates to this list.

Rank	Fund	Web Site
10	Founders Balanced	www.foundersfunds.com
9	McM Balanced	N/A
8	INVESCO Total Return	www.invesco.com
7	ValueLine Asset Allocation	www.valueline.com
6	Vanguard Asset Allocation	www.vanguard.com
5	Vanguard/Wellington	www.vanguard.com
4	INVESCO Balanced	www.invesco.com
3	Vanguard Balanced Index	www.vanguard.com
2	Dodge & Cox Balanced	www.dodgeandcox.com
1	Vanguard STAR	www.vanguard.com

Chart 4.3 Sage's top ten balanced funds as of February 1999.

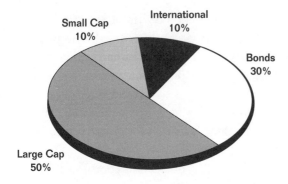

Figure 4.3. Conservative portfolio model.

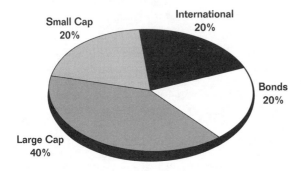

Figure 4.4. Moderate portfolio model.

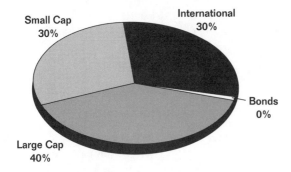

Figure 4.5. Aggressive portfolio model.

Once a client establishes what type of investor he or she is—as you did in Chapter Two—we modify the models slightly to complement the client's needs and goals. If an investor falls between categories, we merge two models together until we find the perfect match.

The allocations were calculated based on historical returns of different asset classes and correlations between asset classes. Based on our experience, the models laid out above provide superb risk-adjusted returns.

The drawback of asset allocation and diversification is that they will not maximize absolute returns. The aim of broad diversification and asset allocation is to offer solid returns with little volatility. A diversified portfolio will never provide a higher return than all other investments.

We love investing and we love watching the market gyrate on a daily basis. But we also recognize the importance of sanity. Highly concentrated, volatile portfolios are just plain tough to live with.

Illustrating that point is an e-mail we received from Taggie911, a member of the Sage community:

"Two months ago I bought my first stock. I had a hot tip that Ciena was fixing to unleash a wave of blockbuster press releases. My cost basis on the stock was $14 3/16. A few weeks later the stock was sitting at $20. I got word that the stock was headed to $60 so I held on. A few weeks later, the stock was back down to $12. Let me tell you, I was cussing something fierce. I sold the stock and bought Amazon.com at $190. Like seven days later, it dropped below $100. And get this: Ciena was back up to $18!

"I am still holding Amazon because I believe in the company, but I have learned my lesson. If I had bought a bunch of stocks or funds, I would not be so affected by the movement of one holding. I have since bought a couple of funds and a few stocks. It is nice not to have to run home every day, turn on CNBC, and wait with shot nerves for the closing prices."

That member's experience is a common one. Each and every day investors flood the Sage chat rooms to chat about their one golden stock. "Why was IBM down $18 today? Should I sell? Should I buy? What should I do? Help me, Sage!"

With a highly concentrated portfolio, you can make or lose a lot of money in a short span. Either way, it is a certainty that it will wear on your nerves and force you to make untimely, rash portfolio decisions at some point. In a later message board post, Taggie911 said that he was literally spending hours a day on the Web just staring at his stocks. He would sign on to his E*TRADE account, type in the ticker symbol for Ciena, and hit RELOAD over and over again to get up-to-the-second quotes. He even went so far as to load a scrolling ticker on his desktop that continuously updated him on the price of Ciena.

. . . Ciena +1/8 . . . Ciena +3/16 . . . Ciena –1/16 . . . Ciena –3/16 . . . Ciena +1/8 . . .

As ridiculous as this situation might sound, it is far from unusual. A portfolio can control you. When the market is suffering from a strong bout of volatility, it is easy to lose perspective and set your long-term plan aside. Learn from Taggie911 so you do not suffer the same fate.

● IMPLEMENTING THE SAGE INVESTMENT PHILOSOPHY

While it is imperative for you to create a well-diversified portfolio that is correctly allocated, you must have the discipline to follow through with your plan. As we mentioned in Chapter Two, the keys to investment success are regular investments, patience, diversification, asset allocation, tax efficiency, dollar cost averaging, and online investing. If you create a sound portfolio and have the time and patience to stay with it, you will do well—no matter what the market throws at you.

● OFFLINE VERSUS ONLINE

It is difficult to understand what is so great about researching and making your investment decisions online if you have done so in the offline world. The following timetable (see Chart 4.4) should put the advantage of online investing in perspective.

More important than the actual days and hours you will save by investing online are the various free services available on the Web, which simply do not have an offline, cost-effective alternative.

Years ago Merrill Lynch created the "wrap account," which put high-net-worth investors in touch with money managers. For a fee of 1.5 percent a year—on top of operating expenses—Merrill would man-

Step	Online	Time	Offline	Time
Screen for funds	Morningstar.net	1 hour	Wall Street Journal	1 day
Obtain fund information	Download from Web	10 minutes	Have information mailed	3 days
Invest in fund	Buy via Web broker	5 minutes	Mail check	3 days
Track portfolio	Yahoo!, AOL, Excite	5 minutes /day	Transfer info to spreadsheet	1 hour /day
Sell fund and get money	Sell via Web broker	5 minutes	Call family, have them mail check	3 days
Total		1:20 + 5 min/day		10 days + 1 hour/day

Chart 4.4. Investing online saves time.

age an investor's entire portfolio under one umbrella. One of the perks of such an account was the quarterly conference call. During this call the client could talk one-on-one with his personal money manager about what his outlook of the market was, what he was buying, and what he was selling. Essentially the money manager would pool all of his clients' money and run that money as if it was a mutual fund. Often this money manager was a mutual fund manager, but with this wrap account, unlike a mutual fund, clients had access to him on a regular basis, and carried the status symbol of having a personal money manager—even though it was far from personal.

The Internet, or more to the point, the online chat room, has duplicated this very setting. On a regular basis, shareholders can talk first-hand with their "personal mutual fund managers." Where the online world diverges from the offline world is that there is no cost involved for the privilege of chatting with the fellow who is watching your nest egg.

Technology advances increased investor mobility. Before the world became wired, the financial industry moved at a much slower pace. In order to invest in a fund from, say, INVESCO, you needed to open an INVESCO account. If you wanted to add a fund from Putnam to your portfolio, you were required to open an account with Putnam. Investing in the best offerings from various fund families required a great deal of paperwork, and frankly, hassle. Pioneers of brokerage supermarkets, which are clearinghouses where investors can buy and sell funds from numerous families, opened up their offline businesses to the Web world. Any investor with a computer and a modem was immediately exposed to thousands of fund family offerings.

No longer was an individual investor chained to a small circle of fund families. In effect, there were no more restrictions placed on the individual online investor. He was free to invest where he pleased, when he pleased, and how he pleased. We tend to take these individual empowerments for granted; but we should remember, they would have not have been possible—at least not with such speed and ease—without the technological advances of the Internet.

Puter5367: "I have become hooked with online, but today I came across what just may be the coolest investment tools site I have seen. SmartMoney.com (www.smartmoney.com) has free tools that allow you to track the Dow Jones Industrial Average, watch the hottest stocks in tons of sectors, and graphically watch what the market is doing or has done over a variety of time frames. It is like nothing you have ever seen. If you are into cool market tools, you have to bookmark this page!"

Over the coming chapters, we will teach you how to maximize your investment experience by using the various online offerings. Chart 4.5 shows an abbreviated list of online perks, which you will soon encounter.

Task	Online	Offline
Chat with fund management	E*TRADE, Sage, Yahoo!	N/A
Interaction with investors from around the world	AOL, Raging Bull, Sage, Yahoo!, etc.	N/A
Instant fund prices	All free quote services	N/A

Chart 4.5. There is no offline alternative for various online services.

If you are a first-time investor, you may never fully appreciate the ease the Internet provides; if you are a seasoned investor who is making the transition to the Web, you will never know how you got by without it.

● CHAPTER WRAP

• Portfolio diversification is used to reduce the risk of one company or geographic area bringing your portfolio down, by combining different styles and sizes of stocks from various regions. When one portion of your portfolio heads south, another part of your portfolio will counteract it with positive returns. Diversification reduces risk and makes for many restful nights.

- Asset allocation, how a portfolio is diversified into stocks and bonds from different sectors and regions, determines over 90 percent of your portfolio's gains. Assessing and monitoring the allocation of your portfolio is critical to investment success.

- Choose an asset allocation mix that is consistent with your investment profile, determined in Chapter Two. Depending upon your makeup, you should have a conservative, moderate, or aggressive mix.

- If you do not have an adequate amount to maintain a well-diversified portfolio of funds, consider a balanced fund, which has a diversified selection of stocks, bonds, and cash in one holding.

- Implement the Sage investment philosophy using the various online sources. Not only will your money spend more time in a fund and less time in the mail, the entire investment process will be cut down from a week or more to less than a day!

IN THE TRENCHES WITH SAGE

KandDGask53: Everyone says invest in stock funds. Do you guys have any suggestions?

Stephen Cohn: It depends on what your objective is. Your allocation to stock funds should change based on your risk profile, expected time horizon, and other factors. Fairly young investors who can stomach short-term volatility should have the bulk of their assets in a variety of solid growth-stock mutual funds. However, more conservative investors with a lower tolerance for risk should have less of their assets invested in equity mutual funds. Remember, nothing is guaranteed. If the market goes down, stock mutual funds go down with it. The benefit of mutual funds is the ability to diversify your assets so that you do not realize the wide fluctuation that can occur with individual stocks.

Selecting Winning Funds

SUCCESS IS TURNING KNOWLEDGE INTO POSITIVE ACTION.

Dorothy Leeds, author of *Powerspeak*

Ask the ninety Sage community volunteers how they choose all-star funds, and you will get ninety very different answers. SageVestor likes low-cost funds, SageMaybe prefers slow and steady churners, SageMitch looks for funds with strong management, and SageCalc seeks out beaten-down laggards on the verge of a turnaround. Under the Sage Online community umbrella there are literally thousands of investment ideologies. In essence, we merged the varied opinions on the Sage Online investment site with our father's traditional asset allocation approach. From the juxtaposition of new-wave online strategies with old-line financial planning, we developed a fund selection process that is a marriage of numerical and subjective analysis.

Numerical analysis, which we will discuss first, is simply a method for looking at funds strictly by the numbers. Because there are so many funds—more than ten thousand—it is impossible to look in depth into each one. Therefore, we have established certain numerical hurdles that funds must overcome to make it to the point where we will spend time analyzing their unique characteristics. Using any one of the free online databases makes this screening process easy.

Once we have run the numerical screen, we can concentrate on a more manageable group of funds. We will apply a subjective analysis to these funds. Subjective analysis requires us to look at specific attributes of funds, such as year-by-year performance, management continuity, and other characteristics that are not easily screenable using online databases.

The goal of numerical and subjective analysis is threefold:

1: Eliminate the thousands of funds that are not worthy investment choices.

2: Spend more time studying funds that are worthy of consideration.

3: Select funds in a manner that is straightforward, consistent, and based only on criteria that are relevant.

We now turn our attention to the numerical portion of the screening process.

● NUMERICAL ANALYSIS

Number crunching can be a tedious task. Fortunately, you need not have a degree in differential equations or vector calculus to be a successful fund researcher. A lot of smart people like Larry Ellison of Oracle and Scott McNealy of Sun Microsystems have created databases, spreadsheets, and online tools to do the numerical analysis for you. There is no need to recreate the wheel. Let their sweat be your equity.

Screen for Returns

The first step in sorting through the fund chaff is to eliminate the perennial laggards. Out of every four funds, three are not worth your Sage dollars. While many critics see poor mutual fund performance as a negative for investors, it is actually a hidden blessing. Screening for poor performers cuts out a huge chunk of funds. Historical laggards become future laggards. By ridding your list of potential deadbeats, you immediately cut your chances of picking a future fumbler.

Ad: "Our fund rules! It beats all other funds over all kinds of time frames."

Fine print: "Of course, this does not mean a thing since past performance has no bearing on future returns."

In the fund industry, this loud and annoying little disclaimer, "Past performance is no guarantee of future returns," is always located at the

Top Diversified No Load Funds

Year	Fund	Return
1976	44 Wall Street	46.50%
1977	Sequoia	19.90%
1978	Value Line Leveraged	27.60%
1979	20th Century Growth	74.20%
1980	Able Associates	56.70%
1981	Hartwell Leveraged	-13.20%
1982	Lindner	27.10%
1983	Tudor	28.00%
1984	Strong Investment	9.70%
1985	Vanguard High Yield	30.10%
1986	Fidelity OTC	11.40%
1987	Strong Opportunity	11.80%
1988	Mathers	13.70%
1989	Kaufmann	46.80%
1990	20th Century Vista	-15.70%
1991	Founders Discovery	62.50%
1992	Montgomery Small	9.60%
1993	Oakmark	30.50%
1994	PBHG Growth	4.80%
1995	PBHG Emerging Growth	48.50%
1996	Wasatch Mid Cap	3.60%
1997	Robertson Stephens Partners	18.10%
1998	Safeco Growth	22.20%
Average Gain Per Year		22.20%

Chart 5.1. Persistency of Performance returns from 1976 through 1998.

bottom of mutual fund advertisements, and for legal purposes is plastered all over fund Web sites, investment literature, marketing kits, and newspapers. But despite lawyers' widespread infatuation with discrediting the value of past performance, what happened yesteryear does have a bearing what will happen this year.

The "Dean of No Loads" and Sage chat regular, Sheldon Jacobs, conducted a study some years back relating past performance to future performance, which he described in his book, *Successful No-Load Investing*. Mr. Jacobs created a mythical portfolio that invested in just one fund a year.

The fund selected for investment each year was the top diversified no-load performer from the previous year. For example, if the Hippie Fund had been the top performing fund in 1973, Jacobs would have bought that fund at the start of 1974. At the beginning of 1975, he would have invested in the top performing fund of 1974, and so on. Mr. Jacobs back-tested this strategy, called "Persistency of Performance" (PoP), from 1976 to 1992 and then real-time ever since.

Had you invested $1,000 using the PoP method, over these twenty-three years you would have accumulated $99,771 after expenses. The same $1,000 in the average diversified no-load fund would have grown to only $25,884 before expenses. Not only did PoP greatly outpace the S&P 500, it also beat every single fund over this twenty-three-year stretch.

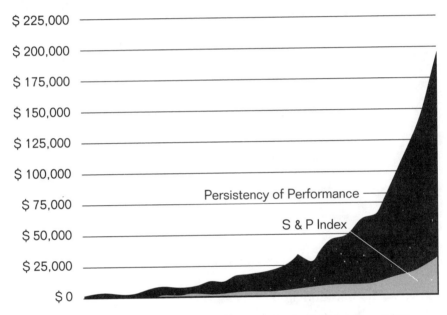

Figure 5.1. Persistency of Performance versus the S&P Index from 1976 through 1998.

If you had bought the worst fund from the previous year, the inverse of Persistency of Performance, you would have dramatically underperformed the S&P 500 Index. PoP is not a revolutionary strategy. Jacobs deserves credit for bringing it to the mutual masses, but this type of momentum investing has been a popular strategy in some circles for years.

PoP is an appealing investment strategy, but it may not fit well in a financial plan. Since asset allocation and diversification are the keys to volatility-adjusted returns, and PoP does not discriminate among large, small, growth, and value, its overall fit into a portfolio is forced. Furthermore, with the frequent buying and selling of funds required by PoP, the tax burden associated with the strategy would be substantial. So it must be used with caution—if at all.

Because past performance, to at least some extent, is indicative of future gains, we employ the past performance screen as a starting point. However, we monitor it very closely.

When you screen for returns, you should compare apples to apples. Small cap funds should be compared to small cap indexes, large cap funds to large cap indexes, and international funds to international indexes. We will get more into indexes later in the book, but the point warrants mention here because so many investors inadvertently screen all funds against one index, the widely known S&P 500 Index. Their pool of potentials is tainted from the beginning because of improper performance measures.

Screen for Expenses

Expenses have a direct bearing on performance. The lower the expenses, the greater the chance of strong returns. Because expenses vary from fund category to fund category, start with the average expense ratio of the category of funds in which you are investing. For example, if you are looking at picking up a small cap fund and the small cap expense ratio average is 1.5 percent, screen out all funds that land above the average.

Fees are considered by the academics to be the most important factor in a fund's success. Unfortunately, there is little incentive for fund families to cut fees. A feature in *Investor's Business Daily*'s "Making Money in Mutuals" sells a fund, a low-cost structure does not. Look at the ads in the *Wall Street Journal*'s "Money" section: "Top Performing Fund over the Past 10 years!!!" "Ranked Highest by Lipper," "Awarded Morningstar's Highest Rating." Sexy returns and sleek marketing garb sell funds, not low-fee structures.

Do not fall into the returns-are-everything trap. They are important, yes, but so are fees.

At the close of 1998, Sage Online conducted a study on fees. The top twenty-five performing growth funds over a ten-year period sported an average expense ratio of 1.03 percent. The twenty-five bottom performing funds had an expense ratio of 1.60 percent. There is an inverse correlation between returns and fees. The higher the fees, the lower the returns. Of course, there will always be exceptions. But in the market, like at the blackjack tables, you have to play the averages. Work with the numbers not against them.

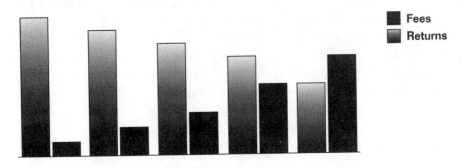

Figure 5.2. As expenses increase, returns decrease.

Early on, you undoubtedly will come across some very appealing stellar performers. Newbies, as we call beginning investors on the Sage Online site, often overlook fees in favor of supercharged returns. For a fund to be successful over a long stretch of time, it should probably have low fees.

Consider the Kaufmann fund. In the fund's first full year of operation it plunged over 37 percent, just about the worst fund in the universe. The market crash of 1987 proved to be the turning point for the hapless Kaufmann. Over the following years the fund diversified into a greater number of high-growth small cap stocks, and the fund rocketed. Once the ten-year crash anniversary rolled around, Kaufmann was the top diversified fund in the land.

The strong long-term performance was actually due to few very good years. Its more recent performance has been lackluster by the rosiest of measures.

Kaufmann, due to strong marketing muscle, ballooned from $1.9 million in 1986 to over $6 billion by 1997. The fund's expense ratio, however, barely budged as assets grew. In the late 1980s, the fund expense ratio hovered around the 2 percent mark (it was as high as 3.64 percent in 1991). By 1997, despite massive asset growth, Kaufmann's expense ratio was sitting at 1.88 percent. Over a ten-year span, the fund's assets grew by 316,000 percent, and its expense ratio dropped by only 0.12 percent.

Part of Kaufmann's early success was due to fund nimbleness, solid stock picks, and favorable market conditions. As assets grew, management failed to take responsible action and cut fees. Small cap market conditions worsened in the late 1990s, and Kaufmann's former small growth stars turned into small cap losers.

The fund, bloated with assets and hundreds of stocks, had turned into a sort of aggressive-growth index fund. But its fees were so high that it lagged its peer group's returns by a wide margin. For the three years ending 1998, Kaufmann placed in the bottom half of all small growth funds.

Kaufmann has become something of a symbol of what excessive expenses can do to performance. When a fund like Kaufmann is hot for a stretch of years, it is easy for investors to neglect the importance of fees. When tougher times come, high expenses can turn a merely average fund into a subpar performer, as was the case for Kaufmann from 1996 through 1998.

"The high costs of expenses and management fees are the biggest threat to investors. When returns of stocks return to more normal levels, these expenses will eat up investor returns."

> *Jeremy Siegel, professor of finance at the University of Pennsylvania's Wharton School, chatting on Sage*

Of course, the importance of expenses is difficult to grasp when you have $500 burning a hole in your pocket. Given two funds to choose from—one that gained 90 percent last year with an expense ratio of 3 percent, and another that gained 25 percent with an expense ratio of 0.20 percent—the newbie will usually select based on performance than fees. Do not do it. Over the long term, the fund with the lower expense ratio has a higher probability for success than the fund that did the best last year.

● SUBJECTIVE ANALYSIS

After you have screened for performance and expenses, you will have a pool of strong candidates. Selecting a fund for investment is not a choice between returns or fees. A fund must have low fees, high returns, and pass our subjective analysis test to meet Sage standards.

Subjective analysis consists of both statistical data and community-gathered information. We tweak the subjective process slightly based on the type of fund we are screening for, but essentially, it is a four-step process:

1:   Screen for management continuity.

2:   Screen to see if expense ratios have decreased as assets under management have increased.

3:   Screen for year-by-year performance.

4:   Screen through an online community.

Screen for Management Continuity

In the 1980s a fund by the name of Fidelity Magellan, managed by Peter Lynch, powered far and fast past the market. The Magellan name became synonymous with market-kicking returns. After Lynch retired, money continued to pour into the fund. Investors bought into the idea that Magellan's success was due to the family's expertise, that Lynch had been somewhat of a tool. Since Lynch's departure, however, Magellan has never come close to recapturing its former glory. This same story repeats itself every time a stud manager moves to greener pastures. As you screen for performance, make sure those gains are due to the current manager's stock-picking ability, not his predecessor's.

> "When evaluating a particular fund it is imperative that the fund's performance is due to current management."
> *Financial planner at Sage Financial Group*

Management is key to fund success. Just as golfers could not possibly duplicate the game of Tiger Woods just by using his clubs, new managers cannot exactly replicate the management style and stock-picking nuances of their predecessor. When a manager leaves a fund, that fund is destined to change dramatically. Historical performance, risk measures, and diversification characteristics are no longer meaningful. It is a new fund.

Fund families go to great lengths to assure shareholders that the family, not the manager, is responsible for a fund's actions. Their motives are obvious. Managers can, and do, leave all the time, but the family must preserve assets and grow corporate profits. If investors departed with each management shift, the flow and ebb of assets would increase fund costs and decrease the bottom line.

With so many funds vying for your dollars, you can afford to be selective. Stick with funds that stick with their managers.

Screen to See if Expense Ratios Have Decreased as Assets Have Increased

Mutual funds are first and foremost a business. Like all businesses, they have expenses. Certain expenses are fixed no matter how big or how small a fund is. As assets in a fund grow, these costs can be spread out over a greater number of assets or shareholders. We call this economy of scale.

For example, suppose a fund's costs were $100 a year. If the fund had just $1,000 in assets, the expense ratio for the fund would be 10 percent ($100 out of $1,000). If the fund assets were to grow to $1,000,000 and its expenses remained fixed, its expense ratio should decline to 0.01 percent ($100 out of $1,000,000). In reality, some expenses will continue to increase, but the total expense ratio should still decline.

This example is not any different from what is experienced in the mutual fund industry. Therefore, as a fund's assets increase, its expense ratio should decrease.

Screen for Year-by-Year Performance

Consider two funds. Fund A has gained 50 percent annually over the past three years, while Fund B has gained 45 percent annually over that span. A numerical screen would rank Fund A on the top of the other fund ten times out of ten. However, Fund B, the lower performing fund, is actually the better fund.

To get a feel for which fund is better, you need to look at year-over-year performance, volatility, consistency, risk, and fund management.

In Figure 5.3, you can clearly see that the lower performing fund was the better investment. They both ended with solid three-year gains (45 percent versus 50 percent), but Fund B's path was smooth whereas Fund A was erratic.

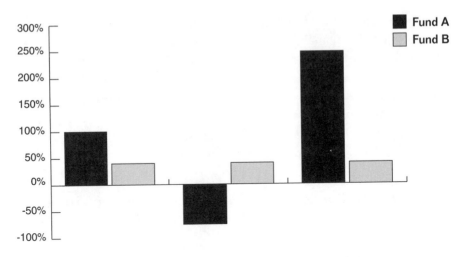

Figure 5.3. Often the lower performing fund is the superior investment.

And although the total return of Fund A would be slightly higher than that of Fund B, the difference would not compensate for the sleepless nights Fund A's year-over-year volatility would cause an investor.

Year-by-year analysis provides insight into a fund that mere numbers will not. Studying a fund's management, its performance, and its volatility will spare you the pain of jumping into or out of a fund for the wrong reasons.

Screen Through an Online Community

Screening through an online community involves both listening to the experts in chat and interacting with investors from around the world in chat rooms and on message boards. In the antiquated past, before online screening tools, we spent many hours reading annual reports and talking with fund management. While we still speak directly with the head honchos and read fund literature, the Internet has cut down the number of fund company visits we must make and increased the number of home-cooked meals we eat. Our online site allows us to chat directly with the fund managers who are making our investment decisions. In addition, we can tune in to other community members' excellent questions. This is truly revolutionary.

Jim O'Shaughnessy of O'Shaughnessy Funds highlights some of his investment strategies on Sage Online: "Price-to-sales proved to be the king of value ratios, with the most consistency on a decile by decile basis. Yet, others also worked well. Here they are in order of my preference: low price-to-cash flow, low price-to-book, and finally, low price-to-earnings ratios. In most instances, however, it works best to marry these low ratios with things like relative strength, or in the case of value stocks, high dividend yield."

Subjective analysis can also be gathered from other people's opinions. For example, on the Sage message boards you can see firsthand the importance of digging deep behind the numbers. The following was written by Sage member BnDConn555:

"Today I did something I swore I would not do five years ago. I sold my entire position in the XYZ Fund. When I bought the fund, its long-term performance and its low fees impressed me. I read the manager's book to learn more about his style.

"His book got me so interested in the fund (although I had already bought it) I decided to do some checking. It turns out most of the strong returns were due to his early years when the fund was small and invested in little-known stocks. Over the past five years or so, the fund has been a real dud. And, despite his long book ramblings of how great small caps are, he currently buys large mid cap stocks like Harley-Davidson and Borders. To top it off, the fund currently invests a ton of its assets in foreign stocks—something it did not do when returns were so good. Now it turns out he is not even doing most of the fund management (you have to dig deep in the prospectus to find this out).

"I bought this fund on what I considered some pretty solid research. But the numbers did not tell the whole story; they merely muddied the water. Had I dug a little deeper I would have never had to sell my entire XYZ holding and I would not be facing a big tax bite come April."

In addition, sometimes the best source of subjective information comes straight from the manager's mouth. When asked in a Sage chat how long he would stay with Franklin as its premier fund manager, Michael Price responded that he was in "a five-year transition period to my senior people. I will be a large investor in the funds through that period. I will always care about the funds. It is time for me to let them do much more of the stock picking and management. . . . "

It was obvious to the Sage audience that night that Price would soon step down from the helm after over twenty years of market-beating performance. Nine months later Price retired as fund manager. In this case, the impact on shareholders was minimal.

A little subjective analysis, such as reading a chat transcript, attending a chat with Price, or talking with those in the know on the Michael Price/Franklin message boards on Sage, would have saved those investors a lot of questions.

Talking with the managers firsthand can give insight into a fund that mere numbers cannot. It can also give you the little extra push you need to purchase a fund.

Jsion840 wrote on the boards that she was hesitant to buy Legg Mason Value Trust. But after chatting with William Miller, the fund's manager, she took the plunge and has not looked back.

> "I was hesitant to buy Legg Mason on the basis of its name. It is called a 'value' fund, but considering the stocks it invests in, it is growth all the way. But then I talked to Bill in chat and he laid out his investment strategy. Not only did he redefine the way I classify growth and value stocks, but also he gave me the oomph I need to get into the fund.
>
> "Essentially Miller buys stocks that trade at discount to their intrinsic value. This method of buying stocks changes the value/growth line markedly. What is important is how fast a company is growing and how that relates to its current market value. If its current value trades at a discount to what the stock is really worth when considering its growth prospects, then it is a value stock. This stock valuing method led Miller to stocks like Dell. When he bought Dell, it was at $14. A little more than a year later, it was more than $80.
>
> "I also appreciated his sense of humor and humility. When asked how he has beaten the market for so many years in a row he responded, 'Luck!' I was expecting some highfalutin sales pitch as to why his firm is so superior. Another chatter asked him what his worst investment was. He said it 'was probably an apparel company named Salant, which managed to go bankrupt twice while we owned it.'

"I appreciated the honesty in his answers. It gave me the confidence I need to invest. Now, a couple years later, Miller and my money are handily outpacing the market!"

From 1990 through 1998, William Miller's Legg Mason Value Trust beat the S&P 500 each and every year by an average margin of 6.4 percent a year. It was the only fund to beat the S&P 500 each calendar year of this time frame. Miller generally chats with Sage Online investors each quarter.

Where numerical analysis is highly defined, subjective analysis is more art than science. To do subjective grunt work you need a bit of a nose for funds. This can be developed over time, or you can use the crack analysts on Sage Online or Morningstar to do the gumshoe work for you.

Now that you have internalized the Sage investment philosophy of asset allocation and diversification and possess a basic understanding of our fund selection process, you are ready to implement our proprietary fund selection techniques within an online environment.

You may be curious why we neglected to talk about risk with respect to fund selection. The beauty of asset allocation, diversification, and the Sage fund selection process lies not only in its simplicity, but in its ability to address risk or volatility. The different portfolio models— or asset allocations—that we have laid out smooth the issue of volatility, and the fund selection process provides you with a stepwise, foolproof method of filling that model with the best possible candidates.

In the coming chapter we take this process to the Internet, allowing you to select, online, winning funds, using the Sage process of numerical and subjective analysis.

CHAPTER WRAP

- Numerical analysis quickly weeds out laggards and high-fee funds. Studies show that historical returns and low fees do matter.

- Subjective analysis requires a little more detective work than numerical analysis. Screen for management continuity, expense ratio sensitivity, year-by-year performance, and online community feedback.

🔵 IN THE TRENCHES WITH SAGE

Max742: I have heard there are more mutual funds than stocks. If this is true, then wouldn't it be easier for me just to pick up a few stocks and forgo funds altogether?

Alan Cohn: It is true there are more funds than stocks on the New York Stock Exchange. But you must remember that funds invest in stocks on the NYSE, the Nasdaq, and in the international markets. Additionally, there are many funds that invest in bonds, currencies, and hard assets like gold and platinum. If you consider all of the different individual securities throughout the world—such as Mannesmann in Germany, Ahold in the Netherlands, Argentinean bonds, and many, many others—there are a vastly more stocks and bonds than funds.

If you are considering one or two or three or four stocks versus a mutual fund, the fund will typically be safer—or, more accurately, less volatile. The alternative would be to buy twenty-five or thirty-five individual stocks, and then you would have the same effect as owning a fund. However, when you own a fund you have hired a full-time manager to work for you to search out new ideas and to actively manage the portfolio. It would be difficult for you to duplicate that thorough approach and comprehensive effort.

Screening for Success

You may not realize it, but you possess a formidable arsenal of fund selection knowledge. In fact, you are just a few hundred words away from turning that theoretical knowledge into practice. By the end of this chapter, you will be ready to do what so many others cannot do: select winning funds!

But before we jump too far into the fray, let us recap what we have talked about:

- In Chapter One we talked about different fund investments such as small and large cap funds. We also looked at stock and bond funds. We related types of funds to different risk levels.

- In Chapter Two we developed an investment profile. This profile will dictate how your portfolio will be assembled and what types of funds you will choose.

- In Chapter Three we looked at dreaded fund expenses and at different measures used to gauge a fund's value.

- In Chapter Four we discussed the effects of asset allocation and diversification. We learned that allocation determines most of the gains of the portfolio.

- In Chapter Five we discussed how funds should be chosen based on numerical and subjective analysis.

Pat yourself on the back; you know more about investing than most who have invested for years. The knowledge you have gained will drive you in the direction of success over your lifetime.

It is time to put aside the theory and get down to virtual reality. Investing on the Web is an easy and fun task. Unfortunately, we talk with investors every day who feel hopelessly lost in a sea of endless dot-coms. It is an easy trap to fall into. If you do not have a plan or a little up-front knowledge, you will waste countless hours surfing through cyber-trash. We know this fact all too well—in our early Web surfing days we would literally waste hours upon hours looking for miscellaneous pieces of financial information. Online investing has changed. It is for both the computer-savvy and the tech-adverse, and it can empower you as an investor as never before. Best of all, mutual funds are a great way to invest online.

Below is a short list of the sites you need to know to get the most out of your online investment experience. It is by no means comprehensive; such a list is impossible to compile. In fact, we describe only three forums in addition to the Sage Online site. These are the sites most referenced by our community members and most used by our staff. These sites deserve special mention for the unique resources they offer the individual investor. This list and the Internet addresses of these sites will be regularly updated on our site.

Investment sites fall into three general categories:

1: Community and Education: These sites are driven to a large extent by the community that populates them. Education provided is practical and easy for the individual investor to apply. The community aspect focuses on message board interaction, live chats with financial experts and money managers, and community commentary. Sage falls squarely into this category.

2: Commentary: Many financial sites act merely as an extension of the newspaper industry. Communication usually travels in one direction: from the experts to you. These sites are useful news and market tools—you can find news on almost any financial event on these sites—but typically offer little investor interaction.

3:   Promotional: A fair number of sites are constructed as marketing tools for financial products. Some of the better sites, like Strong On-line (www.strong-funds.com) and Vanguard (www.vanguard.com), boast unbiased educational content and expert commentary. Promotional sites vary in quality and usefulness.

In addition to the three types of sites outlined in this chapter, there are also so-called portals. These portals to the Web offer Net-goers start pages from which they can easily jump to a range of subjects, from beekeeping to photo editing to mutual fund investing. Portals such as AOL, Yahoo!, Lycos, and GO Network offer many links to investment information and commu-nity interaction.

Since the content of these portals is often the same as that contained in the sites we will soon discuss, there is no need to cover the individual portals. This does not mean they are use-less. Far from it. Portals are indispensable information sources, and you should take the opportunity to surf around a few of them to get a feel for how they are structured.

As we review our favorite sites, we talk about the strength of their offerings in these three categories. Please check out the Sage site for updates to these overviews.

● FUND INFORMATION SITES

Here are three sites, in addition to Sage Online, that we feel boast unique mutual fund information offerings. Other compelling sites, not reviewed in this book, include Quicken.com, money.com, and Smartmoney.com.

Morningstar

"Without exception I use Morningstar every day. The breadth and depth of information they provide is simply indispensable."

> *Stephen Cohn of Sage Online speaking at a fund conference*

Figure 6.1. Morningstar.

www.morningstar.com

AOL KEYWORD: Morningstar

About Morningstar: Chicago-based Morningstar is the leading provider of mutual fund information. Morningstar was founded on the premise that investment information should be widely available. Since 1984, Morningstar has created a variety of computer tools and publications with the goal of "democratizing investment information."

What It Offers: Morningstar is best known for its fund rating information. The firm ranks funds from one to five stars based on risk-adjusted performance. Specific funds and fund families typically use the coveted five-star rating as a marketing tool.

Why You Would Use It: Morningstar houses a huge database that is updated daily. For free, investors can screen for funds based on a variety of criteria such as year-to-date returns and expenses. For a small fee, the screening capabilities are expanded.

Morningstar is, far and away, the preeminent fund screening database. Later in the chapter, we will walk you through the fund selection process using the Morningstar database of funds.

Community and Education: Strong educational material that is slightly academic in nature.

Commentary: Most commentary centers around education, though there is a fair amount of timely news information.

Promotional: Morningstar offers a premium service with an expanded screening and information database.

AOL Investment Research

"Investment Research is one-stop shopping for all of my investment research."

Jennifer Carey of Sage Online

Figure 6.2. America Online's Investment Research.

AOL KEYWORD: Investment Research

About Investment Research: The Investment Research center is an outgrowth of AOL's market-leading Personal Finance channel.

What It Offers: Stock and mutual fund reports, corporate earnings estimates, financial statements, company overviews, and a modified Morningstar fund screening database.

Why You Would Use It: The screening tool allows for multiple screens in one step. For example, on Morningstar's free service you can only screen for funds that meet one specific criterion, such as three-year return. If your goal is to find no-load funds that returned more than 20 percent annually over three years, you would have to run two screens on the Morningstar site, compare the data, and keep funds that met both criteria. Investment Research allows you to accomplish this task in one step.

The advantage Morningstar has over Investment Research is its timely information. Morningstar is updated daily; Investment Research is updated monthly. This is a colossal difference.

Community and Education: No direct community or educational content. Community and education are available via promotion of and links to other sites.

Commentary: No direct commentary. Commentary is available via links to other sites.

Promotional: The site promotes various America Online content providers.

Mutual Fund Investor's Center

Figure 6.3. Mutual Fund Investor's Center.

"MFEA is an all-out advocate for the little guy."
                    BeefNOBroc

www.mfea.com

About Mutual Fund Investor's Center: This site is operated by the Mutual Fund Education Alliance (MFEA), a nonprofit trade association of no-load funds committed to the education of the investor. Alliance members in aggregate serve over 80 million shareholders and manage nearly $2.0 trillion in assets.

What It Offers: The site offers investment education material, financial planning advice, and a fund screening tool.

Why You Would Use It: At first glance, the fund screening tool (www.mfea.com/fundcntr.html) comes off as rather primitive. After a few screens, you will come to realize that its simplicity is its greatest attribute: no learning curve is required to successfully use the tool.

Community and Education: Good, albeit somewhat dry, educational content.

Commentary: There is no commentary.

Promotional: The site promotes no-load fund families.

Sage

"There is one site that has become a 'must click' for both fund shareholders and fund managers: Sage."
                    SmartMoney *magazine*

Figure 6.4. Sage Online.

AOL KEYWORD: Sage
The Sage Online site has the goal of bringing the mutual fund

industry and the mutual fund investor together in a forum where they can interact and learn from each other. We work hard not only to educate and entertain our community members about investing, but also to open the fund industry up. For a century, the mutual fund industry has remained closed off from its investors. Now through message board interaction and live chats, the fund industry is rapidly opening its doors to shareholder accountability.

It is a mutually beneficial relationship for the investors and industry experts. Fund managers have the opportunity to speak with a highly motivated group of potential investors, and our community gets to pick the best and brightest brains in the financial industry. Every week over one hundred financial leaders visit our site to chat with our audience.

We offer complete education departments—Portfolio Strategies, Sage School, Tax Center, Retirement Center—that offer comprehensive, highly focused mutual fund content. Sage also offers a number of free newsletters that discuss a myriad of investment topics. The most important feature of the site, however, is the group of highly dedicated Sages. The Sages answer all message board questions within forty-eight hours, host a number of chats each day, dispense real-time investment opinions, write candid articles, and moderate the community, keeping it a safe place for all.

The content and the community make the Sage Online site the most vibrant mutual fund site on the Internet. The unique blend of educational material, hands-on Sage assistance, and access to leading financial icons has proven to be a virtual magnet to investors. In just a couple of years, the Sage Online site has grown to become the most heavily trafficked online mutual fund forum.

● PUTTING THE PIECES TOGETHER

Okay, now it is time. It is time to put our numerical theory to the test. I hope you are pumped; we sure are. Fire up your computer and let's get going!

For the sake of simplicity we will walk a hypothetical investor through the screening process twice, first with Morningstar and then with AOL Investment Research. The mechanics may have changed by the time you read this book, but the concepts remain the same. If you are still lost, come to the Sage site, page a Sage, and we will help you find your way.

Connect to the Web.

Log on to www.morningstar.com.

Figure 6.5. Navigation banner on Morningstar.com.

Click on "Funds" on the navigation banner

When the page loads, click on "Basic Screens."
You will see a page with two drop-down menus:

- "Select fund categories . . . "

- "Select available screens . . . "

Navigate both drop-down menus until you can select the following:

- "U.S. Stock Funds."

- "Total return %: 3 Year Annualized."

Figure 6.6. View Results button.

Click on "View Results." You will see a list of thirty funds grouped into sets of five. Do not pay attention to the list just yet.

Navigate the top drop-down menu and select the following:

- "Large-Cap Value."

Click on "View Results."
You will see a list of thirty funds grouped into sets of five. These are your start funds. Print this list out, or copy and save the screen to a text file if you have no printer.

You have completed the first step in the numerical screening process. Now it is time to ferret out the lower-fee funds. You will need a pad and paper.

Print this list out or copy the list and paste it into a text file.
Preceding each fund you will see a five-letter ticker symbol that ends in an "X." This is a fund identifier. Investors use these letters to identify the funds

or stocks. Click on one of the symbols and you will be taken to a "Quicktake" page such as this:

Morningstar Quicktake Report   Add JAVLX to My Portfolio

Janus Twenty JAVLX

2.9 % INTRO % APR

◎ Get a 1-page, print-perfect Morningstar Analysis of this fund.

How Has This Fund Performed?

Growth of $10,000
- Fund: Janus Twenty
- Category: Large Growth
- Index: S&P 500

(chart showing values 31.0, 26.0, 21.0, 16.0, 10.0 across years 1996, 1997, 1998, 1999)

Annual Returns

	1996	1997	1998	08-99
Fund	27.9	29.7	73.4	15.1
+/- Cat	-8.9	4.2	39.1	5.6
+/- Index	4.9	-3.7	44.8	6.8

Data through 08-31-1999

View additional performance information

Category Rating What is this?

Worst   Best

Data through 08-31-1999

Return **High**

Risk **Average**

Fund Details

Sales Charge %
| Front: | Closed |
| Deferred: | Closed |

Expense Ratio %   0.91

Manager Name: Scott W. Schoelzel
Manager Start Date: 08-01-1997

View additional fund details information

Quick Stats

NAV (09-28-1999)	$ 63.57
Day Change	$ 0.51
YTD Return %	19.27%
Morningstar Rating	★★★★★
Morningstar Category	Large Growth
Net Assets ($mil)	25,566

View ratings details

Inside Scoop

With a huge asset base and a focused format, this offering is clearly venturing into uncharted waters. Scott Schoelzel has rung up astronomical gains here, but the fund's girth could weigh on its future flexibility. ➡ Read full analysis

What Does This Fund Own?

Style Box What is this?

(Style box grid highlighting Large Growth)

Size
Large
Medium
Small

Value Blend Growth

Investment Valuation

Style Box as of 08-31-1999
View Style Box details

Asset Allocation %		Top 3 Stock Sectors %	
Stocks	81.7	Technology	59.9
Bonds	4.6	Services	16.2
Cash	13.7	Health	9.0
Other	0.0		

Asset data through 03-31-1999
Sector data through 03-31-1999
View complete sector breakdown

Figure 6.7. Quicktake of Janus Twenty fund.

This is a basic Morningstar report. The list on the left side is broken down into four categories: "Total Returns," "Ratings and Risk," "Portfolio," and "Nuts and Bolts."

Under the "Nuts & Bolts" category, click on the "Fees & Expenses" link on the left side of the screen. The following page will load:

Quicktake	Snapshot Risk & Return Portfolio **Nuts & Bolts** News & Views Profile & Analysis

Janus Twenty

Sales Fees (Maximum Potential)		Actual Fees	
Initial (front end)	0.00%	Distribution (12b-1)	0.00%
Deferred (back end)	0.00%	Management and	0.66%
Distribution (12b-1)	0.00%	Administrative	
Redemption	0.00%	Total Expense Ratio	0.91%

Management

Fees & Expenses

Purchase Info

More Quicktakes

- ticker
- name

Figure 6.8 Nuts & Bolts report for Janus Twenty.

The above fund carries an expense ratio of 0.91 percent, which is low for the large growth category of funds. Because this fund was a top three-year performer and sports a low expense ratio, it passes the quantitative, numerical portion of our screening process.

To assemble a list of candidates for subjective analysis, go back to your original list of top performing funds. Move down the list, cross out all of the funds with expense ratios over 1.4 percent. Repeat the process, moving down the list, until you have eight to ten funds that meet the low-expense criterion. Once you have assembled a group of funds, you are ready to conduct subjective analysis. More on that in a bit.

The expense ratio cutoff of 1.4 percent is not an arbitrary one; 1.4 percent is just about the industry average. By choosing funds that fall below this mark, you are statistically increasing the odds that the fund you choose will rank high against its peers.

To assemble a full portfolio of funds, you will have to repeat the process for the large value, small growth, small value, and international categories. Do not stress, you do not have to do this in one sitting. In fact, we recommend that new investors start slowly. Pick a good large value or growth fund. Invest in it for a couple of months, then move on to an additional fund. It may take a year before you have an entire portfolio assembled. Enjoy the process and do not rush.

JennieCarr562: "In the early 1970s I jumped into the mutual fund market with both feet. I was like a kid in a candy shop. I bought it all. After sixteen months, I had a portfolio of eighteen funds. Back then, they did not offer fund supermarkets or consolidated account statements. By 1976 I had a closet full of account statements. One day I got it in my mind that I was going to do a little bit of a portfolio overhaul. Out of those eighteen funds, I only kept four. The fourteen that I tossed back were high cost, near clones of the ones I kept. If I bought those initial four and did not waste time on the others, my portfolio would have been worth several hundred thousand more today than it is. It was an expensive lesson to learn."

Before we jump into the subjective analysis portfolio of the fund selection let's step through an alternate screening tool with America Online's Investment Research.

Figure 6.9. Navigation banner on America Online's Investment Research.

Sort Order:				
Ascending	Descending		**Screen Funds**	**Reset Form**

SORT	SHOW	SCREENING ITEM	SELECT FROM MENU	
O	☐	Fund Category	Large Growth	▼
O	☐	Morningstar Stars	Not Selected	▼
O	☐	Fund Family Name		▼
O	☐	Fund Assets	Not Selected	▼
O	☐	Front End Load	No Load	▼
O	☐	Standard Deviation	Not Selected	▼
O	☐	Minimum Investment	$1,000 to $1495	▼
O	☐	Manager Tenure	Not Selected	▼
O	☐	YTD Return	Not Selected	▼

SORT	SHOW	SCREENING ITEM	LOW VALUE	HIGH VALUE
O	☐	1 Year Return		
O	☐	3 Year Return		
O	☐	5 Year Return		
O	☐	10 Year Return		

Sort Order:				
Ascending	Descending		**Screen Funds**	**Reset Form**

Figure 6.10. America Online's fund screening tool.

On America Online, go to KEYWORD: Investment Research.

You will notice that Investment Research lacks the aesthetic appeal of Morningstar. Do not be turned off by its scarcity of bells and whistles. It is a powerful database.

On the left-hand side of the screen you will notice that Investment Research has stock and fund information consolidated into one massive tool. Click on "Fund Screening."

Navigate the drop-down menus; check boxes and push buttons until your screen matches the picture in Figure 6.10. As you can see, the fund screening tool on America Online lets you display multiple screens in one fell swoop. As your familiarity with funds and fund terms increases, you will come to find that this is a powerful feature. Once you have made your page look like this one, click on "Screen Funds" on the bottom or top of the screen.

In a few seconds, a list of twenty-five funds will be presented in tabular form with the names of the funds hyperlinked.

Click on one of the hyperlinks. An intermediary page will load that will give you two options:

- AOL Investment Snapshot.

- Mutual Fund Reports.

Click on "Mutual Fund Reports" and a Morningstar fund page will present itself. This page, though visually bland, offers almost everything you would ever want to know about a fund in one easy-to-view location.

Note the fund's expense ratio under the "Portfolio Statistics" section of the page. Is it under 1.4 percent? If so, it is a keeper; otherwise, throw it back. Print out each fund that passes this test.

Head back to your list of twenty-five funds, and select another fund and look at its expense ratio. Continue this process until you have eight to ten funds with high three-year performance numbers and low expenses.

You have completed the numerical screening process on two different platforms: Morningstar and America Online. If you think they bear a resemblance to each other, you are right. As we said earlier, Morningstar is the source when it comes to fund data. America Online's fund screening database is merely a modified Morningstar database.

Okay, you have completed the database-screening portfolio of the fund selection process. It is time to move into subjective analysis. But first, take a break; you have accomplished an enormous amount in a short span. Be proud.

Subjective Test

Now we move to the subjective aspect of fund selection. This section merely involves a checklist, and you should move through it markedly more quickly than you did with the numerical screening. You will not be dealing with massive fund databases or quirky online tools. Access to the Morningstar or Investment Research site is all you need. Grab a pen and paper and let's get moving.

Gather your group of potential funds together and fire up your Web browser.

Point to www.morningstar.com (or KEYWORD: Investment Research).

Once you get to Morningstar, enter a fund ticker symbol.

Hit ENTER (or RETURN) on your keyboard. A fund "Snapshot" will load up.

Look at the "Percentile Rank in Category" line at the bottom of the page.

- Has the fund performed in the top 50 percent (a number of 50 or below) most years?

Click on the "Ratings and Risk" category on the left side of the page.

- Is its alpha, under the "Best Fit Index" column, greater than zero?

Alpha is used to measure the value added or subtracted by a fund's manager. A positive alpha generally indicates value added by fund management.

- Is its "Bear Market Decile Rank" 6 or lower?

The Bear Market Decile Rank is a measurement of how a fund holds up under poor market conditions. If a fund performs in the top 60 percent of all funds in a category, it passes the test. If you are screening for ultra-safe funds, you may want to bump the number down to 3 or lower.

Click on the "Portfolio" category. After the page loads, click on the "Sector Weightings" link on the left-hand side.

- Does the fund hold multiple sectors and have less than 40 percent of assets in all sectors?

- Does the fund have at least 80 percent of its assets in stocks?

When a stock fund holds a great deal of cash or bonds in its port-folio, it usually means one of two things: 1) management is attempting to time or anticipate the short-term swings of the market by moving in and out of stocks, or 2) management is letting cash pile up in the fund, waiting for a correction or drop in the market as an entry point. If the former is the case, the continuous buying and selling of stocks increases taxable distributions. If the latter is the case, management lacks the stock-picking abilities needed to run a successful fund. The result in both cases is sub-par performance.

Click on the "Nuts & Bolts" category.

• Is the start date of management at least three years old?

If you answered no to any of these questions, the fund in question does not pass the subjective analysis test. Throw it back and start over.

Do not be discouraged if it takes a while before you find a fund that meets all of the criteria. You need only two funds from each category—large, small, and international—so if it takes some time before you select one, do not worry.

● NEXT STEPS

If you found a fund based on the criteria but still are not completely positive it is the one for you, you should take the following steps.

Call the fund family or visit its Web site and get a prospectus on the fund.

See if the manager has visited a community site like Sage. Many managers are more than willing to talk to shareholders. Ask the manager:

How he picks stocks.

Whatever his method is—and there are many—it should be easily definable and should not include high-powered, confusing financial terms.

What were some of his better and worse picks over the past year?

He should be humble enough to admit some poor stock picks. If he claims he has not had any or cannot recall any, do not buy the fund. All investors make bad decisions, and they are always the ones most remembered.

What would cause him to buy and sell a stock?

The manager should have a clearly defined method for buying and selling stocks.

If he invests his own money in the fund.

He should invest in the fund, though this is not a deal breaker. Some managers simply have different personal investment profiles than the one the fund calls for.

Where he thinks the market is going over the next few months.

This is a trick question of sorts. No one can call the short-term swings of the market with regularity. If he has an answer other than "I do not have any idea," or something to that affect, he is not being truthful.

Get on the Web and look for chat transcripts with the fund's management. At Sage, we have transcripts archived. Other sites, like Morningstar, have interviews with fund managers that provide good subjective insight. If the manager has not chatted on a site like Sage, this is a red flag. There is no excuse for not being accessible to your shareholders.

Talk with other investors about the fund via message boards dedicated to the fund or in chats. Individual investors offer real-world experience that you will not find in a fund prospectus or on a Morningstar "Quicktake" report.

If, after doing all of this, you are still not sure if the fund is for you, leave it alone for a while and revisit later. Picking your core fund can be a daunting process. Spend time reading, researching, and talking to other investors until your comfort level increases and you find a fund to your liking.

● SCREENING SHORTCUT

The subjective analysis component of the screening process is straightforward. Getting past the numerical screen can, we understand, make for a tall task. Because of the frustration many of our community members were having in searching for suitable funds, we developed Top Ten lists. Each week on the Sage site we highlight ten funds from specific fund categories that pass the numerical and subjective aspects of the Sage screen.

The selection process we use is identical to the one outlined here. Funds are screened based on expenses and performance. The ten funds with the highest overall score (performance minus expenses, weighted equally) are ranked in descending order. The highest score receives the number one spot, the second-highest the number two spot, and so on.

Once the funds are ranked into a large spreadsheet Sage analysts conduct subjective analysis on the pool starting with fund number one. If the top-ranking numerical fund fails the subjective test, it is crossed off of the list. They work their way down the list until ten funds are found that meet both aspects of the screening process.

Once the list is compiled, a small write-up is given to each fund with noteworthy information such as sector allocation, risk level, minimum investment, and expenses. Top Ten lists for every fund category have been compiled and archived on the Sage site at KEYWORD: SageTopTen.

Using the online fund selection tools described in this chapter, Sage compiled a list of the Top Ten Large Cap Funds in February 1999 (see Chart 6.1). This list may no longer be valid, but here is what we came up with at the time:

Rank	Fund	Web Site
10	Vanguard 500 Index	www.vanguard.com
9	American Century Equity Growth Investments	www.americancentury.com
8	Vanguard Health Care	www.vanguard.com
7	Fidelity Export & Multinational	www.fidelity.com
6	Fidelity Dividend Growth	www.fidelity.com
5	Janus Growth & Income	www.janus.com
4	Wilshire Target Large Growth Investor	www.wilshire.com
3	Vanguard Growth Index	www.vanguard.com
2	Reynolds Blue Chip Growth	www.reynoldsfunds.com
1	Legg Mason Value Trust	www.leggmason.com

Chart 6.1. Sage's Top Ten Large Cap Funds in February 1999.

The Top Ten list should be used as a starting point, not the deciding factor in whether or not to purchase a fund. The only way to become a successful long-term investor is through education. You need to know how to pick funds on your own. You need to know if a fund is right for you. The Top Ten lists can save you time and point you in the right direction, but they should not be treated as your answer to investment success. Develop your own skills.

● CHAPTER WRAP

- To make money online you need to get connected to helpful investing sites. Most sites have a combination of community and education, commentary, and promotion. The best sites offer investment education, community interaction, and timely information. They bring together like-minded individual investors that share knowledge and bounce investment ideas off of each other.

- Use Morningstar and/or AOL Investment Research to drastically cut down the workload involved in fund selection. Screen for performance and then fees using these powerful online databases.

- Talk with management via an online chat to get insight into the fund that the numbers simply do not supply.

- Cut your screening time down by using Sage Top Ten lists. Treat them as a starting point, not an endorsement.

In this chapter, you transformed theory into practice. You now know how to screen for winning funds using online tools and offline checklists. You are well on your way to becoming an expert in fund selection—the person family members will come to for investment advice.

But picking individual funds is just one aspect of creating a solid long-term portfolio. In the upcoming chapter, we will move from single fund selection to portfolio creation. We will answer the following questions:

How do you select a winning mix of funds for a portfolio?

How do you know if your portfolio is well diversified?

How can you create a low-risk, high-return portfolio?

● IN THE TRENCHES WITH SAGE

PegandRck689: Hey, I need help. About a year ago, I selected what I thought was a great fund. It turns out I was way off. How can I avoid making this mistake in the future?

Stephen Cohn: In the future, use online tools to select your funds. Before investing in the fund, ask an online community about their thoughts on the fund. This real world experience may be just the tool you need!

Designing Your Fund Portfolio

EVERY MAN IS THE ARCHITECT OF HIS OWN FORTUNE.

Appius Claudius

In the past two chapters, we have focused heavily on the cornerstone concepts of diversification and asset allocation. Because diversification will define how risky your portfolio will be and asset allocation will determine the majority of your investment returns, we consider mastery of these two concepts to be most important. A nondiversified portfolio is doomed to endure constant volatility. Poorly allocated assets will undoubtedly result in lackluster performance.

Simply allocate and diversify well, and your portfolio is almost assured success. But how do you assemble a portfolio that can withstand the rigors of day-to-day market wear?

COMMON MISCONCEPTIONS

"Fundamental progress has to do with the reinterpretation of basic ideas."

Alfred North Whitehead, British mathematician, logician, and philosopher

Incompetence is not always to blame for an unsuccessful portfolio; many highly competent investors have created disastrous portfolios. Every day on the Sage site we see common mistakes that effectively kill a portfolio before it has a fighting chance. Understand and internalize these common investor misconceptions, and you will increase the odds that the portfolio you create will indeed be a moneymaking machine.

S&P 500 Index Funds Are All-In-One Portfolios

Index funds have been available to investors since 1976, when the First Index Investment Trust was introduced. The name was later changed to Vanguard Index Trust and finally to Vanguard 500 Index Trust Portfolio. From 1977 through 1979, it averaged in the bottom quarter of funds. Finally in 1983, the fund had a breakout year, gaining 21 percent and outpacing 65 percent of funds. Since that time the fund has not looked back. From 1995 through 1998, the fund outgunned over 90 percent of all funds.

Not surprisingly, its popularity exploded. From 1995 through 1998, assets in the fund jumped over $60 billion, and it is regularly one of the hottest-selling funds in the industry. Vanguard 500's success led to an exponential increase in the number of index funds offered. The bandwagon began to roll, and almost every fund family jumped on.

The indexing boom had mostly positive effects, with investors buying low-cost funds with strong performance. The popularity of S&P 500 Index funds, however, led many investors to a dangerous conclusion. The S&P 500 Index constitutes 70 percent of the U.S. market's value. Investors unwittingly assumed that this equaled a fully diversified portfolio. Nothing could be farther from the truth.

The S&P 500 Index is a market-cap-weighted index, which means large stocks such as General Electric and Microsoft have more bearing on the index's return than do smaller stocks such as Sherwin-Williams and Whirlpool. As larger stocks outpaced smaller stocks in the late 1990s, the S&P 500 Index became increasingly skewed towards larger stocks.

By the end of 1998, the largest fifty stocks accounted for over 50 percent of the index. The smallest fifty stocks, by comparison, accounted for less than 1 percent of the index. So, while technically there are five hundred stocks in the index, the vast majority of the S&P 500 Index returns were driven by the largest stocks in the market. This supposed all-encompassing index, in actuality, only represented a sliver of the market.

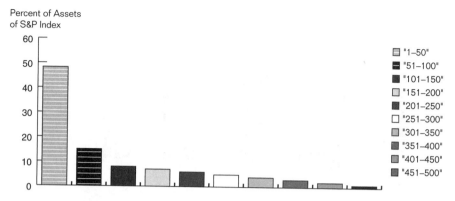

Figure 7.1. Ten groups of fifty stocks in the S&P 500 Index are ranked in descending order in terms of market cap. The largest stocks in the S&P Index have the most bearing on its performance.

During times when small cap stocks fared well, the S&P 500 Index trailed by a considerable amount. Investing via an index fund, such as one that mirrors the S&P 500 Index, results in only limited exposure to the entire market. Even though it does include some small and mid cap stocks as well as several international holdings, it is not a broad market barometer and does not offer adequate diversification.

Value Investing Is Safe Investing

There is a longstanding battle for supremacy between value and growth investors. Both groups possess vastly different investment philosophies and have a fair amount of disdain for each other. The value investor is seen as highly intelligent and analytical. The growth investor is viewed as somewhat roguish with an aggressive demeanor.

Likewise, growth and value funds bear little resemblance to each other on a day-to-day basis. Growth funds are generally more volatile because they favor stocks that are heavily traded and wildly popular. Value managers stick with off-the-beaten-path, occasionally distressed companies.

The daily, even monthly, divergent paths between the two types of funds—with growth funds all over the place and value funds relatively sedentary—has led many market watchers to conclude that value funds are the safer investments. As a result, safe haven seekers flock to value funds over their growth counterparts.

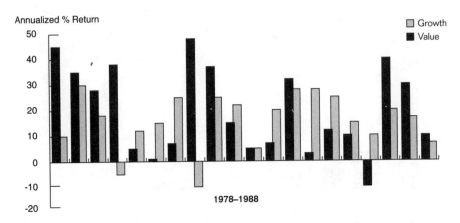

Figure 7.2. Growth and value funds move in and out of favor. (Historical data obtained from Morningstar Principia CD-ROM Research Database.)

This seems intuitively to be a wise move. However, it actually increases risk because the overall diversification of the portfolio is reduced. As Figure 7.2 indicates, value has had more than its share of down years.

In the 1990s, value funds were heavy in financial, real estate, and energy stocks, and light in technology and health care–related stocks. Financial and real estate stocks, though normally stable, can falter drastically during times when inflation is a threat, and energy stocks can do poorly as the result of global economic events, such as a change in oil production rates. When inflation rears its head, the entire market tends to fall. But technology and health care stocks are apt to hold up better than their financial siblings. As a result, in periods of economic strength when inflation is a threat, growth stocks often fare well and value stocks falter. Even during times of economic slow-down, growth stocks, particularly health care stocks, do well because of the strong demand for pharmaceutical products regardless of the economic state.

And because value stocks are often distressed companies in financial trouble, the risk of an earnings shortfall or a financial fiasco is that much greater. However, value stocks are not without merit. When picked by a skillful hand they can increase portfolio returns while decreasing volatility. But safe havens they are not.

The Greater the Risk, the Greater the Return

An unfortunate notion has permeated the investment community for a full century and has led many investors into hairy situations: the idea that increased risk produces increased return.

When it comes to stocks versus bonds, the risk-reward relationship holds. Stocks are much riskier than bonds and return much more. But that's where the risk-reward relationship ends.

Different types of stocks carry different risks. But higher risks do not necessarily correspond with higher returns.

Consider small and large cap stocks. Over the 20th century, small caps have greatly outperformed their larger siblings with more risk. But for the past twenty years or so, small caps have lagged large cap stocks by a huge amount. In effect, small cap investors have taken on about 12 percent more risk annually (as measured by the standard deviation of small and large cap stocks) and have given up more than 6 percent annually in returns.

Voicing frustration over the lack of returns generated by small caps, James O'Shaughnessy of the O'Shaughnessy Funds said during a Sage Live Event, "It has been a long and lonely drought for small stocks. Even though history shows that small capitalization stocks outperform large stocks over almost all long periods of time . . . there are some long periods where the patience of Job is required."

The same scenario plays out in other regions of the market. International and emerging market stocks, considered the riskiest of all stock investments, have posted horrible gains relative to other types of stocks.

In general, large stocks are more stable than smaller and emerging stocks. And in theory, small stocks and stocks from emerging countries should outperform large, slow-growing stocks. But theory does not equate to reality.

Countless investors have poured billions of dollars into small cap, international, and emerging market funds in hopes of outperformance. The result has been missed gains that can never be recaptured. Only one side of the risk-reward relationship holds up in the market. Small,

Low Risk High Return	High Risk High Return
• Well-Diversified Portfolio	• Large Stocks
• Bonds	• Small Stocks • International • Emerging Market
Low Risk Low Return	High Risk Low Return

Figure 7.3. The right portfolio blend can result in high returns and low risk.

international, and emerging market stocks are riskier than larger companies. But that has not always resulted in increased performance. Do not create a portfolio loaded with risky funds in hopes of market-beating returns.

Global Diversification Can Be Achieved Through Large Cap Exposure

The massive rise in large cap U.S. stocks has resulted in market strategists reevaluating the role of international diversification. Many have concluded that international diversification can be achieved through domestic investments.

The thinking goes like this:

- Large U.S. stocks generate most of their revenues from overseas operations.

- An investment in U.S. multinationals, as they are called, is an indirect investment in overseas markets.

- Therefore, investors need not waste time investing directly in foreign stocks when they can achieve adequate foreign diversification by investing in U.S. multinationals.

The first two points make a lot of sense; but the third misses the mark. The purpose of international investing is not only foreign company exposure; it is foreign market exposure. The distinction sounds small, but it is important.

International markets do not correlate perfectly with U.S. markets. This loose intermarket connection acts as a buffer for a portfolio. If U.S. stocks fall, foreign stocks will not follow in lockstep.

Take a stock like Coca-Cola as an example. Coca-Cola generates about 80 percent of its revenue outside of the U.S., yet it trades on the New York Stock Exchange. When the domestic market moves dramatically up or down, Coca-Cola's stock follows. It does not matter that Coca-Cola is to some extent an international corporation. The market treats Coca-Cola like all other stocks and will send it spiraling or surging, depending on the prevailing market mood.

Loose market-to-market and nation-to-nation correlations mean that direct foreign investments dampen volatility. There is no substitute for overseas diversification. Its role is portfolio enhancement through risk reduction. Investing solely in domestic multinationals may result in increased returns but at the cost of vastly increased portfolio risk exposure.

The most common investment errors are the result of a lack of time and attention. Many seasoned investors have spent years in the market, plugging along at a snail's pace, because they have never taken the time or made the effort to look at investing with a fresh eye. The world is a dynamic place, and the fund industry is no different. Rules that held many years ago no longer apply. Investors who continually scrutinize how they invest are the most successful.

Chart 7.1 summarizes the mistakes in thinking many investors commit:

Misconception	Fact
S&P 500 Index is all you need: The index holds 70 percent of the market. Why would you need anything else?	Small caps and mid caps are not represented; the index focuses only on the largest stocks on the domestic market.
Value investing is safer than growth investing: Value funds do not bounce around as much as growth funds, therefore risk-conscious investors should load up on value funds.	Growth funds, though more volatile than value funds over short spans of time, work together with value funds to reduce overall portfolio volatility. A portfolio of only value funds will be more risky than a portfolio of both value and growth funds.

Misconception	Fact
High risk results in higher reward: To maximize gains you should overweight your portfolio in risky small caps and emerging market funds.	Small cap and emerging market funds carry much more risk than larger cap domestic stocks, but that has not always resulted in greater rewards. In fact, oftentimes large caps have greatly outpaced these riskier funds.
International exposure can be obtained through domestic large caps: Because large U.S. companies generate the majority of their revenues from overseas operations, an investment in these companies is an investment in overseas markets.	Domestic large caps trade on domestic stock exchanges and are subject to domestic events, such as political turmoil and stock market crashes. International funds shield investors from U.S. market exposure and therefore reduce portfolio risk.

Chart 7.1. Common investment misconceptions.

● CHOOSING YOUR NEXT FUNDS

Now that we have talked about potholes in thought many investors fall into, you are ready to fully Sage your portfolio. In a moment, you will chose a large cap value or growth fund for investment. In Chapter Six you selected your core fund, and your portfolio looks like either Figure 7.4 or 7.5. Remember, the Morningstar box pictorially tells what size stocks and what type of stocks a fund invests in. A darkened box in the upper right-hand corner indicates a fund is large growth. A darkened box in the upper left-hand corner indicates a fund is large value.

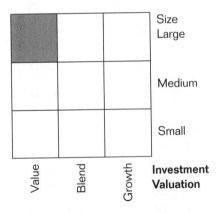

Figure 7.4. Large value style box.

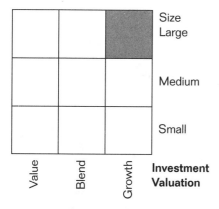

Figure 7.5. Large growth style box.

Now you will build a well-diversified portfolio around your core holding.

In the first few chapters, we dug deep into the theory behind asset allocation and diversification. Remember, at the center of successful portfolio creation is asset allocation. We will spend time selecting funds here, but the result—the portfolio—is more important than the specific funds you choose. You do not have to select the best funds in each category to make your portfolio a winner. So, do not stress.

It is time to find a match for your first fund. The selection process you will follow is similar to the steps you took when selecting your first fund.

Connect to the Web.

Log on to www.morningstar.com.

Click on "Funds" on the navigation banner

When the page loads, click on "Basic Screens." You will see a page with two drop-down menus:

- "Select fund categories . . . "

- "Select available screens . . . "

Navigate the drop-down menus until you see the following:

- "U.S. Stock Funds.

- "Total return %: 3 Year Annualized.

Click "View Results."

Navigate the top drop-down menu until you see one of the following:

- "Large-Cap Value" if your core fund is a large growth fund.

- "Large-Cap Growth" if your core fund is a large value fund.

Click "View Results."

Click on the ticker symbol of the first fund on the list.

A fund "Snapshot" page will load on your Web browser.

Under the "Nuts & Bolts" category, click on the "Fees & Expenses" link on the left side of the screen.

Does the fund have an expense ratio below 1.4 percent? If it does, the fund passes the quantitative screening process. If its expense ratio is higher than 1.40 percent, cross the fund off your list of potentials.

Head back to the list of the thirty top performing funds. Conduct the numerical screening process on each fund until you have eight to ten funds that have passed the screen.

The subjective portion of the fund selection process deviates slightly from the original test you conducted to find your core fund. The core fund you chose worked out to be an ideal offering, the fund around which you will build your portfolio. For this reason it is held to a higher standard than the other funds you will chose, so the subjective test varies slightly.

To pass the subjective test, your core fund had to have the follow characteristics:

It is broadly diversified into many sectors.

It has performed well in down markets.

It has had consistent performance.

It invests nearly all of its assets in stocks.

The remaining funds we select will not be held to quite the same standard. Because your core has the above-described attributes, it will offset the deficiencies found in the other funds you select.

For example, suppose the next fund you choose is heavy in technology. If this were your only fund holding, your portfolio would be subject to a great deal of risk. When the technology sector heads south your entire portfolio would dive with it. But because of your core holding, the poor performance of your tech-heavy fund will be offset by the broad sector diversification of your core fund.

Remember that you are assembling a portfolio based on asset allocation. The style boxes provided by Morningstar do most of the mathematics for you. So long as you assemble a portfolio of decent funds around your core from a variety of style boxes (large value, large growth, small value, small growth, international), you are virtually assured a successful portfolio.

Now, retrieve the list of eight to ten funds that passed the numerical portion of the Sage screen and apply the following subjective test.

Subjective Test

Click on the "Ratings and Risk" category at the top of the page.

- Is its alpha, under the "Best fit index" column, greater than zero?

Click on the "Portfolio" category. After the page loads, click on the "Sector Weightings" link on the left-hand side.

- Does the fund hold less than 60 percent of assets in each sector?

Click on the "Nuts & Bolts" category.

- Is the start date of management at least three years old?

If you answered yes to all of these questions, you have found your second fund. If one or more of the answers was no, cross off the fund and move to your next candidate.

At this point, you have selected two large cap funds: one growth and one value. When you put them together in a portfolio, the style box is transformed into what is called a large blend. A blend fund, as the name implies, is merely a marriage of growth and value stocks under one portfolio.

Intuitively you would think blend results in bland, or average, returns and risk. However, in this case, the sum is greater than its parts. In 1981 large growth stocks (represented by the Wilshire Large Growth Index) dropped 10.9 percent. Large blend stocks (represented by the

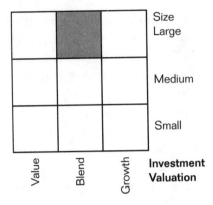

Figure 7.6. Large blend style box.

average of the Wilshire Large Growth Index and the Wilshire Large Value Index) dropped less than 1 percent. During 1993 large growth stocks dropped a little over 0.5 percent. Large blend stocks gained over 6 percent. In 1990 large value stocks (represented by the Wilshire Large Value Index) slid over 7.5 percent; large blend stocks lost just 3.6 percent. The same result repeated itself in 1994 when large value stocks dropped almost 4.5 percent, whereas large blend stocks lost less than 1 percent.

Famous value and growth fund managers frequently define their style in Sage chats.

Michael Price, former manager of Mutual Series, on value investing: "A value investor should be a person who works on what the intrinsic value of a business is and ways to buy a business at a 40 percent discount to its intrinsic value because of some bad news or some event like a down day in the market."

Doug MacKay, assistant manager of White Oak Growth Stock, on growth investing: "We believe strongly that technology is single-handedly enabling the domestic economic environment of rising earnings we see today: strong economic growth with minimal inflation and virtually no pricing power. It comes as no surprise that the U.S., given our massive investments in inventions in technology, remains economically vibrant and the engine that is driving the rest of the world in terms of economic growth."

Placing two dissimilar investment styles side by side in a portfolio—in this case large cap growth and large cap value stocks—results in a dramatic reduction of risk, or as financial types say, increased downside protection. The above example only deals with large cap stocks. Just imagine the risk reduction a portfolio would enjoy when small cap and international funds are thrown into the mix.

Choosing Small Cap Funds

Now that you have two large funds in hand, it is time to select small cap funds. The process of selecting small cap funds is similar to the process you just stepped through when selecting your second fund.

Small cap funds invest in stocks that have market capitalizations of about $1 billion or smaller. In the 1990s small cap growth funds invested the majority of their assets in technology (MEMC Electronic Materials, for example), health care (Capital Senior Living), and service (APAC Teleservices) stocks. Small value funds generally preferred financial (Horizon Group Properties), energy (Titan Exploration), and industrial cyclical (Quaker Fabrics) stocks.

We will start with a small cap growth fund. Of all the funds you will choose, small growth funds are the most risky—even more risky than international funds. The small cap growth universe offers a broad range of funds, with a few very poor funds, a majority of average funds, and a few very good funds. High volatility and rapid gains and losses are characteristic of small cap growth investing. It is not uncommon for a fund to outpace all other small cap growth funds in one year, only to be outpaced by all the following year. Due to the rapid turnarounds common in this type of fund, the standard three-year performance measure used in the numerical portion of the screening process should be pushed out to five years. This lessens the likelihood that any one year will have extreme effects on total performance measures.

In 1997 American Heritage jumped 75 percent, outgaining all other small growth funds. The following year Heritage took a nosedive, losing 61 percent, bad enough to put the fund in last place in the small growth category.

From 1993 through 1995, Govett Smaller Companies surged 245 percent compared to a gain of 62 percent from the average small cap growth fund. Over the next three years Govett slumped 31 percent compared to a gain of almost 50 percent by the average small cap growth fund. In each case, the Sage numerical screening process for small growth funds would have eliminated these funds as potential investments. American Heritage's strong year was a one-time shot, preceded and succeeded by weak returns; and Govett lacked five-year performance numbers.

As you screen for small cap growth funds, keep a keen eye out for unusual performance. When you encounter funds with erratic performance, cross them off of your list. Inconsistent performance is usually a harbinger of trouble ahead. With this thought in mind, let's screen for small cap growth funds.

Log on to www.morningstar.com.

Click the "Research" category.

When the page loads, click the "Fund Selector" category.

On the following page navigate the drop-down menus until "U.S. Stock Funds" shows in the first drop-down menu and "Total return %: 5 Year Annualized" shows in the second drop-down menu. Click "View Results."

When the next page loads, navigate the drop-down menu until you see "Small-Cap Growth." Click "View Results."

Navigate your way through the following funds until you find eight to ten that have expense ratios of 1.4 percent or lower, just as you did with the large cap growth and large cap value funds.

Once you have your funds in hand, conduct the subjective portion of the Sage screens. If you can answer yes to all of the following questions, you have your small cap growth fund.

Is its alpha, under the "Best fit index" column, greater than zero?

Does the fund hold less than 60 percent of assets in each sector?

Is the start date of management at least five years old?

The only screening change we made from large cap funds dealt with management tenure (to five years from three years) and total return (again, to five years from three years). We extended the length of management and annualized return to reduce the likelihood that one or two years would affect total return results and thus lead you into an unworthy or inconsistent fund. Also, it is important that current management is responsible for the strong five-year results.

Now that you have chosen a small cap growth fund, navigate your way back to the "Fund Selector" page. Change "Small-Cap Growth" to "Small-Cap Value" in the second drop-down menu and run through the dual screens to select a small cap value fund.

Once you complete the second small cap screen, your portfolio is almost created. In fact, you only need to select one more fund—an international fund—before your portfolio becomes fully Saged. But before we begin the international selection process, which will differ from domestic fund selection, we need to touch upon mid cap funds.

You might have seen reference to the mid cap category as you perused different investment sites. Mid cap funds are an odd bunch in that very few funds are pure mid cap funds. By definition mid cap stocks have market capitalizations between $1 and $5 billion. In a market where the size of companies ranges from a few million to over one half trillion dollars, mid cap stocks represent a tiny sliver of the overall market of stocks. Most mid cap funds are merely hybrid funds, holding large and small cap stocks. The resultant median market capitalization of these hybrid funds places them in the mid cap category, even though many of them hold relatively few mid cap stocks.

When you buy a large cap growth and a large cap value fund and put them together in a portfolio, you essentially end up with one large cap blend fund. Likewise, when you buy a small cap growth and a small cap value fund and put them together in one portfolio, you have what amounts to one small cap blend fund. Now, if you take that large cap blend fund and place it in a portfolio with the small cap blend fund, you are left with a portfolio that is basically one very large mid cap blend fund.

Adding mid cap funds to the portfolio would only duplicate what you have already created.

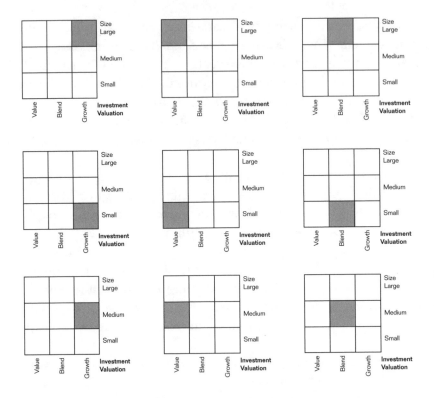

Figure 7.7. As you assemble funds from various categories and styles, your final portfolio will resemble a mid cap blend fund.

Choosing an international fund is the final step in your fund selection. For many years, international investing was considered an integral part of a well-constructed portfolio. Poor performance, political instability, high volatility, and high expenses in the late 1990s prompted many seasoned investors to question the validity of international inclusion. The reason investors brought into question the usefulness of overseas investments is that the intended function of global and international funds was not clearly understood.

True, international funds often offer higher volatility with lower returns than their domestic counterparts, but this should not fool investors into thinking that they are meaningless investments. It is important to keep one point in mind before you invest in an international or global fund.

- International funds will not usually increase the returns of your portfolio. The benefit of an international fund lies in volatility reduction. Because international markets do not flow in perfect harmony with the domestic market, they act as a hedge, countering domestic stock market movements.

Ideally, international markets will rise when domestic markets fall and vice versa. When this happens to a well-diversified portfolio, the overall portfolio remains relatively stable. Unfortunately, there is a partial correlation between the U.S. and international markets, so the markets often, but not always, rise and fall in tandem and do so in varying degrees. Given that there is a slight correlation, no portfolio composed of international and domestic funds is immune from instability. However, the effects of volatility can be greatly reduced with the inclusion of an international or global fund.

Consider how the portfolios in Chart 7.2 fared from 1987 through 1997. Standard deviation, as you may recall, is a measure of volatility. The higher the standard deviation, the more a portfolio has bounced around. For example, Portfolio A is more than two times more volatile than Portfolio C. On a day-to-day and year-over-year basis, Portfolio C would move up and down considerably less than the other two portfolios.

	Portfolio Holdings	Standard Deviation
Portfolio A	100% Vanguard 500 Index	14.33
Portfolio B	100% Vanguard International Growth	15.36
Portfolio C	60% Vanguard 500 Index	
	40% Vanguard International Growth	5.97

Chart 7.2. Volatile funds can work together to create a tame portfolio.

By adding a more volatile component (an international fund) to a domestic fund (in this case Vanguard 500 Index), the volatility of the overall portfolio is reduced. It is important to add enough international exposure to bring volatility down to a comfort zone. International exposure in the neighborhood of 20 to 30 percent is generally considered suitable.

We have talked about global and international funds interchangeably, but in fact, they are distinct types of funds. Many investors struggle to understand the difference between global and international funds and how to choose between the two for inclusion into a portfolio. In everyday conversation, the words *global, international,* and *worldwide* are used synonymously. We say that IBM is a global company, that the United States is an international trendsetter, that Michael Jordan is a worldwide hero.

Within the mutual fund industry, *global* and *international* have specific meanings. A global fund invests anywhere in the world. It might own stocks in Texas; it might own stocks in Thailand. Wherever opportunity presents itself, a global fund will show interest. An international fund invests anywhere in the world outside of the United States. Thailand, yes, Texas, no. You can see that the distinction between global and international funds comes down to the ability to invest in the United States.

Knowing the difference, it is relatively easy to choose between investing in a global or an international fund. Because you have the domestic investment landscape covered many times over, there is no need to select a global fund, unless that is the only way to gain access to an excellent manager, such as Helen Young Hayes of Janus Worldwide.

Choosing an International Fund

The international fund you choose will play a defining role in your portfolio. Because its sole function will be to counteract movements in the U.S. stock market, do not buy into an international fund with hopes of ultra-strong performance. International funds generally have higher expense ratios than domestic funds, and over the long term will likely return less than their domestic counterparts. Nevertheless, not just any old international fund will do.

The ideal international fund is broadly diversified across a number of foreign countries. While we favor more developed regions, such as European countries, your foreign holding should include at least a spattering of developing country stocks. Mature countries have historically performed at about par with the U.S. market. The market success of underdeveloped countries varies greatly, with some vastly outperforming the U.S. and others vastly underperforming. Performance is merely a side issue when dealing with emerging market stocks. Stocks from underdeveloped countries have only a moderate correlation with domestic stocks, whereas stocks from mature regions of the world have a relatively strong correlation with domestic stocks.

Therefore, it is important that your international fund selection holds a broad range of stocks from many countries. An adjustment for this will be made in the subjective part of the Sage screening process.

The numerical rules for selecting an international fund are the same as are used when selecting large cap funds: strong three-year performance and an expense ratio below 1.4 percent. The subjective portion of the screening process, however, differs markedly from the screens we have run thus far. The most important aspect of international fund selection is broad diversification. The subjective test will ensure that the fund you choose will hold stocks from a variety of regions.

Subjective Test for International Funds

Click on the "Ratings and Risk" category at the top of the page.

- Is its alpha, under the "Best fit index" column, greater than zero?

- Is the Sharpe ratio greater than zero?

The Sharpe ratio is used to measure a fund's risk-adjusted performance. The higher the Sharpe ratio, the better the risk-adjusted returns. Because international funds are quite volatile, we use the Sharpe ratio to eliminate poor performing, excessively volatile funds that don't provide a return that justifies their risk.

Click on the "Portfolio" category. After the page loads, click on the "Sector Weightings" link on the left-hand side.

- Does the fund have exposure in at least three of the following regions: Europe, Japan, Latin America, or the Pacific Rim?

- Does the fund have less than 65 percent of its assets in each region?

- Under "Country Exposure Summary" are there more than four countries listed?

- Does the fund hold no more than 20 percent of its assets in any one country?

Click on the "Nuts & Bolts" category.

- Is the start date of management at least three years old?

Cycle through your list of candidates until you find a fund that is a

"yes" in each subjective category. When you find an "all-yes" fund, you have found your international selection.

As a final check on all of your fund selections, you should take the opportunity to visit an online fund community and converse with investors on the message boards and in chats that currently hold the funds that you are considering buying.

Now that you have selected a group of funds, it is time to put them all together in one diversified portfolio. The results from the investment profile test you completed in Chapter Two describe whether you are an aggressive investor, moderate investor, or conservative investor. Given your investment type, all that's left to do is to allocate your group of funds into the right portfolio. Chart 7.3 illustrates the model you should apply to create your portfolio.

Class	Conservative	Moderate	Aggressive
Bonds	30%	20%	0%
Large cap	50%	40%	40%
Small cap	10%	20%	30%
International	10%	20%	30%
Total	100%	100%	100%

Chart 7.3. Sage model portfolios.

You can see that the conservative portfolio calls for a bond fund, yet we have not talked about bond fund selection. Over the long term, you can expect bond funds to gain 6 percent a year. A superb fund will gain as much as 7 percent on a yearly basis; a poor fund will gain as little as 5 percent a year. The range in returns between good and poor funds is incredibly thin. Active management of a bond fund is likely to add little, and what it does add will be offset by expenses. For the bond category we suggest you choose a low-cost index fund such as Fidelity U.S. Bond Index, Vanguard Total Bond Market Index, Schwab Total Bond Market Index, or a similar fund.

There are four ways you can implement the desired allocation: lump sum, partial average, cycle average, or asset build.

1: Lump Sum: If you have a large sum of money and can meet the minimum initial investments for all funds, you could create your portfolio instantly. For example, if you were an aggressive investor with $50,000, you could put $10,000 into each fund in the portfolio. Lump-sum investing is ideal for high-net-worth investors with a long-term holding period.

2: Partial Average: Initial investments are typically $2,000 per fund, with a range from $0 to over $10,000. However, many funds will allow investors into the fund for a lesser amount if the investor agrees to make consistent fund purchases until the account minimum is reached. For example, T. Rowe Price Dividend Growth carries a minimum of $2,500. Investors can circumvent the minimum by using an automatic investment plan (AIP) and contributing $50 on a regular basis until the account balance reaches $2,500.

   Suppose you are a moderate investor with $500 a month to invest. Using an AIP approach, you could put $200 (40 percent of $500) in the large cap portion of your portfolio, $100 (20 percent of $500) in the small cap portion of your portfolio, $100 (20 percent of $500) in the international fund, and $100 (20 percent of $500) in the bond fund. This would allow you to achieve a model allocation from the outset. The partial average investment is appropriate for investors starting from scratch with no assets.

3: Cycle Average: Because many banks charge for automatic drafts, it can be costly to have five withdrawals deducted from a checking or savings account on a monthly basis. Most funds allow quarterly, as well as monthly, investments drawn from your bank account. To cut down on the total number of transactions, invest in different funds at different times.

   If you were an aggressive investor with $200 a month for fund investments, you could cycle your purchases across a different fund each month. After a few months you would have a fully diversified portfolio set up with minimal transactions. Cycling is suitable for investors with little money or restrictive bank accounts.

4: Asset Build: Most investors simply do not have the money to create a full-fledged portfolio. If you are strapped for cash, consider an asset builder account. With an asset builder you concentrate on one fund at a time, investing small amounts until the minimum investment is reached. Once the minimum is reached you move on to another fund. It will take some time before you create an entire portfolio, but it is a great way to start putting small amounts of money to work for you in the market.

At this point, you are just a couple of steps away from becoming a full-fledged market maven. You have the tools and knowledge necessary to become a Sage investor.

First Jen: "They said it could not be done. I called up a broker, from what I now know was a less than reputable firm, to open up an account.

First Jen   Yes, I am looking to open an account.

Broker: Okay, what are you looking for?

First Jen: Well, I wanted to start putting some money aside, you know, for later on in life.

Broker: Okay, great! We have some great new products just coming out. Can I get your annual income and net worth?

First Jen: Sure, I make $30,000 a year and really do not have much of a net worth. But I am looking to put away maybe $200 a month.

Broker: Oh, I see. Well, at this time you do not fit our requirements. Generally, you need a *minimum* of $10,000 to get started investing.

"As you might imagine, I was a little ticked off. I mean, isn't it this guy's job to help me make money? If I had money, why would I need him?

"So I called up Strong Funds and had them send me some material on a fund I learned about on your [Sage] site. I figured that since I was starting on my own, without the help of a broker, I had better start small. So I began with $50 a month in Strong Blue Chip 100—a nice, solid large cap fund. It went pretty well so I decided to open up another fund with $50 a month. This time I chose Strong Dow 30 Value. To make a long story short, I opened up three more funds—one international with Strong and two small caps with T. Rowe Price. I am currently investing $250 a month and have a fully diversified portfolio. But what is best is that I have done this all on my own and I have not paid a cent in commission to some better-than-me broker."

CHAPTER WRAP

- Common misconceptions keep most investors from creating winning portfolios. The S&P 500 Index is not the end-all, be-all; value investing is not always safe investing; higher risk does not necessarily result in higher returns; and U.S. multinationals do not provide adequate overseas diversification.

- Value, growth, small, large, and international funds create a portfolio whose sum is greater than its parts.

- Online tools help you conveniently pick the funds that are right for you based on the numerical and subjective processes we have outlined in this chapter.

- Implement the process reviewed in this chapter using either the lump sum, partial average, cycle average, or asset build method of investing.

In the coming chapter, we will highlight different time-saving avenues you can take to buy funds and create a portfolio. We will delve into online prospectus clearinghouses and fund supermarkets that make investing incredibly easy. You have the opportunity to set up a portable portfolio for free and learn how to paper trade. These are the same practices that we use in our financial planning practice and that we advocate online. You are almost there!

IN THE TRENCHES WITH SAGE

MCLarge DC: Recently I heard an analyst talking about trouble in overseas markets. Do you think I should sell my global fund?

Alan Cohn: Absolutely, unequivocally not! You should expect international markets to fall, and you should consider the drop a buying opportunity. The markets are all about volatility. Each and every year some far-flung region gets hit hard. If you look at a long-term graph of any nation's market, you will see many peaks and many valleys. Sometimes the troughs persist for years, but they are always followed by a massive surge in prices. In 1994 the Mexican market collapsed. Over the next three years, it gained 300 percent. In 1987 Hong Kong's Hang Seng was rocked. Over the next nine years, it jumped almost 1,000 percent.

Markets are made to be broken every now and then. What separates the average investor from the great investor is how he reacts when the doomsayers are out in full force. When international markets take a dive, do not run, do not hide. Buy!

Purchasing Funds and Tracking Your Portfolio

IF YOU WANT TO ACHIEVE A HIGH GOAL, YOU ARE GOING
TO HAVE TO TAKE SOME CHANCES.

Alberto Salazan—A three-time winner of the
NYC marathon and a former world record holder

● HOW TO BUY A FUND

You know how to pick winning funds and assemble a strong portfolio. But you may not be fully aware of how you go about actually buying funds. Before the Internet and America Online eclipsed the *Wall Street Journal* as the cutting-edge investment sources, before the birth of Sage, there was really only one way to buy a fund—dial an 800 number, receive an application, and snail-mail a check. But now there are simple e-methods that can link investors and investments in days, sometimes minutes.

There are four primary methods to get you on track to becoming a fund holder:

1:   Dial the digits.

2:   Surf the Web.

3:   Shop till you drop.

4:   Go for broke.

Dial the Digits

The Web has not rendered the telephone useless. As you become an expert online investor, your need to talk one-on-one with fund family representatives will diminish. But in the beginning, your comfort level will not be as high as a seasoned investors will. More than likely, your first fund purchase will be conducted over the phone. You will call and talk with a fund rep and make your purchase with a friendly voice on the other end.

Phone numbers for all funds are available all over the Web. Sites such as Sage and Morningstar provide phone numbers for all mutual funds. AT&T's Toll Free Directory (www.tollfree.att.net/tf.html) is one of the more useful Web tools available for finding numbers for funds. Once you have the phone number, call the fund family and have them send you a prospectus.

The prospectus will come via regular mail. The total time it takes to call up a fund, have them send you a prospectus, and mail off your check should be about two weeks or less. Once your check is received and processed, you become an official shareholder, after which—if you did not initially do this when filling out the application—you can set up an automatic investment plan over the phone. With an AIP, you invest regularly with a predetermined amount automatically deducted from your bank account.

This method has pros and cons.

Pro: You do not need a computer to make any of your transactions.

Con: It can be painfully slow waiting for the requested material to arrive.

Surf the Web

Most fund families, all of the larger ones, have Web sites that allow you to download prospectuses and applications. The download takes just a few minutes. Once these are downloaded and printed, simply fill out the application and mail a check.

Pro: It is fast. Clearinghouses such as E*TRADE (www.etrade.com) or the Lipper Mutual Fund Fan Club (www.lipperweb.fundclub.com) allow you to download prospectuses, though you may have to register.

Con: You need a printer and a little patience to wait for the download and print process to run its course.

Shop Till You Drop

Fund supermarkets offer investors hundreds, sometimes thousands, of funds from different fund families. Once you open an account, you are free to shop and buy until your heart is content. In most cases you can download an application and send off a check to the supermarket of your choice. For financially qualified investors looking for instant gratification, many supermarkets allow for immediate setup and account access. Simply fill in the blanks and shop away.

Well-known fund supermarkets include:

American Express Financial Direct (www.americanexpress.com/direct).

Charles Schwab (www.schwab.com).

DLJdirect (www.dljdirect.com).

E*TRADE (www.etrade.com).

Fidelity Investments (www.fidelity.com).

National Discount Brokers (www.ndb.com).

We will cover fund supermarkets in depth in Chapter Ten.

Pro: Supermarkets offer huge numbers of fund options and a consolidated fund statement. Most offer promotional incentives to get your business.

Con: The number of options can be daunting.

Go for Broke

Full-service brokers and financial advisors offer individuals personal service and expertise. Choosing a financial advisor is a personal decision. This is someone you will entrust with your life's savings. Be picky in your selection process. Set up a consultation so that you can interview the advisor and get a feel for him or her. Take your time and find an advisor with whom you mesh. You should ask your prospective financial advisor the following questions:

Are you a licensed financial planner?

How long have you been in practice?

How many clients do you have?

Will you be the only person working with me?

Do you invest in stocks or funds?

What method do you choose to select funds or stocks?

Can you provide references?

Have you ever been publicly disciplined for any unlawful or unethical actions in your professional career?

Can you put a detailed agreement in writing?

After you interview your candidates and make your selection, you will set up an appointment where investment options are discussed. The entire process should not take more than a few weeks.

Pro: Professional assistance, relatively little work after initial consultation.

Con: There is no guarantee of better investment performance than if you did it yourself and there is greater expense.

No method is perfect. Your choice should be based on your financial comfort level, investment knowledge, and your specific investment needs and goals.

Sage advocates that you invest online and that you take the same precautions online that you would offline. Namely:

1: Read the prospectus. Yes, a prospectus makes for drab reading, but it is very important that you know how specific funds operate.

2: Get other people's opinions. You can do this easily via online community tools such as message boards and chat rooms.

3: Consider the sources of information. Are they credible or do they go by a name like "Joe's Broker"?

4: Do your own research. Use sites such as Morningstar.

5: Transact with established firms. Ask how long the firm has been in business, and by all means, get references!

6: Consider the opinion of a professional. Educational designations such as CFP or CFA are practically a must.

Once you have decided which method you will use to buy funds, you need to set up a portfolio. It is not necessary to hold funds or stocks to set up a portfolio. One of the beautiful features of the Internet is that you can set up a mock portfolio using play dollars. The purpose for creating a portfolio now, maybe before you own any investments, is to get a feel for the daily movements of the market and how it will affect your money. The long-term trend of the market is upward; however, on a daily basis and even monthly basis, the movements of the market are seemingly random. The sooner you come to terms with the fact that funds do not rocket straight up every day, the less stressful your investment experience will be.

As recently as a few years ago, the only way to set up and track a model portfolio involved either a cumbersome spreadsheet or a pencil, paper, and calculator. Early pioneers of the Web realized the purchasing power of the online investor. In a mad rush to capture investor eyeballs, savvy Web sites created complex portfolio tracking services and made them available to the Web public. Some of the better sites allow investors to create twenty or more portfolios, holding stocks, funds, and cash, which update continuously throughout the day in 3-D. Web sites are so desperate to get your attention that they have spent millions of dollars creating incredible Web portfolio applications. Not too long ago, portfolio tracking applications, such as the ones available on the Web today, would have cost over a thousand dollars a year. Today they are all free!

RNTCne1: "I must say, the convenience of online portfolio tracking and trading became kind of like a video game for me. It was addictive. The fact that you can change your mind and go and buy and sell so easily became a bit of a compulsion for me. I think everyone has to be aware and a little careful of it. Sure it is fun, but not when you lose all your money, as I did."

Of course, there is always a catch. In order to use the free portfolio trackers available on the Web, you must register. Fortunately, the questions asked during the registration process are unobtrusive, albeit annoying. Most simply ask for a user name (a Web "handle"), gender, and a few other incidentals. Once registered, you are free to create as many portfolios as you please.

Figure 8.1. Excite.

Figure 8.2. Lycos.

YAHOO!. FINANCE▦

Figure 8.3. Yahoo! Personal finance Web site.

America Online (KEYWORD: quotes), Yahoo! (quote.yahoo.com), Lycos (investing.lycos.com/portfolio), and Excite (quicken.excite.com) offer some of the better portfolio tracking Web tools you will come across. All allow for multiple portfolios, update continuously through-out the day, and offer news from major news services. And of course, they are all free!

● SETTING UP A PORTFOLIO

Although each site has its unique look and feel, they are all quite simi-lar. To set up a portfolio you will need the following information:

- Fund ticker symbol (all sites that offer portfolio creation have search features for the symbol).

- Purchase price.

- Share amount.

At this point in the game, you may not have actual investments. We will create a hypothetical portfolio to give you a feel for the creation process.

Here we use Excite's portfolio tool to create a portfolio. Almost all portfolios are assembled in the same stepwise fashion with only minor tweaks. You could use Yahoo! or American Online as your primary portfolio tool, and the setup and implementation would be almost identical.

Log on to Excite's financial page (quicken.excite.com).

Click on "Your Portfolio."

If you are not registered, do so now—it will only take a minute.

Once you have registered, create a new portfolio by clicking on the "New Portfolio" link.

Name your portfolio. We will call it "Sage Funds."

Enter fund ticker symbols. We will use two funds, Janus Overseas (JAOSX) and Vanguard 500 Index (VFINX).

Click "Save Changes."

Your Web browser will load up a page the contains your newly created portfolio.

At this point, your portfolio contains funds, but it does not hold any shares in the funds. In other words, it is a shell. Click "Adjust Shares."

A new page will load with each fund placed in tabular form. Next to VFINX in the "Current Shares" column, enter 100. Under the "Average Price/Share" column, enter 10. Use the same numbers in the column to the right of JAOSX.

Click "Save Changes."
A page will load that will look similar to this:

Symbol	Price	Change	% Change	Shares	Value	Gain/Loss
VFINX	115.31	1.09	0.95%	100	$ 11,531.00	10,531.00
JAOSX	20.25	0.13	0.65%	100	$ 2,025.00	1,025.00
Total			0.91%		$ 13,556.00	11,556.00

Figure 8.4. Customizable online portfolio.

You can customize this view, adding and subtracting a multitude of options.

Earlier we mentioned that you could set up twenty or more portfolios on a single account. At this point in your newly launched investment career, it is difficult to imagine the need for so many portfolios. However, as your investment knowledge increases, you will find yourself tracking potential stock and fund investments. The ability to create multiple portfolios makes the tracking of multiple investments a snap.

TRJohnnyLou: "Every six months I head to an industry-related conference located in Las Vegas. One day when I was at the craps table my friends and I started talking about investing (quite an ironic location). We were all boasting about what great investors we all are. The conversation quickly transformed into a fish story contest. 'I did 30 percent last quarter.' 'That's nothing, my portfolio was up 42 percent.'

"I suggested we put our money where our mouth is. We were each given $100,000 of fake money and allowed to pick a five-stock/fund portfolio. The portfolio that fared the worst over the next six months—by the time of the next convention—would buy the top performer dinner. That night we picked our investments, I logged on to AOL and created seven portfolios—one for each of us. I am sure a use such as this was the furthest thing from the software maker's mind when they created multiple portfolios, but it sure is a handy tool.

"Now, about eighteen months later, I have yet to win a free dinner and it does not look like that will change anytime soon. However, I did manage to lose not once, but twice, picking up the tab both times. Thank goodness for cheap Las Vegas buffets."

Before the Internet achieved mass appeal, computer tracking of portfolios was relegated to computer software packages such as Quicken. Information was downloaded, often for a fee, at the close of market trading. Breaking news stories and intraday portfolio values were luxuries that only privileged institutional investors enjoyed. The Web changed all of that. Online portfolios allow for up-to-the-second corporate news, stock quotes, and portfolio information.

In addition, portfolio portability—the ability to obtain portfolio information anywhere, anytime, from any computer—was made possible by the Web. You do not need to be sitting at your "home base" or be talking with your broker to get portfolio information or even place trades. All you need is a computer with an Internet link (now widely available anywhere, even coffee shops) and you are totally connected with your financial investments.

● MONITORING YOUR PORTFOLIO

Of course, setting up a portfolio is only part of the process. To invest successfully you must monitor your portfolio with a watchful eye.

A large part of your investment plan is supervision. To invest properly you must monitor your portfolio. This does not mean you must check the Dow Jones Industrial Average's level twelve times a day (or even twelve times a year) or watch CNBC or Bloomberg regularly (or at all). It is nice to know how the market is doing and how your portfolio is behaving, but it is not necessary to micromanage your investments.

There are two key components to successfully monitoring your portfolio: relative performance and allocation.

Many investors think they are getting a great deal when they see their fund jump 30 percent in a year. They think, "The long-term average of the market is 10 percent. My fund did 30 percent last year. I have a good fund." This is investing in a vacuum.

How good is Buffett?

Warren Buffett, a legendary value investor, has run Berkshire Hathaway for more than thirty years. Berkshire is similar to a mutual fund in that it pools its assets and invests in stocks. Over the ten years ending 1997, Berkshire returned 31.6 percent annually. A one-time $10,000 investment in Berkshire in 1987 would have grown to $156,000. That's a great return, is it not? Consider this: The same $10,000 investment in insurer Conseco over that ten-year period would have mushroomed into $671,000.

Berkshire Hathaway's return over that span is great, but it is far from the top. In fact, according to *Fortune* magazine, twenty-three other companies posted better gains during that period.

The market does not go up in a straight line. Yearly returns are volatile, but long-term results are rather consistent. Figure 8.5 depicts how long-term returns can mask year-over-year volatility.

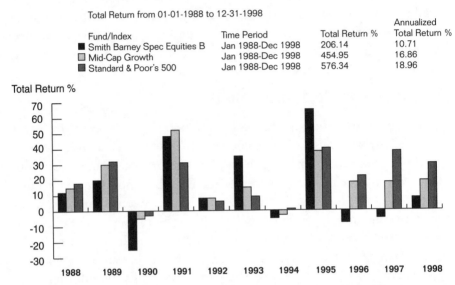

Total Return from 01-01-1988 to 12-31-1998

Fund/Index	Time Period	Total Return %	Annualized Total Return %
■ Smith Barney Spec Equities B	Jan 1988-Dec 1998	206.14	10.71
☐ Mid-Cap Growth	Jan 1988-Dec 1998	454.95	16.86
■ Standard & Poor's 500	Jan 1988-Dec 1998	576.34	18.96

Figure 8.5. Returns of Smith Barney Special Equities compared to its peer group.

Smith Barney Special Equities returned just under 11 percent over the eleven years ending 1998. However, its returns ranged from a loss of almost 25 percent in 1990 to a gain of over 62 percent in 1995. By itself, this fund looks like a winner. After all, it beat the historical average market return of 10 percent. However, over the above span in the graph it lagged the market (the S&P 500 Index) and its peer group (mid cap growth funds) dramatically.

As you can see, it is important to monitor your portfolio versus the market and other fund peers. A fund's gain is meaningful only when looked at in the context of a like index and a like fund.

Beginners, and oftentimes experts, mistakenly compare all mutual funds to the S&P 500 Index. As we discussed earlier, the S&P 500 Index is a large cap domestic index and should be compared to large cap growth and value funds. Small cap and international mutual funds should be compared to small cap and international indexes. The following discussion introduces you to the relevant investment indexes. In the coming chapter we will show you how to compare fund returns and risk measures to index benchmarks.

We have heard mutual fund commentators say it time and again: "Fund XYZ has over- (or under-) performed the index." What does this mean? To which index are they referring? This section will make you as savvy on benchmarks as if you were a close friend of Charles Dow, the inventor of the Dow Jones Industrial Average, himself. Remember, this is important because your mutual fund portfolio will frequently be compared to an index.

THE STANDARD BENCHMARKS: THE DOW JONES INDUSTRIAL AVERAGE, S&P 500 INDEX, NYSE

Steve Harmon, Internet analyst, chatted with Sage: "I think the Dow and those sort of indexes have had their day. The Dow Jones Industrial Average? I don't know about you, but the industrial era is pretty much over; this is the information age and that is why I created the Internet Stock Index in 1995, to track the next one hundred years."

The Dow Jones Industrial Average

The Dow Jones Industrial Average, referred to as the "Dow" in common speech, or abbreviated DJIA, is the granddaddy of all indexes. Created in 1896 by Charles Dow, it tracks thirty blue chip, or large cap, stocks. The Dow Jones Industrial Average measures price. Originally, Charles Dow simply added up the prices of the Dow Jones Industrial Average stocks and divided by the total number of stocks to find the average. Then came a problem: what happens when a stock splits?

Let us take a simple example. Say you are averaging four stocks priced at $2, $4, $6, and $8. The first time around, you add up the numbers and divide by four to get your average: $2 + $4 + $6 + $8 = $20; and $20 ÷ 4 = $5. That's your simplified Dow Jones Industrial Average. The next time around, your $8 stock splits and is now worth $4. (Companies do this when the stock price gets too high. Investors now have double the number of shares for their original value.) So, you replace $8 with $4 and repeat the process of summing and dividing, this time with your new price: $2 + $4 + $6 + $4. This gives you $16; and $16 ÷ 4 = $4. After the split, your Dow Jones Industrial Average is worth $4, one less than before.

That is the problem. In real life, a split generally increases the stock's value. Something had to be done to compensate for this artificial lowering of the Dow Jones Industrial Average

The solution was to modify the divisor. After years of modifications, the divisor is currently a fraction! In effect, when you divide a number by a fraction, you increase its value. This means that the divisor has become a multiplier.

There are definitely some problems with using the Dow Jones Industrial Average as the benchmark for a garden-variety fund. For one thing, with the divisor now a multiplier, each time the stocks in the index increase or decrease by one dollar, the index as a whole moves many points. Thus, a small move by the stocks making up the Dow Jones Industrial Average moves the Dow average by a large amount, which can unnecessarily cause investors to worry.

In addition, the stocks in the Dow Jones Industrial Average are price-weighted: stocks worth more count for more in the averaging. This is simply a holdover from the 1800s, when that was the easiest thing to do.

As a benchmark, the Dow Jones Industrial Average should be used to compare conservative funds mostly invested in large blue chip stocks.

Examples of Dow Jones Industrial Average stocks include General Electric, Coca-Cola, and Exxon. Usually all of the Dow Jones Industrial Average stocks are also included in the S&P 500 Index.

In the late 1990s, after a hundred years of operation, the once venerable Woolworth was kicked out of the Dow Jones Industrial Average and replaced with Wal-Mart. Some time afterwards, the company closed all of its Woolworth stores and changed its name to Venator (*venator* is a Latin word for sportsman or hunter). Almost a year after the company changed its name, it was kicked out of the S&P 500 Index and its stock price had fallen nearly 70 percent.

S&P 500 Index

The S&P 500 Index measures market value. The five hundred companies included in the S&P 500 Index are the larger companies listed on the New York Stock Exchange and the Nasdaq. The value of the stock is weighted by market capitalization. The larger a company, the more influence on the index it has: A percentage change in the market value of a large cap company will affect the index more than an identical percentage change in a company with a smaller capitalization.

As of February 1999, the largest fifty companies make up approximately half of the index's value. About 20 percent of the S&P 500 Index's assets are located in America's ten largest stocks, and about 50 percent of the index's assets are located in the largest fifty stocks. In contrast, less than 12 percent of the index's assets are located in the smallest 250 stocks. The S&P 500 Index is a top-heavy index, with the largest names generating most of the returns.

That is the problem with these indexes. Since the S&P 500 Index, like the Dow Jones Industrial Average, is highly influenced by a small number of stocks, it does not typify the "average" stock. This is not a bad thing; however, it is something about which you should be aware. Do not be alarmed when your fund underperforms the S&P 500 Index by a little in certain times of large cap dominance, especially when the S&P 500 Index cannot even lay claim to representing the "average" stock.

Examples of S&P 500 Index stocks include Dell Computer, Lucent Technologies, and Schering-Plough.

Kevin McDevitt, analyst at Morningstar, chats about the benefits of indexing with Sage Online: "For large cap stocks I think indexing makes a lot of sense, but if you're talking about small caps then I think active management is often the way to go."

NYSE Index

The New York Stock Exchange indexes include all stocks listed on the NYSE. Like the S&P 500 Index, the NYSE is a capitalization-weighted index—the larger a company, the more it influences the index. It should also be used for growth or growth-and-income style funds that invest in large cap companies.

Examples of NYSE stocks include BellSouth, Pepsi, and Motorola.

● OTHER MAJOR INDEXES: RUSSELL, NASDAQ, AND WILSHIRE

Russell Indexes

There are three Russell indexes. The Russell 3000 tracks the three thousand U.S. stocks having the largest market capitalizations. The Russell

1000 looks at only the largest one thousand out of the Russell 3000, while the Russell 2000 comprises the smaller two thousand stocks remaining. The Russell 2000 is by far the most popular small cap benchmark against which to measure small caps.

Examples of Russell 2000 stocks include Seaboard, Amtran, and Kinross Gold.

Nasdaq

The National Association of Securities Dealers Automated Quotation index is composed of all companies trading on this exchange. Unlike the NYSE, the Nasdaq exchange has no centralized floor; rather, all buy and sell transactions are done by phone and computer. The Nasdaq is gaining in prominence. Recently, more than three-fourths of new stocks chose to be traded on the Nasdaq because of its lower fiscal requirements.

The Nasdaq Index is market-value weighted, and most of the large Nasdaq companies are technology or telecommunications oriented, so the index itself is quite technology weighted. The Nasdaq 100 is a large cap technology-dominated index that has grown in prominence in recent years.

Examples of Nasdaq stocks include Amazon.com, Yahoo!, and Intel.

Wilshire 5000 Equity Index

Although it now includes more than seven thousand stocks, Wilshire Associates continues to call this index the Wilshire 5000. The Wilshire 5000 index averages most U.S. common stocks that report price data daily. It is a broad-based, market-capitalization-weighted index that is useful for comparison with domestic mutual funds.

The Wilshire 4500 is a sub-index. It is composed of the Wilshire 5000 minus the S&P 500 Index stocks.

● USEFUL INDEXES FOR SPECIALIZED FUNDS: VALUE LINE, LEHMAN BROTHERS, EAFE

Value Line Index

Unlike the others, the Value Line Index is not capitalization weighted. Instead, large companies are put on the same footing as smaller companies. Since it is not heavily weighted in high capitalization companies, the Value Line Index is a useful, albeit somewhat little known, benchmark for growth funds.

Lehman Brothers Aggregate Bond Index

There are several Lehman Brothers Indexes that track bonds by type, including Corporate, Government, High Yield, Municipal, Treasury, and mortgage-backed securities. A common index is the Lehman Brothers Aggregate Bond Index (LB Agg), which is a compilation of the Lehman Brothers Government, Corporate, Mortgage-Backed, and Asset-Backed Securities indexes. To track the performance of your bond funds, use the appropriate Lehman index.

MSCI EAFE Index

The Morgan Stanley Capital International Europe, Australia, Far East Index is a widely accepted index that tracks securities abroad. It is a market-weighted aggregate of the indexes of twenty individual countries. The more developed a market is, the more influence it has on the index. Japan accounts for the most stocks, followed by the U.K., then the U.S. Canadian stocks are excluded. International fund managers often reference the EAFE Index when stating that they are under- or overweighted in a particular country. The EAFE Index is useful for tracking international funds.

Although the Dow Jones Industrial Average and the S&P 500 are the indexes heard most often in the news, they are not the best benchmarks for every mutual fund. A benchmark should be chosen based on the fund's holdings. A quick way to find an appropriate benchmark is to scan through Chart 8.1 and choose a benchmark based on fund type.

Index	Fund Comparison
Dow Jones	Large caps
S & P 500 Index	Large caps
NYSE	Large caps
Nasdaq	Technology/Aggressive
Russell 2000	Small caps
LB Aggregate	Bonds
EAFE	International

Chart 8.1. Market indexes and comparable funds.

Knowing the right benchmark is important not only for accuracy—it saves you from comparing apples to oranges—but for your personal sanity. Should the Dow Jones Industrial Average drop 50 points in one day, rather than spending a day fretting over the consequences to your emerging growth fund, you can check your benchmark and then lean back and relax, after finding out that the Nasdaq was not so badly affected.

It is extremely important to compare your fund's performance to the appropriate market indexes. You can manually add many of these indexes to your America Online, Yahoo!, Lycos, or Excite portfolios, but if you still need to get a better description of how your funds are faring against the appropriate indexes, you should monitor your funds periodically on Morningstar.com or SmartMoney.com. These sites update performance figures daily and accurately compare funds to the correct index.

Steve Goldberg, associate editor at *Kiplinger's Personal Finance Magazine*, chatted with Sage Online about index investing: "An index fund is an ideal first and last investment for those who want to keep things simple. It requires no thought afterwards, no monitoring. Buy it and forget it. Look for Vanguard Total Stock Market, which invests in the Wilshire 5000, a broader index than the S&P. Schwab has good index funds, too. The Schwab 1000 is a fine fund."

If you are looking for in-depth information on indexes, Index-Funds.com has developed an exceptional site dedicated to index education and index fund investing, "designed for the investor who wants to participate in the many advantages that index funds offer." The goal of IndexFunds.com is "to provide a one-stop, unbiased site about index funds" and stock and bond index information.

Figure 8.6. IndexFunds.com.

In the coming chapter we will discuss the tracking of funds relative to indexes and show how it can help in your selling decisions. At this point, however, you have likely just bought your funds or are in the process of assembling your portfolio. The last thing you want to think about is poor relative performance and selling strategies.

COST AVERAGING

Once you have assembled your portfolio, you will need a strategy for investing new money. In the previous chapter we talked about partial averaging, cycle averaging, and asset building. All of these strategies fall under the umbrella of dollar cost averaging.

> "Press on. Nothing in the world can take the place of persistence. Talent will not: nothing is more common than unrewarded talent. Education alone will not: the world is full of educated failures. Persistence alone is omnipotent."
> *Calvin Coolidge*

Dollar cost averaging is the process of investing equal dollar amounts regardless of what the market conditions are or what the gurus predict. When you dollar cost average, you buy more shares when prices are low and fewer shares when prices are high. This gives you, the investor, a cost basis that reflects the fund's average NAV (net asset value, the fund's share price). It also protects against investing a lump sum in a market that is at a peak. Dollar cost averaging is usually most suitable for the long-term investor who seeks to accumulate wealth by systematically putting money into the market.

Many fund families offer a lower minimum amount to open an account if you agree to contribute a given monthly amount. With T. Rowe Price, for example, you can open a fund with $50 if you agree to add $50 per month. This is one form of dollar cost averaging.

Another form of dollar cost averaging that many investors use is a 401k plan or similar retirement plan. While most people do not think of this as dollar cost averaging, it is the most prevalent form of dollar cost averaging out there. When your paycheck is debited, you are automatically adding to your funds every month. You do not sit back and say to yourself, "Hey, self, I do not think I am going to have any money deducted from my paycheck this month, the market is not doing what I want." That would be a foolish response and unfortunately a common one. The purpose is to keep adding to your holdings to achieve your ultimate goal, whether it is retirement funding, a house purchase, or a vacation.

While dollar cost averaging is the process of investing fixed dollar amounts regardless of market conditions, value cost averaging is the process of investing for a fixed portfolio value.

Value cost averaging, a new investment strategy altogether, is aimed at investing when prices fall or are flat, holding steady as prices rise, and selling some shares when the market is rising rapidly. It is the flip side of dollar cost averaging, where the investor puts money in every month to amass wealth, regardless of market swings.

Suppose your goal is to increase your portfolio by $300 a month. If after one month your fund did not gain value, you would add $300. If the next month your fund gained $300, you would add nothing. If after the following month your fund rose $500, you would redeem $200. While value cost averaging is not a foolproof investment strategy, it does provide investors with a disciplined investment plan—an attribute lacking in all but the most successful investors.

Keep in mind that value cost averaging could involve considerable buying and selling of funds during times of heightened volatility. This "trading" of funds can result in a larger tax burden, since you must pay taxes on your capital gains. Value cost averaging is most appropriate for risk-averse investors with little concern for taxes. It works best in a volatile market and inside tax-sheltered plans such as IRAs and 401(k)s.

As your portfolio motors along, you will notice that the leaders will start to dominate your portfolio. As legendary investor and former fund manager Warren Buffett said, the Bulls would never have traded Michael Jordan, because he is too valuable a player. Likewise, you should not pare down your strong leaders because they do so well that they start to command a large portion of your portfolio. Let the winners run a bit, and keep allocation in line by adding new money to those areas of the portfolio that are underweighted.

If, for example, you are a long-term investor (as we encourage all investors to be) and your allocation has shifted towards large caps, add new money to your small cap holdings. If you feel your portfolio is too heavy in small caps, add to the large caps. Above all, always consider selling to reallocate as a last option.

CHAPTER WRAP

- The Web has eclipsed traditional communication methods such as snail mail and telephone calls, making for faster dissemination of fund material. Just a few years ago, it took weeks to set up a fund account. Today it can be done in a few minutes.

- Portfolios can be set up and tracked for free using any one of the various online services or Web portals. In an effort to get your eyeballs on their site, Web site creators have spent millions inventing complex and interactive portfolio tracking tools that provide news stories, investment performance, and analysis of portfolio holdings. The global nature of the Web gives investors the ability to create a portable portfolio that can provide up-to-the-second information on your investments from anywhere in the world.

- Compare your funds to the appropriate large cap, small cap, and international indexes. Look at your portfolio regularly to see how your funds stack up against these indexes. Careful observation of the indexes will help you understand and appreciate why your funds perform the way they do. We will use these benchmarks as a determining factor in the selling process later in the book.

- Dollar cost and value cost averaging are strategies that successful investors use to keep allocation in check and assure that a portfolio continuously grows.

Your primary goal over the next week or so is to set up an online portfolio and begin funding your funds. It is time to get on the ball and start investing!

IN THE TRENCHES WITH SAGE

PTMater Dei 92: My small cap fund has been trailing the S&P 500 Index for some time. What do you suggest I do?

Stephen Cohn: Sell! Sell! Sell! Just kidding. Frequently, when it seems as though a small cap fund is lagging the market, it really is not lagging the market. Investors tend to compare the S&P 500 Index to everything investment-related under the sun. The S&P 500 Index is a mega-cap index that really only measures how the largest fifty or so stocks are faring. Small cap funds should be measured against small cap indexes, such as the Russell 2000 Index (www.russell.com/indexes/us) or the S&P Small Cap 600 Index (www.spglobal.com). Many small cap funds outpace their respective indexes year after year. Measure your small cap against one of these indexes and see where it stacks up. You may be pleasantly surprised.

When to Sell Your Funds

Breaking up, as they say, is hard to do. Most mutual funds are designed as long-term investments: "Buy and hold" is the fund investors' mantra. In an ideal world, a fund would be bought and held through retirement. In the olden days, when our parents entered the fund market, the industry was quite static and lacked choices. Today the mutual fund industry moves at breakneck speed, with managerial shifts, new fund offerings, and performance figures changing daily. The dynamic nature of the industry has forced financial planners and individual investors to remain on alert mode.

There are times when it is in the best interest of a portfolio for you to sell a fund. The following circumstances are the greatest sell indicators and the easiest for the average investor to identify. These are selling indicators that we use to evaluate funds on our online site and to analyze funds for our financial planning clients.

POOR RELATIVE PERFORMANCE

A number of factors typically lead to poor performance. Keep your eye out for any of these circumstances, and you will easily identify future laggards.

1:   A failure of expenses to decline as assets increase.

2:   A rapid rise in assets.

3:   Selective advertising.

4:   A management shakedown.

5:   A change in management.

Performance, or lack thereof, is the number one reason for investors to sell funds; and because it is the most widely cited reason for selling investments, we have devoted special attention to performance evaluation. Unfortunately, how to measure and track a fund's performance versus a benchmark is a poorly understood task. We aim to change that!

As we discussed in the previous chapter, different funds should be evaluated against different indexes. Compare a small cap fund to a large cap index, and you are likely to be frustrated in your fund's supposed poor performance. We provided you with a table that showed the appropriate index by which to compare a fund, and we repeat it here (see Chart 9.1).

Index	Fund Comparison
Dow Jones	Large caps
S & P 500 Index	Large caps
NYSE	Large caps
Nasdaq	Technology/Aggressive
Russell 2000	Small caps
LB Aggregate	Bonds
EAFE	International

Chart 9.1. Market indexes and comparable funds.

It is important that you understand, at least on a cursory level, what these indexes mean and stand for. But the actual number crunching involved in calculating an index's return and measuring it against a fund is somewhat tedious and time consuming. Fortunately, there are many sources on the Web that cover funds, assess which index they should be compared against, and run comparison tables. For example, the following Morningstar.com data summary compares Legg Mason Value Trust (LMVTX) to the S&P 500 Index; but what is more important, compares it to an index that coincides with the fund's objective, in this case the Wilshire Large Value.

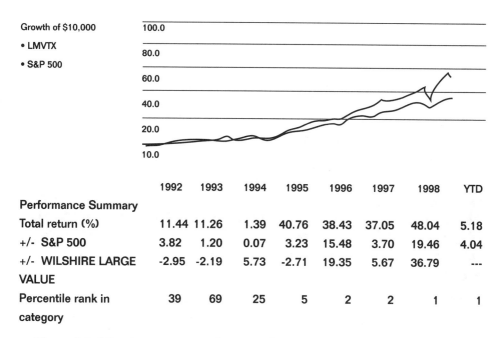

	1992	1993	1994	1995	1996	1997	1998	YTD
Performance Summary								
Total return (%)	11.44	11.26	1.39	40.76	38.43	37.05	48.04	5.18
+/- S&P 500	3.82	1.20	0.07	3.23	15.48	3.70	19.46	4.04
+/- WILSHIRE LARGE VALUE	-2.95	-2.19	5.73	-2.71	19.35	5.67	36.79	---
Percentile rank in category	39	69	25	5	2	2	1	1

Figure 9.1. Morningstar.com performance figures for Legg Mason Value Trust.

The S&P 500 Index is included as a market measurement. Legg Mason Value Trust beat the S&P 500 Index over each period listed above. While this was quite a feat, it is entirely irrelevant. Since this fund falls in the large value category, it should be compared to the Wilshire Large Value Index.

In 1992 the fund recorded a gain of 11.44 percent, but lagged the Wilshire Large Value Index by 2.95 percent. The following year it again lagged its index, this time by 2.19 percent. Other than these two years, the fund has been remarkably consistent and successful. In fact, although the graph does not show this measure, Legg Mason Value Trust outperformed the Wilshire Large Value Index by more than 100 percent over the above span.

Because the fund consistently kept pace with, and even outperformed, its benchmark, there is no cause for concern. However, the next fund typifies a serious performance-based sell candidate.

Frontier Equity, quite possibly the worst fund in existence, has performed miserably over its relatively short life span. From 1992 through 1998, the fund lost almost 70 percent of its value compared to a gain of almost 134 percent by its comparable index, the Wilshire Small Growth Index.

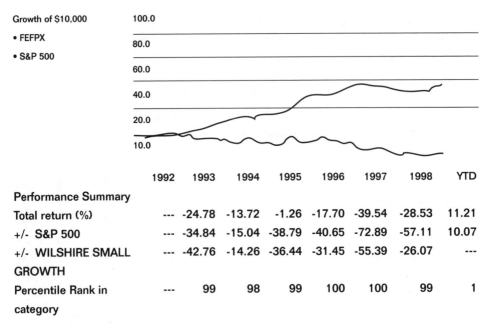

	1992	1993	1994	1995	1996	1997	1998	YTD
Performance Summary								
Total return (%)	---	-24.78	-13.72	-1.26	-17.70	-39.54	-28.53	11.21
+/- S&P 500	---	-34.84	-15.04	-38.79	-40.65	-72.89	-57.11	10.07
+/- WILSHIRE SMALL GROWTH	---	-42.76	-14.26	-36.44	-31.45	-55.39	-26.07	---
Percentile Rank in category	---	99	98	99	100	100	99	1

Figure 9.2. Morningstar.com performance figures for Frontier Equity.

From Figure 9.2, it is exceedingly obvious that this fund is a strong sell candidate. During each calendar year, the fund trailed its index by a wide margin.

You have seen two funds from each end of the spectrum. It is safe to assume you will never come in contact personally with a Frontier Equity–like fund. Likewise, there is a good chance you will never hold a fund that performs as well as Legg Mason Value Trust. The funds that you will have to make hold or sell decisions about will fall somewhere in between Legg Mason and Frontier.

While we chose to use Morningstar.com fund snapshots here, many sites provide fund information with fund-to-index comparisons. The snapshot in Figure 9.3 of Frontier Equity was taken from Yahoo!.

As you can see, Yahoo! chose to compare the fund to the Russell 2000 as opposed to the Wilshire Small Growth Index. Both are small cap indexes and suitable for comparison.

Eyeballing a fund's performance, as we just did, usually will not cut it. The two guidelines that follow should help you decide if you should or should not sell a fund.

- A fund trails its index over the past three and five years.

  Prolonged consistent underperformance is a harbinger of rough times to come. Rarely does a formerly great fund regain its footing from a five-year slump.

- A fund loses to its index three out of four years.

  Past inconsistent performance is a sign of future inconsistent performance.

Looking at Figures 9.1 and 9.2, you see in the last row "Percentile rank in category." Not only are funds ranked against indexes, they are also ranked against peers. For example, Legg Mason Value Trust beat anywhere from 31 percent of large cap value funds in 1993 (100% — 69% = 31%) to 99 percent in 1998 (100% — 1% = 99%). Frontier Equity, on the other hand, lost to just about all other small growth funds each year of its life.

Relative or peer-versus-peer performance is interesting when comparing two funds to each other. But it is not a good sign of success or failure of a fund.

Suppose 80 percent of funds in each category lose to their respective indexes. It is conceivable that a fund could outperform 30 percent of its peers or more and still underperform its index. Measuring success against a peer group only makes the task of measuring success or failure more difficult.

A good fund? At the end of 1998, Pioneer Growth sat proudly atop 92 percent of large cap growth funds over the past five years. Moreover, the fund was awarded Morningstar's highest rating, five stars. Sound good? Even with its better than 25 percent annual gain over the past five years, it still trailed the Wilshire Large Growth Index by almost 3 percent annually. And although it outpaced 80 percent or more of its peers over the previous ten- and fifteen-year periods, it underperformed the Wilshire Large Growth Index by a fair amount. A peer comparison places this fund near the top. But a fund-versus-index comparison indicates that this fund is a slight underperformer.

Dismal performance is the easiest fund sore to spot. Poor performance is typically due to an underlying problem in the fund. As time goes on and the investment climate changes, it is not uncommon for a fund to lose its way. Quite often, one-time leaders transform themselves into perennial losers due to a change in the fund's investment strategy.

A successful manager does not become incompetent overnight. Oftentimes external factors force a manager to change his hand. For example, many times when a fund outpaces the averages for some time, it gains a fair amount of notoriety. A debut on CNBC, a reference in the *Wall Street Journal*, or an appearance in Sage Online's chat lineup can all lead to a massive influx of new assets into a fund.

As assets increase, particularly in smaller nimble funds that invest in micro cap stocks, the fund is forced into a corner, and must engage in one or more of the following practices.

1: It can hold cash.

2: It can invest in a great number of stocks, mixing great stocks in with merely good stocks.

3: It can invest in larger or smaller stocks than it normally invests in.

4: It can invest in different types of stocks than it typically invests in, such as foreign equities.

5: It can close the fund to new investors to stave off the rush of new cash.

If the fund manager takes any of the first four courses of action, the result is usually poor performance due to the following reasons:

1: Cash does not appreciate at the same rate as stocks.

2: Dilution of great stocks with good stocks results in average performance.

3: Managers of small caps are knowledgeable in small cap companies, but when they invest in larger stocks, they are taken out of their circle of competence.

4: Domestic funds that venture off into foreign funds usually fail. The world is a large place, and understanding fully the currency exchange rates and the many accounting methods that are employed throughout the world is a tall task for even the brightest of minds.

The most responsible course of action is to close the fund, at least temporarily. Faced with the economics of running a fund, however, it is easy to understand why closing the fund is not an appealing alternative.

If the fund closes to new investments, asset growth will decelerate and fee growth will slow. If the fund remains open, assets will continue to grow and fees will continue to increase. Suppose a red-hot fund has assets of $100 million. With an expense ratio of 1.5 percent, the fund will bring in $1.5 million a year in fees. Now imagine the fund receives favorable mention in the *Wall Street Journal*, which pushes its assets up over $500 million during the next year. The fund is looking at $7.5 million in fees a year, assuming no asset growth.

The vast majority of fund families are corporations created to generate profits. Ultimate success, unfortunately, is not measured by how well a family fares against the benchmarks, but by how much profit its funds generate. Of course, fund families are not out to take advantage of shareholders. But they must balance what is in their best interest with what is in yours. Given the choice between great performance and minuscule profits and decent performance and outstanding profits, the decision is an obvious one.

Because of the economic circumstance, investors must be on the lookout for signs that a fund is changing its style or practices. The result will be poor performance, which is easy, and costly, to notice after the fact. Keep a sharp watch for the following kinds of dubious happenings:

Case I: A Failure of Expenses to Decline as Assets Increase

Acorn

Figure 9.4. Acorn Funds.

Acorn is arguably one of the best examples of a good thing gone bad. From the early 1970s though the late 1990s, the fund respectably cut expenses as assets climbed. By the end of 1997, the fund's assets crested above $3.6 billion, from under $30 million in 1976. As the funds assets grew, the fund transformed itself from a small cap growth fund into a mid cap global fund. Performance, though from a long-term perspective was impressive, began to look less and less impressive as assets ballooned and foreign dilution took hold.

In 1997, on the heels of another year of lackluster performance, the fund sent out a proxy statement calling for the increase of fees. Investors, not fully understanding what effect the increase would have on fund performance, voted in line with management to increase fees. Since that time the fund's performance has been far from stellar.

Sage investor XOHDIDell had this to say about the fund:

"I am currently a shareholder in the Acorn Fund. Today may be my last as one, though. I just received a proxy vote notice in the mail today. Wanger and Company wants to raise expenses from 0.57 to 0.87 per year. This is coupled with the fact that fund has taken in OVER one billion dollars this past year. The asset base has swelled to close to 4 billion dollars. Too darn big for a small cap fund. Should have closed long ago. Greed, greed, greed. A standard rule of thumb is to never invest in a fund that raises rates as asset base increases. They are already reaping benefits of increased asset base. When a fund gets this big, it will move almost in lockstep with the Russell 2000 index. Real creative, eh? Not for me, anymore, that is."

What to do?

There is no excuse for a fund failing to reduce fees—or to go so far as to increase them—as assets grow. When a fund takes in assets and fails to drop expenses, start asking questions. When a fund with growing assets hikes fees, sell your shares, and move to a more shareholder-oriented fund family.

Case II: Asset Increase Affects Performance

An increase in assets due to favorable press or other reasons can force a manager to either hold cash, invest in a great number of average stocks, invest in larger than normal stocks, or venture into foreign holdings, any one of which will negatively affect the fund's performance.

ᴛᴛF Fasciano Fund, Inc.

Figure 9.5. Fasciano Fund.

In 1992 the Fasciano Fund had just $13.0 million in assets, and only 4.3 percent of that amount was in cash. After years of better than average performance and favorable write-ups in major national publications, the fund accumulated almost $300 million in assets by the end of 1998. The cash level of the fund increased to just about 49 percent. Over that span, the size of the stocks the fund invested in more than doubled in size. Not surprisingly, the fund reverted to merely average performance.

BTJoeWill60 on Sage Online had this information on the fund:

"I was interested in the Fasciano Fund even four years ago and did not get it. I should have. I have heard also that small cap funds are not doing too well, but I recently sent away for a prospectus and also received with it an article of reviews on the Fasciano fund.

"*Money* magazine wrote, 'Here's another fund that does not get the attention it deserves. Take a look: Manager Fasciano scoops up reasonably priced small firms with the potential to double earnings or sales within five years. He's topped about two-thirds of his small blend peers over the past 10 years while taking less risk than 99 percent of them.'

"And *USA Today* wrote, 'Small firm funds hang tight—Small company stocks have had a rotten few years. But these small company funds have performed admirably. Fasciano Fund heads the list for five-year annualized returns.'"

What to do?

An increase in assets usually occurs when a fund is in the midst of a strong performance stretch and the journalistic cheerleaders are egging it on. During bouts of euphoria, it is almost impossible to let a winner go. Fortunately, you do not have to. A strong increase in assets is just a flag that alerts investors to be on the lookout for a dramatic change in investment style.

Case III: Selective Advertising

Sometimes a fund will fail to disclose fully its performance results in its advertising.

The Securities and Exchange Commission watches the industry to assure that funds are honest and forthright with their literature and advertising campaigns. The rules are rigid and the penalties are stiff. But within all legal-speak there are creative ways to push the envelope.

What to do?

If you suspect a fund is not disclosing all it should, conduct a little research. Some digging through its prospectus and a brief look at a fund snapshot will tell you all you need to know. There are numerous families that operate with a full-disclosure policy, going out of their way to make their Web sites useful investment tools rather than marketing devices.

Avoid funds that operate in secrecy from the onset. If you happen to own one currently, watch it closely, with one hand on the trigger. An increase in fees, a change in investment practices, or a lack of strong consistent returns are all reasons to sell the fund.

Case IV: A Management Shakedown

An internal management struggle, often for power or control of a firm, usually results in a disruption to fund operations.

Figure 9.6. Yacktman Funds.

Donald Yacktman of the Yacktman funds entered into a bitter fight with board members over the fund's investment objective. Some fund directors wanted his funds to move to larger cap stocks and abandon his successful investment approach. The battle lasted better than six months and resulted in a shareholder vote to remove four of the fund's six directors.

While Yacktman was in the right and ultimately prevailed, the fund suffered markedly. Over the course of 1998, the Yacktman fund was outpaced by its respective index by over 18 percent and lost over $700 million in assets. Its sister fund, Yacktman Focused, trailed its index by over 14 percent and lost over half of its assets.

The defection of so many shareholders during the dispute forced the fund to sell stocks to meet investor redemptions. When stocks are sold at a gain, taxable gains are passed on to investors. By the close of 1998, the largest taxable gain in the fund's history was distributed to shareholders. Those who had stood next to Yacktman during the bitter fight lost in the end. Although the Yacktman fund posted a gain in 1998, after taxes were calculated, the fund posted a loss.

DFWarmSprngs had this to say:

"I think a lot of investors were disappointed with the funds over the past year. I am sure the power struggle with the board of directors did not help matters either. In short, they had a tough year all around. I do not blame investors for selling out, but that does not mean the fund will not rebound. Still, once you have made up your mind to move on, there is no reason to delay."

What to do?

While internal power struggles are a part of doing business in a high-energy environment, rarely do matters escalate to the point that was witnessed with Yacktman. In case of a public management tussle, the fund usually suffers. Frankly, it is not worth the time or strain to stick with a situation where there is internal strife. We invest in and advocate the use of funds because of the simplicity they offer and the peace of mind they provide. The last thing any fund investor should be subjected to is intra-fund upheaval that will affect these attributes.

Case V: A Change in Management

What happens when the brains behind a fund leaves the family?

In early 1996, after three years of blistering returns for Govett Smaller Companies, Garrett Van Wagoner left the fund to form his own firm. What later turned out to be smart money followed Van Wagoner.

Figure 9.7. Van Wagoner Funds.

Immediately after Van Wagoner left the Govett family, the fund he formerly managed languished. His newest offering, Van Wagoner Emerging Growth, on the other hand flourished. Over the six months following the defection, Govett Smaller Companies gained slightly less than 13 percent compared to Emerging Growth's 56 percent. The performance differential continued for some time and ultimately resulted in many management shifts for Govett, though the fund could never quite capture the thunder (or assets) that Van Wagoner provided.

HDPtnJC followed Garrett from the Govett Smaller Companies fund in 1996:

> "I invested in Govett Smaller Companies in 1993 at the advice of a friend, who at that time suggested a dollar cost average approach. . . . This fund [Van Wagoner Emerging Growth] is and always will be very volatile. It is this fact over any other that led me to choose this fund. With the wide price swings Van Wagoner Emerging Growth exhibits, it creates opportunities to have dollar cost averaging work very well. I am fortunate to say that it has worked well for me."

What to do?

In the case of Govett Smaller Companies, Garrett Van Wagoner *was* the fund. When the manager is the sole driving force behind a fund's gains, it is best to leave when he does. If, however, the fund takes a team-managed approach or relies heavily on analysts for stock selections, you should stick with the fund, but keep on guard.

It will be evident after reading a quarterly shareholder report how the fund operates and who plays what role in the firm. There are only a limited number of fund manager superstars with whom it behooves an investor to immediately flee. Van Wagoner just happened to be one of those select few.

FundAlarm
Know when to hold 'em, know when to fold 'em, know when to walk away, know when to run

Figure 9.8. FundAlarm.

FundAlarm (www.fundalarm.com) is a free site that alerts investors when it comes time to sell funds. Using an alarm rating system, FundAlarm looks at relative performance and management tenure to conclude whether a fund should be sold or not. The site also tracks management changes and offers insightful commentary.

● ALLOCATION SHIFTS

Many times the reason for selling a fund is not based on poor relative performance or a massive run-up in assets, but a change in your investment style or comfort level. As you age or as your investment goals change, your portfolio must also change, which usually results in some sort of fund sale. Likewise, as you commit money to funds, invariably you will make the mistake of investing in something with which you are not entirely comfortable. As a result, you often have to unwind or sell a fund to regain a level of comfort.

As you recall, in Chapter Three we established portfolio models based on your investment profile. These portfolios were based on allocation models that have been time tested and mathematically determined. Setting up an initial portfolio allocation and maintaining it is straightforward. But as you progress from allocations that are more aggressive to models that are more conservative, fund selling will be involved.

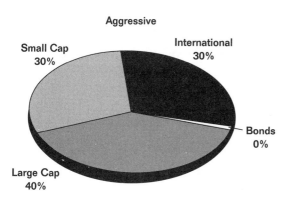

Figure 9.9. Aggressive portfolio model.

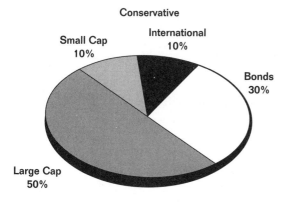

Figure 9.10. Conservative portfolio model.

The sell decisions you make when reallocating your portfolio will be largely mechanical. You will simply roll out of smaller cap, international, and aggressive investments and into large cap funds and conservative bonds.

Class	Aggressive	Conservative
Bonds	0%	30%
Large cap	40%	50%
Small cap	30%	10%
International	30%	10%
Total	100%	100%

Chart 9.2. As your investment profile changes, you will adjust your portfolio allocation.

In fact, the selling does not have to occur in one radical cut. As your goals and investment profile change, you will gradually work towards a new model through periodic reallocations or shift in the direction of new investments.

● MINIMIZING THE TAX BURDEN

Each time you sell a fund at a gain, you must pay taxes. To minimize the tax burden, take the following steps:

- First, sell the funds in your IRA, Roth IRA, 401(k), or other retirement plans. Sales within these plans are not subject to capital gains tax.

- During a transition period from one allocation model to the next, do not invest in a fund that will be sold in the near future. For example, if you are an aggressive investor who invests $500 a month (using the above allocation model) and you want to move to a conservative allocation, cut off your investments to the small cap and international funds.

- Divert all future investments towards funds that will dominate your new portfolio. For example, if you are making the transition to a conservative investor, invest only in the large cap and bond funds prior to making the transition.

- Cut off any capital gains and dividend reinvestments into funds that will be sold during the transition from one model to another.

Funds regularly make distributions throughout the year in the form of cash. Although most investors reinvest this cash in the fund, it is considered a taxable gain. In the early stages of your transition period from one model to the next, stop automatic reinvestment in funds that will be sold in the near future. Reinvest those proceeds into funds that will dominate your new portfolio model.

Even after you take these tax-saving steps, you may need to make sales that result in taxable gains. Do not let the fear of taxes deter you from making the proper allocation shift. Most likely, your portfolio will grow from more aggressive when you have a long-term horizon to more conservative as your timeline shortens. Your portfolio shift will result in a reduction of risk that will ensure your portfolio will be there when you need it.

It is common for an investor to get wooed into a fund, only to find out later it that does not fit into their financial plan or lies outside of their comfort spectrum. Impressive performance over a short span is a seductive force to the inexperienced investor.

In 1993 gold fund gains were up as much as 270 percent! Investors flocked to these funds, not fully understanding the function they serve or the risk they pose. The following year gold funds lost as much 27 percent, and in 1996 they lost another 25 percent. In 1997 gold funds fell as much as 50 percent, and in 1998 some of the poorer performing funds dropped 33 percent.

This example is extreme, but it does highlight the need for investors to identify funds that fall outside of their comfort levels or do not meet their investment objectives. Gold funds are used as a hedge against inflation. Long ago they proved to be successful portfolio stabilizers, but during periods of low inflation, they are horrendous investments. Many investors, blinded by the stunning gains, jumped onto the gold bandwagon in hopes of striking it rich. Those that held lost much more than they invested.

If you have fallen prey to an overly enticing fund that is outside of your investment needs or wants, do not despair. Simply sell the fund the moment you realize it is not what you thought or hoped it was.

RobBobVic7: "Midway through 1997 I bought Wright EquiFund-Mexico after reading some article about the potential of the Latin America region and Mexico in particular. It was flat for a couple months, then it took off—only, in the wrong direction. Over the first four months of 1995, the fund fell over 60 percent. I held, hoping the fund would rebound, but it did not. Today I am down over 50 percent. If I would have sold at the bottom and bought a good index fund, I would have made my money back and then some. But here I sit, with a healthy loss and no hope for a rebound.

"Ironically I am somewhat of a nervous investor, with about half of my portfolio in bonds. I thought a Mexican fund would enhance my returns. It set my portfolio back by about three or four years and forced me to put off retirement. . . . "

● HOW TO MAKE MONEY FROM LOSING IT

With so many funds available, many duplicate each other. For example, most of the Van Wagoner funds are nearly identical: They invest in small, rapidly growing stocks in the technology and health care sectors. When you hold a fund that suffers a severe loss in assets, you could sell the fund, creating a tax loss. This loss can be used to offset any other capital gains you may have. However, if this fund still fits in your investment profile and you have faith in management, you may not want to let the fund go. Ideally, you could sell the fund and buy it back immediately, creating a tax loss while still holding the fund.

Unfortunately, the tax codes forbid this practice. The regulation against a "wash sale," as it is referred to, states that investors cannot sell a fund for a loss and buy it back within thirty days. If the sale takes place, the loss cannot be deducted or offset with other gains.

Fund duplication, however, allows for a sneaky way around this rule. Many savvy investors make it a practice to sell a fund at a loss and invest the proceeds in a similar fund.

For example, suppose you bought Van Wagoner Emerging Growth and it dropped 50 percent. You have faith in Van Wagoner as a manager and desire a small cap aggressive growth fund in your portfolio. To capture the tax loss, you would simply sell Van Wagoner Emerging Growth and roll the proceeds into another of his funds, such as Van Wagoner Post-Venture.

In the end, you are left with a portfolio that is virtually unchanged and a healthy tax loss that will limit the amount you will be required to pay at tax time, or even result in a refund.

● WHEN YOU SHOULD NOT SELL

There will be many times when your portfolio will not act as you would hope. Usually this is not a sign that you should hit the panic button and unload all of your holdings. The market is a fickle place, where uncertainty is the only certainty. There are times when you should hold and times when you should sell. Sell for the reasons previously stated, *not* for any of the following reasons:

- The fund fails to match its peer group.

    Peers are groups of like funds. ABC Small Cap Fund has peers that fit into the small cap category. Due to the variety of different funds within many objectives and styles (large, mid, small, growth, blend, and value) peer-to-peer comparisons can be misleading. Large growth funds compared favorably to large value funds over the late 1990s. Following a peer-to-peer comparison on almost all large cap value funds would indicate poor performance and result in a sell. Compare funds to their respective indexes to obtain a clearer measure of a fund's performance.

- The market outlook becomes murky.

    The market is impossible to forecast. Since the inception of mutual funds, not one fund has been able to successfully employ a strategy that has consistently posted above-average returns. There are literally thousands of economists and market forecasters. Most fail to call the direction of the market with any degree of consistency. (For a scorecard on market strategist's predictions, see www.smartmoney.com/punditwatch.)

- There is a better performing fund that looks more appealing now.

    Individual funds experience varying degrees of success over time. Constantly rolling your money into the flavor of the month will result in a portfolio in disarray, holding funds that do not fit into your investment profile, and high taxable gains.

Selling an investment is arguably the hardest act an investor will ever commit. Second-guessing and a slew of what-ifs typically follow a new investor's first few sales. To reduce the pain involved in selling funds, keep emotions out of the decision process. Try not to be emotionally attached to any fund. Yes, we admit, it sounds rather ridiculous to become emotional with a fund, but it can and does happen.

You spend time reading fund manager reviews and annual reports. On Sage, we offer community members the ability to talk firsthand with fund managers. After spending years with a fund that has made you a lot of money, emotional ties are hard to break.

But the more attached to a fund you become, the more difficult it is to evaluate it objectively. Stick with the numbers and the facts—do not let a gut feeling or an emotional tie dictate your sell decisions. Above all, do not look back once you have unloaded a position in a fund. Have confidence in your convictions and stick with them. Over time, they usually bear out.

● CHAPTER WRAP

- Poor relative performance is a primary sell indicator. Use sites such as Yahoo! or Morningstar.com to evaluate a fund's performance next to its respective index. Sell a fund if it trails its respective index over the past three and five years or it trails its respective index three out of the last four years.

- If the fund changes its philosophy or deviates from it greatly, sell the fund. Your portfolio was created on the basis of allocation. When a fund deviates in its investment style, it alters the allocation of your portfolio, which can result in increased risk or decreased returns.

- Five reasons to consider selling your fund include:
  - A failure of expenses to decline as assets increase.
  - A rapid rise in assets.
  - Selective advertising.
  - A management shakedown.
  - A change in management.

- If any of these circumstances take place, conduct more research to determine if the fund should be sold.

- If your investment needs change, sell a fund that is not consistent with your current plan. Holding funds that are not consistent with your investment needs increases the likelihood that your money will not be there when you need it most.

- As you transition from one allocation to another, reduce the tax bite by selling funds held within IRAs, Roth IRAs, 401(k)s, 403(b)s, and other retirement plans. Sales within these tax deferred/sheltered vehicles are not subject to taxable gains.

- Consider using the "wash sale" rule to your advantage. Sell a losing fund, lock in the tax loss, and buy a similar fund. The integrity of your portfolio remains intact and you reduce your year-end tax burden.

IN THE TRENCHES WITH SAGE

BAtlHglds13: I have been paying taxes on my mutual fund dividends and capital gains distributions for the ten years that I've owned the fund. Upon sale of this fund this year, would the only gains be from this year, 1999? Do not you just subtract capital gains and dividends paid from sale price? The fund is MDBAX, an underperformer over time.

Alan Cohn: No and yes. You will have a gain not just from 1999 but from unrealized gains from prior years. But yes, you just subtract from the sale price all amounts you paid into the fund, including all reinvestments of distributions. This assumes that you sell the entire holding at one time.

By the way, most mutual fund companies now provide the cost basis to their customers. In that case, your gain is just the difference between sale price and cost basis.

Online Brokers

Online brokers are the tools that turbocharge our mutual fund investment strategies. Like any powerful device, they must be handled with care. Our mission in this chapter is to make you a savvy online brokerage customer. We will review the history of online brokers, the benefits and risks of online brokers, steps to reduce the risks, and give an overview of the leading online brokers, how to choose a broker, and the state of the industry. At the conclusion of this chapter, you will be equipped to point your Web browser toward the broker of your choosing.

THE HISTORY OF ONLINE BROKERS

In the late 1990s, eToys began peddling cute toys, Amazon.com sold shelves of books, and eBay opened up a wildly successful auction site. Then NetGrocer opened shop and offered, among other items, Kellogg's cereal, TDK tapes, and Fancy Feast cat food. The concept was a powerful one: offer Internet-jetters a virtual supermarket that would allow them to complete their entire shopping list from the comfort and convenience of their own home.

Charles Schwab saw early the need for supermarket ease in investing. Initially Chuck opened up a number of walk-in brokerage shops. Then he took his act on the road—the Internet road, that is. Schwab hung out a shingle that proudly displayed his domain name, www.schwab.com. Initially business was slow, but as investors took to the idea of making transactions via a computer, the dynamic little company blossomed. Soon others, such as DLJdirect, E*TRADE, Waterhouse, and Ameritrade, took Schwab's lead and made the leap to the Internet. Under the umbrellas of the respective online brokerage houses, investors could invest directly in stocks, bonds, and mutual funds for a fraction of the cost of going to a full-service firm such as Merrill Lynch or Smith Barney. In its spring of 1998 Internet Broker Scorecard, Gomez Advisors ranked different Web brokers.

Dan Burke of Gomez Advisors chatted with Sage Online about the boom in Internet transactions: "I see commerce as we know it going through significant changes, almost a metamorphosis in a sense of how our daily lives are structured looking at them today versus ten years from now. Ten years from now I think we'll look back and say, gee, I can't believe I had to wait on a phone call or go to a bank to get a cashier's check issued when I could've done it online. I think it'll radically change the way we do business."

As the number of Web brokers grew, competition for investors' assets became fierce. Initially Internet brokers dropped commissions (the cost of buying or selling a stock) from $40 to as low as $5. Then they offered incentives such as Quicken's TurboTax, six months free of America Online, and even checks for $75!

Eventually there was a divergence between the various Web brokers. Most brokers opted to cater to the rapid-fire day trader looking for the lowest possible commissions. Others, such as Schwab and Fidelity, took the high road, offering a full range of services and branch offices at lower than full-service commission rates. In the middle fell the E*TRADEs and DLJdirects—brokers that offered a range of services but lacked physical investment locations that investors could visit and talk with an investment professional or transact business.

In addition to offering thousands of third-party funds from the likes of O'Shaughnessy, Rydex, SAFECO, and many others, most of the Web brokers opened their own funds. Typically these funds focused on index investing, such as the E*TRADE S&P 500 Index Fund and the Waterhouse Dow 30 Fund. Others fell into the "funds of funds" category. These funds, in effect, invest in other mutual funds, like the Schwab MarketManager Small Cap, which holds other actively managed small cap funds.

"Do not worry about people stealing your ideas. If the ideas are any good, you will have to ram them down people's throats."
Howard Aitken, inventor of the Automatic
Sequence Controlled Calculator built by IBM

All ranges of Web brokers flourished to varying degrees, with the bare-bones, low-cost shops capturing day traders and the larger, service-driven firms attracting more traditional investors. The only losers in the Web investment game were the traditional full-service firms that have dominated Wall Street for decades.

In less than a year the industry had come full circle—from detesting the existence of low-fee Internet brokers to retooling their business plans to keep pace with them. High fees and a relative level of secrecy had been hallmarks of the larger brokerage houses. "An uninformed client is a good client," was a commonly heard saying in the back rooms of brokerage offices. The exponential rise in the Web's popularity and the continued acceptance of online investing forced the industry to compete within itself like never before. In the end, more Internet brokers and financial institutions were forced to give more services and offerings for lower fees, and the consumer has benefited.

THE BENEFITS AND RISKS OF ONLINE BROKERS

Suppose two investors have $100,000 to invest. Investor A chooses a full-service firm; Investor B chooses a discount Web broker. They both buy $50,000 in five stocks, and $50,000 in five funds, Investor A in load funds (assuming 5.75 percent load) and Investor B in no-load funds. (Investor B's discounts are based on DLJdirect's commission schedule as of April 1999. Investor A's full commissions are based on published schedules of other brokers by DLJdirect in 1999.) Chart 10.1 illustrates the cost or commission savings a Web broker offers:

As the market blossomed in the late 1990s, many investors mistakenly equated their investment success to talent, when in reality the gains they enjoyed were due to the steep and steady rise of the market. A growing number of so-called investors centered their lives on trading stocks online. Ultra-low commissions and ease of use made it

	Commissions Investor A	Commissions Investor B
Stock 1	$ 200.21	$ 20.00
Stock 2	$ 200.21	$ 20.00
Stock 3	$ 200.21	$ 20.00
Stock 4	$ 200.21	$ 20.00
Stock 5	$ 200.21	$ 20.00
Fund 1	$ 575.00	$ 0.00
Fund 2	$ 575.00	$ 0.00
Fund 3	$ 575.00	$ 0.00
Fund 4	$ 575.00	$ 0.00
Fund 5	$ 575.00	$ 0.00
Total	$ 3,876.05	$ 100.00

Chart 10.1. Investing with discount Web brokers can save you thousands.

almost too easy to jump on the Internet and day trade, holding a stock for just a few hours or less, trying to make money off of eighth-of-a-dollar swings. (Stocks typically trade in $1/8 or $1/16 point "ticks," or increments.)

Literally thousands of investors quit their jobs to take up day trading. The mania became so addictive that 1-800-GAMBLER (www.800gambler.org) went so far as to publish the following ten questions for online investors:

1: Do you have specific investment goals?

2: Are you investing money in the market that you cannot afford to lose?

3: Are you risking more money than you intended to?

4: Are you lying to your significant other regarding your investments?

5: Are you risking retirement savings to try to get back your losses?

6: Has anyone told you that you spend too much time online?

7: Is the way you are investing affecting other areas of your life (relationships, vocation pursuits, etc.)?

8: Are you investing frequently (day trading) for the excitement and the way it makes you feel?

9: Are you becoming secretive about your online trading?

10: Do you feel sad or depressed when you are not trading in the market?

A yes answer to any of the questions, according to 1-800-GAM-BLER, may indicate that an individual is "moving from investing to gambling."

HGrundel88: "Online investing was the biggest boost for my portfolio I have ever experienced, but it did not start out that way. I got the idea that I could day trade in and out of tiny stocks and make a ton of money. I still remember the night I picked my first stocks. I sat with a local paper on my desk and read though the Nasdaq Small Cap section. I was looking for anything that looked volatile and was cheap. I picked three stocks that had big moves the day before, figuring they would bounce around the next day, giving me an opportunity to sell them at higher prices.

"I was still in college at this point, so I had a tendency to sleep in late. I remember running down the stairs, jumping on the computer, and connecting to the Internet. I logged on my brokerage account and was confronted with a screen that announced all of my purchases. I was shocked. I had put in a market order, which simply buys stocks at the current market price, and bought these very cheap stocks for a 15 percent premium. I did not understand spreads (the difference between the bid and ask price on a stock) or limit orders (a buy or sell order that is executed at, and only at, a price the investor sets). And I sure did not understand liquidity (the ability to get in and out of stocks; usually highly traded stocks are liquid and thinly traded issues are illiquid). By midafternoon the only shares that traded in each of the stocks were the shares that I bought.

"I grew frustrated and sold the stocks at the current bid price. I lost another 15 percent, plus commissions! I started the day with $500 and ended the day with $110, after losing $150 in the stocks and another $240 in trading commissions. In the early days, 'deep discount' meant $40 to buy or sell a stock.

"Talk about a tough lesson learned! Over the next few months I changed my ways and settled into more of a buy-and-hold pattern. Every now and then, the market jarred me and I sold stocks. But luckily the urge to trade abated over the next year. Then it happened. My mother sold her house and gave me $60,000 to invest. I made a commitment to myself that I would not squander the money away, that I would act responsibly.

"I bought three stocks that headed almost straight up. In four months $60,000 (plus the $15,000 I had in the account) exploded into a little over $160,000. Had I treated my brokerage account like a Las Vegas casino, as so many do today, that $60,000 could have easily vanished over those four months."

The greatest danger online investment brokers pose is the freedom they provide. How you react to it will determine the health of your portfolio. It is exceedingly easy to lose focus on the long term and dwell only on the here and now. As you become plugged into the Internet investment world, you cannot help but know how the Dow Jones Industrial Average or the S&P 500 Index are performing every few minutes. The information is there, right in your face, wherever you turn. Because of the greater market awareness and ease of use that come with online investing, restraint is sometimes difficult.

With Web brokers offering hundreds of NTF (no transaction fee) funds and charging only a few dollars to flip in and out of stocks, cost is no longer a deterrent. Before the days of the discount broker, commissions to buy and sell funds and stocks ran in the hundreds of dollars, sometimes more. The knowledge that a sale of a fund or a stock would cut deeply into your portfolio's value was the little edge investors needed to stay in the market, riding the ups and downs and keeping focused on long-term goals.

Ted Allrich, founder of the Online Investor AOL site (KEYWORD: OLI), chats with Sage Online about the dangers of trading: "I've found that trading is stacked against you, with the spreads and commissions. You can start trading with very little money, I'd say $1,000 or less, but you'll probably lose it, so the less you start with, the better."

STEPS TO REDUCE THE RISKS OF ONLINE BROKERS

Now that costs are taken out of the equation, self-restraint is necessary if you want to become a successful investor.

Warren Buffett, the legendary investor behind Berkshire Hathaway, said once that the best thing an investor could do was to forcibly limit the number of trades made. He gave the hypothetical example of a punch card with a limited number of punch spaces available. Each time an investor made a trade, he was required to punch the card. Now, suppose you had such a card with only twenty punch spots. With such a limit, you would tirelessly scrutinize each trade you made. With a self-imposed restriction like this, you will force yourself to be 100 percent positive about each buy and each sell decision you make.

Most unsuccessful investors whom we encounter on the Sage site are actually very smart folks. They can analyze a balance sheet or study a mutual fund with the best of them. Furthermore, the investments they ultimately decide upon are usually sound choices. So why do they fail? By and large, they are herd dwellers. They sell when the market is bad and buy when it looks good. Their overreaction to every broker recommendation, political event, or economic piece of data invariably takes them out of the market exactly when they should be in the market—not to mention that their hyperactive trading increases their taxable gains.

FJulieCW: "I bought America Online in 1994 and sold a little later for a 100 percent gain. Obviously, I was pretty excited by the $10,000 profit I made, but I thought it was time to move on. AOL was going through trouble with all those busy signals. Analysts began to downgrade the stock and I thought Microsoft was going to crush America Online. If I would have held that stock, today my investment would be worth about $1,800,000!

"Funny thing is, if there is really anything about my situation, America Online beat Microsoft, and all of the naysayers have turned positive on the stock."

SManyunkBr: "I purchased Dell many years back after reading a positive story on the company. Right after I bought, it suffered a huge drop in value. I held tight and within a little over a year, I was ahead of the game. I then read a story about Compaq and how it was going to figuratively crush Dell. I sold, figuring I was lucky to get out with a small gain. Over the following five years the stock has gone to levels no one ever thought was possible. I lost out on a huge gain because I listened to someone that I had never met, but recklessly assumed was smarter than me."

Make a commitment to yourself that you will limit the number of trades you make. Do not become a slave to the market's every whim. Force yourself to stay the course and change your investments as your goals change, not based on the current movement of the Dow.

Thomas Byrne, president and CEO of Periscope Analytics, chats with Sage Online about the dangers of becoming a slave to the market: "I have read dozens of academic and professional studies that look at market timing and market timers. I have yet to find one that yields positive results, especially versus buy-and-hold long-term strategy. Market timing is a loser's game."

OVERVIEW OF THE LEADING ONLINE BROKERS

Charles Schwab

Figure 10.1. Charles Schwab.

www.schwab.com
1-800-435-4000

What makes Schwab special:

- Nearly full service, such as retail brokerage offices located throughout the country.

- Proprietary Schwab funds that maintain different allocations, such as growth, balanced, and conservative.

- Proprietary Schwab funds that invest in other funds to maintain broad diversification.

- Access to many non-Schwab funds.

Schwab is suitable for:
- Investors who like a little hand-holding and are willing to pay a little extra for it. Commissions are up to three times higher than deep discount brokerages, but are still considerably less than a full-service firm.

Figure 10.2. Fidelity Funds Network.

www.fidelity.com
1-800-544-6666

What makes Fidelity special:

- Similar services as Schwab, with offices located throughout the country.

- A broad range of proprietary Fidelity funds that specialize in every-thing from the automotive sector to the Latin American region.

- Access to many non-Fidelity funds.

Fidelity is suitable for:

- High-net-worth individuals who desire a full range of services and are willing to pay a little extra.

Figure 10.3. DLJdirect.

www.dljdirect.com
1-800-825-5723

What makes DLJdirect special:

- Strong customer service and a broad range of services, though not as comprehensive as Schwab and Fidelity.

- Low commissions given the range of offerings.

DLJdirect is suitable for:

- Investors looking for a balance between services and price.
     An added bonus is that, because DLJ (DLJdirect's parent company)

engages in underwriting, high-net-worth members (those who meet certain requirements) can purchase initial public offerings (IPOs) at the subscription price while nonmembers must pay a premium to buy the stock.

The first mutual funds built for the online investor ™

Figure 10.4. E*TRADE.

www.etrade.com
1-800-786-2571

What makes E*TRADE special:

- A full range of investments, from mutual funds to municipal bonds.
- Low commissions considering the breadth of investment offerings and services.
- Proprietary E*TRADE funds that focus primarily on indexes.
- The firm offers special incentives for active traders, such as Nasdaq Level II quotes (typically available only to stock brokers) and a priority customer service hotline.

E*TRADE is suitable for:

- Do-it-yourself investors who do not need a lot of hand-holding.
- Low service, low commissions.

Other Online Brokers

There are a number of "third tier," as we call them, Internet brokers that are virtually indistinguishable from one another. Commissions are as low as the single digits, but services are almost nonexistent. Beware: Many of the cut-rate online brokers have limited fund offerings, and do not offer investors the ability to purchase funds online.

We recommend that you stay far away from these little brokers until you are firmly comfortable with online investing. Unless you trade often, something we do not advocate, the low commissions offered by these dime-a-dozen firms will not outweigh the service shortfalls you will have to deal with. If you intend to be a buy-and-hold investor, the costs associated with making one or two trades a year with a higher-priced broker will not have much of an effect on your overall returns.

Different types of investors should opt for different types of brokers. Aggressive investors, for example, will not need all of the perks that are provided at the more established, higher-price firms. And conservative investors who are looking for an array of conservative investments and hand-holding should be willing to pay a little extra for a higher degree of service.

● CHOOSING A BROKER

The online brokerage industry is a dynamic one. Brokerage firms are constantly retooling their sites, cutting commissions, and sprucing up their offerings to attract new customers. Because the industry is still emerging, no clear leaders or "best brokers" have emerged. Certainly Schwab, Fidelity, DLJdirect, and E*TRADE boast strong services and competitive fees, but the ultimate leaders on the Web have yet to pull fully away from the pack.

Figure 10.5. Gomez is the leading Web rating service.

www.Gomez.com

To choose a broker, you must stay on top of what services are offered and how well a brokerage house fulfills its customers' needs. Fortunately, the selection process is incredibly easy, thanks to Gomez.com. "The mission of Gomez Advisors is to be the single best source of insight for consumers when selecting e-commerce services." As such, the site is an objective third-party watchdog of all places where the Web and money come together.

Using Gomez.com, you can find:

The cheapest airline ticket prices.

The easiest auction site to make a bid on.

The best online bookstores.

The best investment supermarket.

The easiest online auction.

Other useful Web consumer information.

Gomez assembles information on Internet brokers in three ways:

- Through direct examination of the site.

- Via questionnaire.

- By telephone interviews with the brokers and customer service representatives.

They then rate brokers in five key areas. With the exception of "Overall Cost," each of the major categories includes three subcategories, and each subcategory has as many as five separate criteria. These get lumped together to determine how the broker rates overall, as well as in each of the five major categories.

To determine what firms are best suited for each customer profile, Gomez developed a proprietary process to weight scores in each category and subcategory most relevant to each customer type. Scores range between 0 and 10, with 10 as the best score (10 is the least cost in Overall Cost).

Using Gomez's rankings you can easily pick a broker based on your needs. And because Gomez updates information regularly, you can be sure that the results you get from the site are reliable.

Let's walk through the process of selecting a brokerage account.

Point your browser to www.Gomez.com.

Click on the "Personal Finance" button.

Click on the "Internet Broker Scorecard" link.

Firm	Score
DLJdirect	7.65
Discover	6.83
E*TRADE	6.80
Datek	6.77
Schwab	6.75

Chart 10.2. Sample Gomez ranking of brokers.

Once this page loads, you will see a list of brokers ranked in descending order in terms of "Overall Score." (Gomez updates the scores regularly; scores in Chart 10.2 are as of February 1999.)

To find the brokerage house that fits your needs, use the drop-down menus on this page.

If you are a new investor, and are looking for wide range of services at reasonable costs, navigate the "Profile" drop-down menu to "Serious Investor."

If you are Netaphobic, still slightly uncomfortable using the Internet, navigate the "Category" drop-down menu to "Ease of Use."

If costs are your primary concern or you plan to trade stocks actively, navigate the "Profile" drop-down menu to "Hyper-Active Trader."

Block off an hour to spend on the Gomez site, reading reviews of the different online brokers. Once you have pared down the list of potential brokers to three or four, head to the actual brokerage Web sites (they are all linked from Gomez) to get a feel for their layout and ease of navigation. Most if not all brokerage sites offer demonstration accounts that let you practice trading stocks and funds. Play with the demo account so you understand how you will be executing trades.

Once you have made your selection, head back to the brokerage site of your choice and click on "Apply Online," or "Open an Account."

You will be prompted to enter personal information such as birth date, Social Security number, current employer, and salary. Once the forms are filled out, you will be given an account number, which in many cases is activated instantly. If you meet certain financial requirements, you can make a purchase at this time, so long as you send a check to cover the amount within three days.

It is that easy. In less than five minutes you could open an account and begin trading stocks or investing in funds.

If you prefer not to sign up right away, you can download and print the application or have the Internet broker of your choice mail you an application.

When choosing on online broker, watch for the following six Sage red flags. An online broker that engages in any of the practices below is not worth the paper their application is not printed on.

1:. Requests your personal information before you open an account.

2: Offers hot tips.

3: Publishes inflammatory statements.

4: Pressures you to open an account immediately.

5: Promises high returns.

6: Sends you junk e-mail.

As a final step in choosing an online broker, go to moderated Web message boards and chat rooms, like those at Sage, and ask other people their opinion about a particular broker. There is nothing like learning from the school of hard knocks when making a decision.

> Chuck Carlson, editor of *DRIP Investor* and manager of the Strong Dow 30 Value fund, advises Sage Online community members: "Make sure your online broker allows you to make phone trades . . . online brokers do have their share of technological difficulties. It is always best to have multiple options when trying to contact your online broker."

● THE STATE OF THE ONLINE BROKERAGE INDUSTRY

The transition from high-fee, offline brokers to cheap and easy online brokers has not gone without its hitches. Almost all of the most popular online investment supermarkets have experienced system outages. The number of new investors and active day traders surprised even the most optimistic industry leaders. Consequently, online brokers scrambled to beef up the computer infrastructure used for placing trades and powering the Web sites. During some of these upgrades, it was common for the systems to become overloaded and crash.

During these outages, access to personal accounts and the ability to place trades was severely restricted or eliminated altogether. Imagine what it must feel like to watch the market fall rapidly and not be able to to sell your holdings. After a string of system outages at Schwab and E*TRADE in early 1999, the attorney general from New York stepped in to investigate.

The online brokers scaled back advertising and quickly increased telephone representatives and built up computer infrastructure to meet demand. Currently it is rare to experience an outage; and when one does occur, it is usually fixed within a few minutes. While the technological shortcoming made for great journalistic stories on CNBC and in the *Wall Street Journal,* the effect they had on the average investor was quite limited.

Most long-term buy-and-hold investors who do not engage in hyperactive trading tactics were not inconvenienced. Still, the negative publicity was enough to get the industry to straighten up and become more driven by customer demands.

Now that most of the technological shortcomings of online brokers have been all but eliminated, there is no reason for an investor, any investor, not to use an online broker. That is, unless you do not have a computer. But even so, Web brokers are making a big push into the offline world. With automated telephone "touch tone" trading, the Web-based broker can now deliver the same low costs and range of services to nontech types that previously were offered to Internet investors. So do not let the lack of a PC deter you. Explore what's out there and get started now. Armed with your investment profile, Sage's fund investment strategies, and an online broker, you are ready to profit from online communities described in Chapter Eleven.

CHAPTER WRAP

* Online brokers have taken the brokerage industry by storm, forcing traditional brokerage houses to rethink their business models and investment offerings. The result has been a steady decline in fees associated with maintaining a portfolio and an increase in the services offered as the major brokers fight to sign on new clients.

- Online brokers present both opportunities and risks. Proper care should be taken to make sure you do not fall into the traps of many unsuspecting online investors. Define your objectives, watch out for red flags, and do not do anything online that you would not do offline. Self-imposed restraint is a necessary ingredient of all online investors.

- Within the online brokerage industry there are basically three tiers of brokerage offerings:
  - High-service, relatively high-fee houses such as Schwab and Fidelity.
  - Moderate-service, moderate-service firms such as DLJdirect and E*TRADE.
  - Low-fee, low-service shops that cater to day traders.

- Choose the type of broker that best meets your needs. Use the Gomez.com Web site to determine which online brokerage house is right for you. Confirm your conclusions with other online investors via moderated Web chat rooms and message boards.

- Brokers have made online investing easy to implement. Do not let the lack of a PC or general computer knowledge deter you. Explore what's out there and get started now.

- Updates to the sites covered within this chapter will be provided on the Sage site.

● IN THE TRENCHES WITH SAGE

HHAdmirals: I am considering opening up an online brokerage account and thought E*TRADE looked good. I know they have had some technological problems but how do they look beyond that?

Stephen Cohn: There are a lot of things we like about E*TRADE. Despite the service problems that most of the online brokerage industry has faced in the past few months, E*TRADE has fantastic offerings for the online brokerage customer. In particular, E*TRADE's services, like loans, mortgages, institutional quality research, IPOs, are significant product differentiators.

● SELF-HELP TEST

The following test should help you choose the right online broker for you. Give yourself one point for each answer A, two points for each answer B, and three points for each answer C.

I. What is the most important feature for you?

A. Cost.

B. Ease of use.

C. A full range of options.

II How often do you plan to place trades or check your brokerage portfolio?

A. Daily.

B. Monthly.

C. Quarterly.

III. How comfortable are you with the Web?

A. Very comfortable.

B. Somewhat comfortable.

C. I'm just getting started.

IV. What services are you looking for in a Web broker?

A. Stocks first and then funds; I do not need assistance.

B. Funds and stocks; I would like the ability to get assistance over the phone.

C. Funds, stocks and bonds; I would like the ability to talk with a financial planner.

Results:

Four through six: Start your search by looking at the lowest-cost, barest-bone offerings. Screen for these feature in Gomez.

Seven through nine: Look for a firm with an established footing in the Web broker market, such as DLJdirect or E*TRADE. Costs are important, but you need to be able to get assistance via the phone if necessary.

Eight through twelve: Service is key for you. Avoid cut-rate commission outlets that lack a full range of offerings. To satisfy your investment goals and needs, you will have to pay a little extra, but it will greatly enhance your investment experience.

Enhancing Your Investing Through Community

Community: A group of people living in the same locality and under the same government (*The American Heritage Dictionary of the English Language*).

Community: Online message boards, chats, live events, and other interactive communication forums (Sage).

Communities are a critical element of online investing. The Web is bursting at the seams with useful investment information. However, without an avenue to transfer information and share ideas, investment decisions can become terribly difficult. Without a helping hand, the Web can be a cold and lonely place to invest.

During the early development stages of the Internet, traditional media outlets such as television stations and newspapers used the Web to distribute static content—news stories and dry editorials. At that stage in the game, the Internet was merely a toy, not a serious business tool. Soon some very proactive minds in Silicon Valley figured that if they could reach enough Internet surfers, they could make money via direct sales and advertising. Once this realization came to light, everyone and his brother opened up a Web site peddling goods from furniture to fertilizer and in between. The sheer number of Web sites pushing product became overwhelming. Suddenly this barren land, ripe for e-commerce pillaging, became thick in supply and light in demand.

Site creators realized they must work to attract and keep viewers, who to that point had been taken for granted. To increase the "stickiness" (how long users would stay tuned into a Web site), sites that were centered on community interaction developed a "read about and talk about it" model. An article would be written and a bulletin board would accompany it, through which readers could post their viewpoints on the article to the authors and other "posters."

As trivial as the read-about-it-talk-about-it model may sound, it was a driving force behind the early success of the Internet. One-way talk-to media (sh)out-lets such as *Barron's* and CNBC, where editors and commentators merely shouted at their viewers/readers, were blindsided by two-way talk-with forums. Not surprisingly, some of the establishment balked at the idea of lowering themselves to the same level as common Web-goers. The thought of communicating and debating one-to-one with the average reader was, to say the least, somewhat demeaning.

Tiny upstarts such as America Online and Yahoo! jumped at the chance to open up community forums where Web-surfers could talk about virtually anything they wanted to.

Over time, community sites such as Sage (online investing), iVillage (a women's forum), and BikeNet (an online motorcycle magazine) focused on specific segments of the online audience and teamed up with some larger sites, like AOL, Yahoo!, and Prodigy, to provide a one-stop community. If Web-goers wanted to learn and talk about pets, they could go to Pets.com via Yahoo!'s Animals, Insects and Pets channel.

With respect to investing, initially the traditional media sources publicly wrote off the likes of the Motley Fool as rumor mills where investors hyped-up or pushed stocks using false and misleading information. What they failed to realize or acknowledge was that the information, though sometimes misleading, was often insightful and knowledgeable.

While the large one-way media conglomerates sat on the sidelines, the smaller upstarts took a huge leap forward, amassing loyal community members who numbered in the hundreds of thousands. Eventually the Web's popularity gained such mass appeal that General Electric (the owner of NBC), Disney (the owner of ABC), and CBS were forced to swallow their pride and pay millions of dollars to acquire stakes in community sites. Likewise, the *Wall Street Journal* and *The New York Times* were forced to increase their respective Web offerings to bolster their distribution.

Sage's first chat bore only a slight resemblance to chats today. Christine Baxter, a noteworthy manager at PBHG Funds, agreed to be our guinea pig. Although there were only forty or so chat participants, the back-end work involved in the chat required six Sage volunteers, a typist, and a host. The chat was only an hour long, but the entire process took more than forty hours in planning.

Once the big-money media giants stepped into the online community ring, they were forced to play a game of catch-up. Collectively they unleashed a massive print, television, and radio campaign aimed at winning over new online customers. About this time, Asian economies imploded. In a move of desperation, Asian technology companies flooded the market with cheap computer components. Computer prices came down from over $3,000 to under $1,000.

At one end, the media giants were pushing heavily their online offerings; and at the other, computer prices hit an all-time low. The Web was too cheap and too tantalizing to pass up. Non-technology-savvy computer users hit the Web with little knowledge and a lot of questions. Within the various segmented forums, communities took on a life of their own and actually began dictating site navigation, layout, and content.

While the larger media giants merely duplicated their offline content on the Web, smaller, more nimble sites listened intently to their community.

Though the Motley Fool's initial thrust was its real money portfolio, it soon developed message boards that allowed investors to talk about particular stocks based on community feedback. Soon the site opened up message boards for investors located in different states and for those interested in different types of investment philosophies.

Initially Sage was set up in a similar manner as the Fool. We provided, in addition to investment education, a message board for each fund. Through various message board posts we learned that most fund investors felt distanced from their fund managers. In response, we set up periodic chats with well-known fund managers. As community demand for chats grew, we added more and more guests. By the end of

the first quarter of 1999, we were featuring about seventy fund manager, financial journalist, and Wall Street analyst chats a week, and a
total of ninety hours of scheduled financial chat programming.

FMapesGen: "During October of 1998, the technology sector
took a major hit. Many stocks were down almost 30 percent. I
had a holding in Dell Computer at the time and was understand-
ably shaken. I turned to a message board to consult some fellow
community members. I remember one individual, who I knew to
be perennially negative on the stock, talking about the oblitera-
tion of the company. Asia, competition, falling computer prices,
and scores of other potential problems were going to kill the
stock, according to him. He almost pushed me over the edge. I
signed on to my brokerage account and was putting in an order
to sell the stock.

"Just then, I got a phone call from a friend who works in the
technology sector. He was commenting on the fall in the stock
market and talking about how crazy it was. From his end,
demand for PCs, especially Dells, was strong. I hung up the
phone and quickly changed my order from sell to buy. Now, just
four months later, the stock has gone from $44 to $90."

Financial chats and message boards at first were met with a lot of
skepticism. Because the Web provides anonymity, it seemed easy to
promulgate misinformation. However, as close-knit communities grew
roots, a sort of self-policing took hold. When members came across a
message board post that seemed dubious, the community would
demand proof. When a chatter pumped up a particular investment or
stock, community members would step forward with questions. Over
time, a checks and balances system took hold in many of the highly segmented communities.

Over time, community developed into a highly sophisticated two-
way medium. Whereas one-way financial media outlets only offered a
platform for a pundit to stand on and preach, the community embraced
the rapid exchange of ideas and debate. The offline financial industry was
taken aback by the force of the individual investment community.

In reality, the online financial communities began to model the
information flow of a trading department in a large, well-established

Wall Street firm. Thanks to online brokers and other financial destination sites, the online investor had access to the same databases and financial information as the Wall Street firms. As financial communities developed online, investors had a means to discuss investment ideas and talk about global economic developments in real time. Where a group of Morgan Stanley traders would meet before the opening bell in the firm's trading pit, online community members would assemble in chat rooms and message boards before the market opened.

Other than a lack of physical contact, there was little difference between the Wall Street trader and the savvy online financial community member.

● TYPES OF COMMUNITIES

While no two communities are the same, they all fall into the unmoderated or moderated camps. Unmoderated communities are open forums with little or no expert supervision. Investors are free to say what they want, when they want, how they want. Because they lack supervision, unmoderated communities come under the most scrutiny and ridicule. Much of the cynicism is unwarranted, but there have been cases where damaging information has been passed via message board posts.

Midway through 1999, Yahoo!'s unmoderated message boards came under fire when purported Raytheon employees (Raytheon operates in three areas: commercial and defense electronics, engineering and construction, and aircraft) posted insider information on the message boards. Raytheon pleaded with Yahoo! to release the names of the posters, and eventually the matter went to court.

Though this example is far from the norm, it is not unheard of. Unmoderated communities such as Yahoo! are subject to a fair amount of suspect, and sometimes illegal, information. However, the unpatrolled territory makes for a highly active community. After a shareholder class action suit was filed against Compaq midway through March of 1999, Yahoo!'s Compaq message board logged over three hundred posts in one day. The Motley Fool's Compaq message board logged under a quarter of that amount the same day. The Motley Fool's moderated board generated fewer, albeit higher quality, posts than Yahoo!'s unmoderated board. Yahoo! was littered with promotional, derogatory, and incoherent posts:

Promotional:

"Forget Compaq. Take a look at this stock. It's selling for just a couple bucks but it is going to be huge!"

"GGNC Sports Book and Internet Casino Show a Continuing Rise in Combined Online Wagering Revenues."

"The Price Waterhouse audit of the Second Acquisition of an established, operating and profitable operation is expected to finish within this month . . . "

Derogatory:

"It is good ignoring some of the ignoramuses on this board. I have learned the best way to fight them is to ignore them. I do not even click on their messages. Leave them alone and the windshield wipers scrape them off. We will be hearing less and less of them as they are proven dead wrong!"

Incoherent:

"I bought Compaq at $48 and again at $35. I am down about $20,000 in 3 weeks. At least I also own SNMM."

Of course, interspersed throughout the message boards were lucid, insightful, and well-thought-out posts. But without oversight, inflammatory and off-topic message board posts were left unchecked. No doubt this wild and often juvenile type of action has led many from the old school to write off message boards as the stomping grounds of penny stock pushers and unschooled investors.

Moderated communities go to great lengths to assure that information stays on topic, solicitations are removed, and personal attacks are eliminated. Each piece of communication is monitored, interaction is supervised, and intelligent conversation is facilitated. Consequently, serious investors tend to gravitate towards moderated communities where discussion remains pure:

Following is a typical post:

"I would not let this shortfall deter investors. Look at the long-term fundamentals of the company! Compaq is growing at a rate of around 20 percent. Compaq management is moving the company towards higher margin businesses and is embracing the Internet. On a valuation basis, Compaq is one of the cheapest tech companies around. I believe we could see $100 per share in the next couple of years. Worst case, with the price around the low thirty range and no debt, growing at 20 percent there is such a margin for error built into this stock that long term you should at least do as well as the market and own a tech stock that allows you to sleep well at night."

While posts like this are typical in a moderated community, the higher standards set and upheld by the community scare off many would-be posters, resulting in a lower number of total posts on any given subject.

Moderated or unmoderated? Which should you choose? It is not a mutually exclusive decision. Moderated and unmoderated communities both have a lot to offer. Moderated communities typically require a little more from the poster, such as an initial registration. The conversation is generally very focused on the topic of the day, and quite often industry experts such as fund managers and other volunteers join in the discussion. Posts that do not meet the standards outlined by the community can and will be taken down and deleted by community leaders. Unmoderated communities typically have a wide range of quality in posts, and oftentimes discussion can become overly heated and sometimes personal.

Each has its pluses and minuses. Most new investors feel more comfortable in moderated communities due to the additional handholding and purity of the information. More aggressive, seasoned investors split time between moderated and unmoderated communities.

1: Communities should be moderated by individuals with credible credentials.

2: Financial experts and professionals should provide much of the information.

3: There should be definite rules for behavior.

4: There should be a privacy policy.

No matter which kind of community you visit, you should use caution. The Web is a massive, anonymous place where investors can hide in relative secrecy behind screen names. Although the vast majority of the fellow investors you will come across have honest intentions, occasionally you will encounter suspect individuals.

It helpful to keep the following things in mind about message boards:

- Never let them scare you.

    The beauty of the market is that it is constantly in flux, reacting on mass emotion. If everyone felt the same about each and every stock and mutual fund, investing would be simple—and highly dull. We would all buy a few stocks and a few funds and make millions. But the market is full of tens of thousands of stocks and funds. And depending on how hard you are willing to look, you can find an investor with a strong opinion on each and every one.

    Money and emotions never part, and it is not uncommon for a message board post to emotionally unwind you, scaring you out of an investment. During times of increased volatility or corporate distress, investors often turn towards communities for support and guidance. Invariably there will be folks who suggest selling all of your holdings or a particular fund or stock to limit further losses. The rational thing to do is step back, evaluate the situation, and focus on your long-term needs. It is all too easy—because of the emotional aspect of investing—to succumb to those who are pushing you to sell.

Each market day, Sage hosts AOL MarketTalk, where we allow community members the chance to talk with at least twelve different market pundits and multiple Sage commentators. Typically these forums are heavily monitored with a number of Sages to guard against the hyping of stocks or other dubious behavior. In contrast, the Market News Center on America Online holds an open chat with no moderation. The open chat offers investors one-on-one talk in a fast-paced environment with like investors. The monitored chat focuses more on communication between individual investors and pundits in a managed format.

- They are only a starting point.

    A message board is simply a means of communication. All too often, however, newer investors see a message board as the place to go and get all of their fund and stock questions answered. Just as we hope you would research any investment even if it was recommended by a qualified professional, you should always research everything you read on a message board or chat room before you make any decision.

- Call a bluff.

  If it sounds too good to be true, it probably is. Yes, this is a tired old cliché, but true. When you come across a message board post that boasts a get-rich-quick scheme or pushes a particular investment product strongly, question the poster on all fronts to see if the opinion is legitimate. More often than not, other community members will smell out the skunk.

REAL-TIME HELP

The message board was the earliest form of online investment communication. It offered investors a tool to converse freely, but lacked a certain personality. When you peruse through and post on the message boards, you are out there alone. On a dead board with very little activity, it can be difficult to get answers or opinions from other investors.

Soon Web sites such as Excite, Yahoo!, and AOL started offering real-time chats. Chats allowed investors to communicate en masse instantly. If the Dow Jones Industrial Average crossed 10,000, scores of investors could jump in a chat room and talk about the momentous occasion—which they did. If an investor needed an opinion on the Elfun Global Fund, he could simply throw out the question in the chat room and get immediate feedback. The chat room took the online community to a new level.

Financial industry experts quickly signed up with the likes of Sage and others to gain access to potential investors, shareholders, and readers.

This type of instant gratification was a massive boom for the online community. Suppose Boston Chicken filed for bankruptcy one morning. An online community would call up the company and schedule a chat with a corporate officer within a matter of minutes. Investors could then talk firsthand with the officer to better understand the situation of the company and make informed investment decisions. Meanwhile the offline world would be handcuffed until the story broke the following morning when the latest addition of the *Wall Street Journal* was published. Furthermore, readers of the *Journal* would not have the opportunity to ask corporate officials the questions they want answered; rather, they would hear only what the author felt was relevant.

The chat room, however, like the message board, has its limitations. Like the message board, there are unmoderated and moderated chat rooms. Moderated chat rooms generally have regularly scheduled chats each day. Unmoderated chats are typically large open rooms where investors congregate regularly to discuss and debate the topic of the moment.

On the message boards, the community members fielded questions from distressed investors:

PlumpSqeek7: "Help! I am debating on whether or not to sell this fund. I have held it since September 1997 and to date my profit is only $136.00. I have done dollar cost averaging till I started seeing my money disappear, of course I have more shares, but this is not a IRA, I am on permanent disability so I really need my money to work for me. I also have Oakmark, which is not doing well either. I recently opened Vanguard 500 Index and Janus Twenty. I wonder if I should close out all of my funds since the market is spiraling lower. I am saving for the long term, have about ten years or so till I will need income. Should I move to a money market fund for three to four months until the hemorrhaging stops?"

Sage response: "In a nutshell, by the time we can all be certain the bloodletting is over, most of the recovery and even some profit may be lost to those who sat it out.

"If you are a short-term trader, you can set limits on what loss you will take on any single investment, and those limits should apply regardless of the market. But to arbitrarily pull it all out after it has crossed that threshold and sank a lot further is more often than not a losing proposition. Especially if it creates tax issues, which makes the situation worse.

"Most of the people who panic do so after most of the damage is done. Odds are pretty good that although today is not likely to be the last big drop day, the overall market probably is not going to go that much further down."

One type of chat is not better than another. If you are looking for professional opinions, a moderated chat room is the place for you. If you have a quick question or want to bat around the topic of the moment, an unmoderated chat room should suit your needs.

Frequently the difference between a moderated and unmoderated chat room is like the difference between the Oprah Winfrey and Jerry Springer shows.

PUTTING IT ALL TOGETHER

"Left to themselves, people will elaborate, not simplify solutions."

> *Chester Barnard, author of* The Functions of the Executive

Successful communities have interwoven chats, message boards, educational material, and financial commentary to provide investors with various ways of communicating, interacting, and learning. The sound financial community will act as a center for education, and what is more important, support. When the market experiences a bout of turbulence, as it tends to do at least once a year, investors need a place to turn. Talking with those who have been there helps a great deal when the stock market is in a steep decline.

When the market fell sharply over the summer of 1998, strong communities across the Web sprang into action to quell investor fears. Through a series of articles, message boards, polls, and chats, communities quickly launched so-called investor support centers.

Industry leaders stepped up in short order to handle the flood of chat questions from worried participants. Here is what some of them had to say:

"I believe the 1930s were great for learning how not to handle a crash. True, there are similarities, but our country is older and wiser and we will not make the same mistakes now."

> *Tom Thurlow, Thurlow Growth Fund Manager*

"Trying to time and predict the markets is not, in my opinion, what the average investor should be doing at this point. They should keep the course and not try to time the market."

> *SageABC, Sage Online community leader*

"We have been calling the daily telephone hotlines this week of the 160 or so newsletters we track and what impresses me is that most of them did not use this week's action as a reason to reduce exposure."

Mark Hulbert, editor of the Hulbert Financial Digest

"Whenever I hear of a panic I think of an old saying: The word 'crisis' in Chinese is composed of two characters: the first, the symbol of danger; the second, opportunity."

Stephen Cohn, Sage Online cofounder

"It is really crucial that you continue to employ dollar cost averaging through thick and thin—and that means especially when the market is tanking."

Manny Schiffres, editor at Kiplinger's Personal Finance Magazine

"The 20 percent correction brought the overall market to quite attractive levels. But that does not preclude the market going down another 10 or 20 percent."

William Miller III, fund manager, Legg Mason Value Trust

"It may be several more months before markets around the world are able to operate with less volatility. Our market may continue to be volatile during this time frame."

Larry Kantor, executive vice president, Lexington Management Corporation

The market was in fact volatile for the coming months, but rebounded strongly over the ensuing months. By the second quarter, the Dow Jones Industrial Average crossed the 10,000 mark—a gain of 36 percent from the summer swoon.

The message boards and expert chats were accompanied by articles that focused on teaching investors what was happening in the market and how to interpret the rapid-fire chatter on CNN and CNBC. We also put the "crash," as it was dubbed by the media, in a historical perspective, showing that in terms of the market's long life the drop was insignificant; and we highlighted funds that have historically shown strong returns coming out of a market dive.

In the end few community members sold. Unfortunately, the same cannot be said of others without a support net. AZJohnnyJJJ, a financial advisor and regular community contributor, wrote on the message boards:

"When the market bellowed on October 8, my office was inundated with phone calls. One of my older clients could not get through to me so she panicked. She circumvented me and called her fund family directly. The next day she called back and told me she sold all of her investments. Well, as you all know, the market has since gone up a good amount and a couple of her funds would have almost doubled. But that is not the end of the story. Now she will owe no less than $80,000 in taxes. I figured out the other day what her portfolio would have been had she stayed with her funds and avoided the tax bite. All told, her portfolio is a little over $200,000 less now because of the rash decision."

AZJohnnyJJJ's client's reaction is typical of how investors feel. An integrated community such as Sage, the Motley Fool, TheStreet.com, and BuckInvestor.com provide investor support against a backdrop of market uncertainty.

Communities are a tremendous tool. You can gather information from informed investors and investment pros with only the click of a mouse. All information disseminated within a community is public, so there is a natural system of checks and balances. Moderated communities such as Sage offer additional safety measures. Finally, you can ask questions and/or voice your opinions anonymously and not feel stupid. For all of you who were embarrassed to raise your hand in class, isn't there a lot to be said for that?

● CHAPTER WRAP

- Communities are a critical element of online investing. Communities offer investors an outlet for group learning, like-minded interaction, and the sharing of ideas.

- There are two types of communities, unmoderated and moderated. Unmoderated communities are open forums with little or no expert supervision. Investors are free to say what they want, when they want, how they want. Moderated communities are more structured. Each piece of communication is monitored, interaction is supervised, and intelligent conversation is facilitated. Consequently, serious investors tend to gravitate towards moderated communities where discussion remains pure.

- During times of heightened market volatility, the community can act as a support center that will keep investors from committing inopportune buying or selling, which is a common action that investors take when left on their own.

- How do you make money from community? Ask questions, gather useful information from financial experts, and participate. You will profit both financially and intellectually. And if you are anything like SageMaybe, your love life may get a boost.

● IN THE TRENCHES WITH SAGE

ORSigma6: Alan, I am interesting in learning more about Legg Mason Value Trust. Where should I start?

Alan Cohn: Legg Mason Value Trust certainly is a popular fund. It is one of the few large caps that consistently beats the S&P 500 year in and year out. The fund manager William Miller is a regular guest on Sage Online, so the first place you should start is in our Sage Voices department. In Voices, you can find chat transcripts from past Live Events we have hosted with industry pundits including William Miller.

Go to AOL KEYWORD: **SageVoices.**

In the list box on the Sage Voices page, click on "Funds A-L."
Scroll down until you see "Legg Mason Value Prime." Double-click on one of the dates.
A transcript will open. Print the transcript for easy offline reading.

Once you have read Miller's comments, head to the message boards.

Go to AOL KEYWORD: **SageBoards.**

Double click "Fund Families."

Scroll down and double-click "Legg Mason Funds."

A message board page will open that houses individual message boards for all of the Legg Mason funds.

Double-click on "Legg Mason Value Prime."

Within this message board you will see many posts, typically more than a hundred.

Our message boards have a format with a community member question and Sage answer.

Questions have a headline; answers have that headline preceded with "Re:".

For example, the message boards will look something like this:

Confused	User Name	Date
Re: Confused	SageLouh	Date

Double-click on some of the message board questions and answers to get a feel for how the message boards flow.

When you are ready to ask a question, click "Create Subject."
A page will open where you can type in your question.

Within forty-eight hours, a Sage, such as SageLouh from above, will answer your question. You can come back to this board in a day or two to read the answers to your questions. The Sages who patrol the Legg Mason Value Prime message boards either hold shares in the fund or follow it closely. This is the case with all of our fund-specific message boards.

Once you are through with the message board, you can check out the chat room.

Go to AOL KEYWORD: SageChat.

Look through the schedule on this page to see when William Miller will be appearing, and mark your calendar.

Each day we have Sage-monitored chats. Find one that is currently running and click on the hyperlink to enter the chat. Once you are in the chat, you will see a number of screen names of people who are talking away.

When you feel comfortable, ask your questions, preceded with "Sage." For example, if you wanted the phone number for Legg

Mason Value Trust, or the Web site, you would simply ask, "Sage, what's the phone number (or Web site address) for Legg Mason?"

Within in a few moments you will get an answer.

We have found that chats can be a little intimidating. Since they tend to run fast, and generally the investors in there know one another, it can be daunting. Do not worry, Sage is here to help. The sole purpose of the site is to help investors. Do not be shy; just jump right in! If you have trouble, a Sage will be available to assist you.

After you have taken these steps, you will have a better feel for Legg Mason Value Trust. I still do not have enough information about you to determine whether it will make a nice addition to your portfolio. For that answer, you will have to discuss your objectives with another Sage community member.

Tax-Efficient Investing

Proper management of your potential mutual fund tax liability will increase your after-tax returns. In 1997, for example, according to a Morningstar report, taxes ate 2 to 3 percent of annual stock fund returns, compared with about 0.2 percent for tax-managed funds.

Everything else being equal, Sage advocates investing in tax-advantaged funds when available. There are two general ways to reduce your taxes with mutual funds: investing in tax-efficient mutual funds and investing in qualified retirement plans. In this chapter we will cover the pros and cons of tax-efficient funds, discuss tax-qualified investment plans including IRA, 401(k), and 403(b) plans, and introduce you to ways to control your taxes. In addition, messages from our online community will point out tax-saving tips that you may never have known existed. Managing your funds' taxes is going to take some time, but the money saved will make it worth your while.

● TAX-EFFICIENT FUNDS

Tax-efficient funds reduce your tax bite by focusing on high after-tax returns. These funds really excite us, as they are advantageous regardless of what the government does with future tax laws. Types of tax-efficient funds include low-turnover funds, index funds, municipal bond funds, and tax-managed funds.

Low-Turnover Funds

Turnover is the fund's level of trading activity, or the number of times the fund buys and sells its holdings. For example, if a fund has a portfolio turnover rate of 100 percent, it holds each stock in its portfolio for a year on average. A turnover rate of 200 percent would indicate an average holding period of six months, and a turnover rate of 25 percent would point to an average holding period of four years.

Turnover is important to an investor because it is directly correlated to two factors: tax efficiency and fund expenses. Usually, the higher a fund's turnover, the higher its tax inefficiency and its expenses. Of course, there are exceptions, such as PBHG Growth fund, but this general rule holds throughout the fund industry.

The more a fund trades, the more money it can accrue in taxable capital gains. More capital gains can mean more taxes for the investor unless that fund is in a tax-sheltered vehicle, such as a 401(k), variable annuity, or IRA.

To reduce your tax burden, look for funds that have a low turnover ratio, generally under 50 percent. Turnover ratios can and often do exceed 100 percent. Some funds even reach 1,000 percent. Obviously, this could be disastrous from a tax standpoint. The amount of trading done usually depends on a manager's personal investment style. Some funds, however, lend themselves to lower turnover rates than others. Which leads us to index funds.

Index Funds

Index funds, as we have seen, are passively managed funds that aim to replicate a market index or barometer, such as the S&P 500 Index. These low-cost, low-maintenance funds are often run by a computer that insures that the fund's holdings replicate the index. An S&P 500 Index fund, for example, would hold the same five hundred large cap companies as are in its corresponding index. Since the specific stocks that are listed in an index change infrequently, index funds are notable for low turnover. They avoid the frequent buying and selling that generates taxable capital gains distributions in mutual funds.

Tax-Managed Funds

Tax-managed funds are run with taxes as a driving force behind the fund manager's actions. Tax-managed funds buy and sell stocks infrequently because this action would generate taxable gains. When a manager does sell stocks for a gain, he will look to offset this gain with a loss in other stocks. If the manager can successfully offset gains with losses, there will be no capital gains distribution to fund shareholders.

Joel Dickson of Vanguard Group chats with Sage Online about tax-efficient investing: "What you would want to do is maximize the after-tax return on your total portfolio. That can be done by putting relatively tax-efficient funds, like index funds, in taxable accounts, and actively managed funds in a tax-deferred account, where they will not do as much damage."

Additionally, tax-managed funds avoid stocks that pay dividends, since dividends are income, which generally is taxed at a higher rate than capital gains are.

Tax-managed or index funds? For large caps, tax-managed funds might be the real deal after all. According to a study in December 1998 of about a thousand large cap and about five hundred small cap mutual funds, Charles Schwab's Center for Investment Research found that:

- In the large cap universe, tax-managed funds offer the greatest degree of tax efficiency, followed by index funds.
- Small cap index funds tend to be more tax-efficient than actively managed funds over a one-year period ending December 31, 1997, but equal over the three year period.

Why might this be? Both index and tax-efficient funds have low turnover, but actively managed tax-efficient funds have two additional advantages:

- Index funds do not weed out dividend-producing stocks; tax-managed funds do.
- Tax-smart managers can use losses to offset gains in a choppy market. As stocks fall from their highs, fund man-

agers of tax-efficient funds can sell out of losing stocks and book tax losses from the sales. The tax losses can be used to counterbalance any gains in the portfolio, which ultimately leads to a reduced capital gains tax burden.

Small cap index funds, on the other hand, do not enjoy the same low turnover as large cap indexes. Given the nature of small businesses, benchmarks like the Russell 2000 change often as small companies become large, or large ones shrink back to small size. This might help explain why, over the long term, small cap index funds lose their tax advantage; they turn over just like their peers. For now, there are too few tax-managed small cap funds to make a comparison, but it's a safe bet they'll do better than their tax-careless peers as well.

Municipal Bond Funds

Investing in municipal bond funds is one of the easiest ways to shelter more of your income. They can offer this special advantage because, in order to encourage investments in debt obligations issued by cities and states, income from these bonds is usually exempt from federal income tax; and depending on the state you live in, state and local income tax may be avoided as well. Be careful, a municipal bond fund may not be completely tax-free. Funds that buy municipal bonds at a market discount may generate taxable income when those bonds are sold. Municipal bond funds pay a low rate of interest and are best suited for investors in high tax brackets who are in serious need of tax-cutting help.

Other Tax-Efficient Funds

In addition to low turnover funds, index funds, municipal bond funds, and tax-managed funds, there are funds within variable annuities and variable life plans that may save you taxes. Popular low cost variable annuities are offered by companies such as AnnuityNet and Charles Schwab. The appropriateness of these kinds of funds depends on your financial planning needs and should be evaluated on a case by case basis.

● TAX-DEFERRED RETIREMENT PLANS

Retirement-intended money should be placed in tax-friendly plans before any other taxable investments are made. Based on favorable tax treatment and government incentives, a person below the age of forty could essentially make all of her retirement investments without ever paying taxes on any gains until she retires.

Cutting back on taxes does not mean you must sacrifice returns. With respect to tax-deductible/sheltered investments, the funds you use are the same; they are just housed under the retirement plan umbrella.

Uncle Sam gives you incentive to invest your funds in tax-deferred retirement plans such as IRAs, Roth IRAs, 401(k)s, and 403(b)s. The following is a brief description of the most popular plans. The rules and regulations spelled out below are as of 1999. Consult tax-specific Web sites such as Quicken.com or the Sage Tax-Smart Center for updated information.

Traditional IRA

The Individual Retirement Account lets you accumulate money without paying taxes until you take your money out. Hence the description "tax-deferred." With deductible IRAs, you get to write off the money you add to your account as a tax deduction.

Here is how a Traditional IRA works:

- Earnings grow tax-deferred, but are taxed at your ordinary income tax rate upon withdrawal.

- Maximum annual contribution is $4,000 for couples ($2,000 per individual), $2,000 for singles.

- A deductibility provision applies for "nonworking" spouse and individuals who do not participate in their employer plans.

- Adjusted gross income (AGI) limits to qualify for full deductibility are $50,000 for couples, $30,000 for singles. (Your adjusted gross income is the amount on which you calculate your income tax; it appears on line 31 of federal tax form 1040.)

- AGI deductibility limits will increase over the coming years to $80,000 for couples, $50,000 for singles.

- AGI deductibility phases out at $100,000 for couples, $60,000 for singles by the year 2007.

- You have to start taking money out by age seventy and a half.

- Early-withdrawal penalties may apply for withdrawals prior to age fifty-nine and a half.

- New laws allow you to take IRA money out before age fifty-nine and a half for first-time home purchase, tuition expenses, and some medical needs.

Roth IRA

A Roth IRA is not tax-deferred; it is virtually tax-exempt. With a Roth, contributions are never deductible, but you do not have to pay any taxes once you take the money out.

Here is how a Roth IRA works:

- Maximum annual contribution is $4,000 for couples ($2,000 per individual), $2,000 for singles.

- Annual contributions are not tax-deductible.

- Earnings grow tax-deferred.

- Tax-free withdrawals are allowed at age fifty-nine and a half if the account is at least five years old.

- Adjusted gross income (AGI) limits are $150,000 for couples, $95,000 for singles.

- Eligibility phases out at $160,000 AGI for couples, $110,000 for singles.

- There are no minimum required distributions at any age.

- Rollovers from Traditional IRAs are permitted if AGI is less than $100,000, married or single. People who are married filing separately are not eligible.

- Taxes are due in the year of conversion if rolled over from a traditional IRA.

- Withdrawals for special purposes such as first-time home purchase and college expenses may be permitted prior to retirement.

How to open a traditional IRA or Roth IRA? Mutual fund companies, online brokers, banks, and other financial institutions offer both Roth and Traditional IRAs. Essentially, an IRA is a special account that can be filled with anything you like, such as mutual funds, stocks, and bonds. The only way they are different from a typical investment account is how they are taxed. Of course, the Sage philosophy is to open up your IRA investments online. That way you are guaranteed to never lose your paperwork.

Skittles64: "I didn't think the paperless office was possible. And maybe it is not, but this week I made a great stride in this area. I jumped onto DLJdirect and opened up an IRA in less than five minutes. Once I got a confirmation that my account was active, I logged on to my NetB@nk account and transferred money into my new IRA. Then I took the money and invested in two funds. I did not have to write any letter, leave my home, or even take a shower. I did it all right here, from my office desk."

401(k) and 403(b) Plans

401(k)s and 403(b)s are retirement savings plans set up by your employer that allow you an easy way to accumulate tax-deferred savings. There are other similar plans, but since 401(k)s and 403(b)s are the most popular, we will limit our discussion to those types of plans here.

Following are six good reasons to participate in your company's 401(k) or 403(b):

1: You can sock away more than you can in an IRA. Contributing to an Individual Retirement Account is a good way to build retirement assets. However, you are limited to setting aside only $2,000 a year. Compare that with the $10,000 (the current maximum allowed) you can contribute annually to your 401(k) or 403(b) plan. And if you contribute to both an IRA and your company's plan, you can really boost your tax-deferred savings, although both contributions may not be tax-deductible.

2: You may get an automatic return on your money. Some employers match the money you put away in your 401(k) or 403(b) retirement plan (usually 25 to 50 cents on every dollar you put away, up to 6 percent of your income). Because of this match, it is generally recommended that investors maximize employer-sponsored plans before they contribute to IRA accounts.

3: You pay less in taxes. Because your contributions are made with pretax dollars, you do not pay income taxes on the money you contribute to your 401(k) or 403(b). That means every dollar you contribute reduces your taxable income and your current tax bill as well. The result? It actually costs you less to save.

4: You can often take out a loan against your 401(k) or 403(b) money, without penalties.

5: You do not pay income taxes on the earnings, so your savings grow faster. With tax-deferred plans you do not have to pay capital gains taxes on distributions while your money accumulates.

6: You save before you spend, since 401(k) or 403(b) contributions are automatically withdrawn from your paycheck on a regular basis. You do not need to write a check, find an envelope, or lick a stamp. And there is no burdensome paperwork to worry about. You can relax knowing that each pay period you are paying yourself first.

A 403(b) plan is a retirement plan for employees of selected non-profits, schools, and certain charitable organizations, whereas 401(k)s cover the wide range of for-profit businesses. Although both plans are permitted to include loan provisions, after-tax con-tributions, and matching employer contributions, each of those features is more commonly found in a 401(k) than in a 403(b).

Simplified Employee Pension-IRA (SEP-IRA)/Keogh

These plans are often set up for small companies or self-employed indi-viduals. The maximum employer contribution is 15 percent of compen-sation or $24,000, whichever is less. Employee contributions are not allowed. Contributions may be based only on the first $160,000 of com-pensation as adjusted. These plans are complicated, and more detail is beyond the scope of this book. If you are self-employed, and/or deemed an independent contractor, look into these plans. They are uncomplicated to set up and they can save you significant taxes.

● CONTROLLING TAXES

Control taxes, do not let taxes control you. In general, taxes on mutual funds are levied at two points: redemption and distribution. Effective management of redemptions and distributions can save you money and increase your after-tax rate of return.

Redemptions

When you redeem, or sell, shares from a mutual fund, you are taking cash out of the fund, and you must pay taxes if there are any realized gains (if you made any money). Your principal, or initial, investment is not taxed, but your earnings are. The way to avoid paying too many taxes is to cash in your shares only when you absolutely must. By developing a sound financial plan and by avoiding the emotions of the market, you will reduce the need to sell shares frequently, and consequently you will reduce your tax burden.

Distributions

When mutual funds generate realized capital gains and dividends within their portfolio, they are required to pay annual distributions to shareholders. Unless your money is in a tax-sheltered vehicle such as a municipal bond fund, an IRA, or a 401(k), you will be taxed on the distributions.

● FIVE DEADLY FUND TAX SINS

In addition to redemptions and distributions, other tax-related scenarios can cause problems for mutual fund investors. Here are five of the most common tax sins:

Not Including Dividend Reinvestments when Calculating Your Cost Basis

Most mutual funds pay dividends and/or capital gains. Investors typically have the option of reinvesting these distributions to purchase additional shares. Whether you elect to reinvest your distributions or choose to receive cash, these distributions are still subject to tax in the year they were paid. Once you pay taxes on these distributions, you increase your cost basis by the amount of the distributions.

For example, suppose you bought shares of a fund for $10. A year later the fund distributed $2, on which you subsequently pay taxes. Your initial cost basis in the fund was $10, but after you pay taxes on this distribution, you have a new cost basis of $12. If you fail to adjust your cost basis upwards, you run the risk of paying taxes twice. If you were to sell all of these shares at $12, you would owe nothing, since you already paid taxes on the $2 distribution. If you sold all of your shares at $12 and failed to adjust your cost basis, you would again pay taxes on $2 per share ($12 sale price minus $10 unadjusted purchase price).

Reinvested dividends can also be important when you sell. For example, say you originally purchased 450 shares of XYZ Mutual Fund at a cost of $4,500 and over the years you reinvested $750 worth of taxable dividends to acquire an additional 50 shares. You currently own 500 shares. The cost basis of your 500 shares is $5,250, which is the sum of your original cost plus the reinvested dividends.

If you fail to include reinvested dividends when you calculate the cost basis of your holdings—and many investors do—your gain on the sale of XYZ shares will be larger or your loss will be smaller. Either way, you shortchange yourself. Also, if you fail to report the dividend income in the year the dividend was reinvested, you now must go back and amend your tax return for that year. And as a result, you will more than likely owe more taxes and penalties.

VVWilliams: "I got hit with taxes twice. Each year when my fund paid distributions I dutifully paid my taxes. But I made one very major mistake: I forgot to adjust my cost basis in my funds for the amount that I paid taxes. According to my incorrect accounting method, I had made more in each of my fund holdings than I actually had. So when I ultimately sold my fund holdings to buy a house, I had a low cost basis—since I never adjusted upward for the taxes I paid each year. Due to the low cost basis, I had a huge taxable gain. I now have a tax expert and he caught the problem. I have spent the past two weeks with my accountant going over old tax filings and account statements. Do yourself a favor: do it right from the onset. If you are the least bit confused, see a tax expert."

Switching Funds Regularly

Many mutual fund companies offer a family of funds, and investors are often allowed to switch between funds within a family. Many brokerages exacerbate the problem by offering multiple families of funds. If an investor purchases the funds through a fund supermarket, he or she can often switch among funds in different families. If you switch funds, remember that a transfer from Fund A to Fund Z is actually a sale of one fund and a purchase of the other. In a taxable account, the sale side of every switch must be reported on your tax return and any capital gain or loss will be taxed according to the rules of Schedule D of the federal tax code. One way to guard against frequent switches and excessive taxes is to always ask your online community its opinion of your planned move before you do it.

BAruLizard: "I thought I developed one of those elusive black boxes—a failproof way to beat the market. I developed a method of switching in and out of Fidelity sector funds. As fund performance would weaken, I would sell. When a fund would do well over a given period, I would buy. On average I was holding a fund for a month. When it came time to pay taxes, all of a sudden my 30 percent gain was just about cut in half due to short-term taxable gains. Many advanced investors use strategies such as this and I may very well go back to it in the future. Only, this time, I will do it inside my Roth IRA."

The Wash Sale

The only laundry we are talking about here is dirty laundry. If you reinvest your dividends, you should also be careful not to stumble into a wash sale. A wash sale is the sale and purchase of the same fund within thirty days. A perfectly legal transaction, a wash sale has nothing to do with money laundering.

Suppose you sell some, but not all, of your shares in ABC Fund at a loss. Assume that ABC Fund pays a dividend within thirty days before or after your sale, and you use that dividend to purchase additional shares of the fund. Since you have sold ABC shares at a loss and repurchased shares of the same fund within thirty days, all or part of your loss will be disallowed as a wash sale. (However, the loss can be later used when you sell the shares you purchased within the thirty days before or after.)

To avoid the problem, plan your loss sales so that they occur more than thirty days before or after a dividend distribution, or buy another fund of similar investment style.

As you can see, the wash sale is somewhat confusing. Unless you are dealing with large sums of money, the negative result of a wash sale on mutual fund distributions will result in just a few extra dollars come tax time. Certainly, you never want to pay any more taxes than necessary, but it is not something to lose sleep over.

Writing Checks Against Your Account

Some mutual funds, especially bond funds, come with check-writing privileges. Every time you write a check, you are instructing your fund to sell shares, and every check must be reported as a sale on your tax return. Even if you keep good records, check writing can create extra work at tax time, especially if the wash sale rules apply. In addition, unintended capital gains may result.

Too Many Capital Losses, Not Enough Capital Gains

If the market tumbles and you take a big hit, we usually advise that you hold on tight unless you need the money within three years. If you must sell at a loss, it is good to know that the first $3,000 of capital losses realized through your sale of fund shares can be deducted against your income. After that, any investments that are sold at a loss can be used to offset any capital gains on a dollar-for-dollar basis.

It is actually possible to make money during a year and still claim a loss. Only realized gains are taxed. (Realized gains occur only after you or your fund manager sell an investment for a gain.) However, the actual annual return of your portfolio includes realized and unrealized gains and losses. If all of the sales you make over the course of a year result in a net loss and your unrealized gains are greater than your loss, you in effect get to claim a loss—and reduce the amount you owe or even get money back—while still increasing your portfolio's value. Tax-savvy investors often sell their losing investments over the course of a year and hold on to their winners. The old Wall Street adage, "Let your winners ride and cut your losers short," is actually a tax-shrewd move. By managing your investments with taxes in mind, you can greatly defer taxes to well into the future.

Reaching the point where you actively manage taxes, gains, and losses takes time if you do it the old-fashioned paper way. Online investing helps you manage your tax efficiency by providing more convenient access to tax information and by facilitating accurate record keeping of all the transactions you make.

If you have some shares of a stock or mutual fund that have run up in price, you can donate them to a nonprofit, or even a private, foundation such as a family trust, and get a double tax break. Not only will you get a tax deduction for the current value, you will not be taxed on the appreciation.

Even better than just giving money to charity is setting up a Charitable Remainder Unit Trust. These splendid little gizmos benefit you three ways: first, you turn over stock or mutual fund shares to a charity and get a tax write-off; second, you do not pay taxes on the appreciation of your assets; and third, the money goes into a trust that pays you or your heirs a steady income stream later in life.

If you are going to manage your fund's tax liabilities online, you might as well go the whole nine yards and file your taxes online. While a detailed discussion of online taxes is beyond the scope of this book (heck, we are CFPs, not CPAs!), an overview of some of the more popular online tax services is below. Check out our online site for frequent updates.

You can easily download all tax forms from most financial sites, or for just a few dollars, you can file your tax forms electronically using an IRS "e-file." E-file is a system developed by the IRS and corporations that make the filing of taxes electronically—over the Web—easy, fast, and guaranteed. The Internal Revenue Service has partnered with various private companies to bring taxpayers affordable, convenient, user-friendly e-file options available from home or through an authorized

IRS e-file provider. Some companies offer free services for qualifying taxpayers. The following group of Web sites offer IRS e-filing.

- America Online—KEYWORD: Tax.

- Block Financial—www.taxcut.com.

- H&R Block—www.hrblock.com.

- Intuit—www.turbotax.com.

- Jackson Hewitt—www.jacksonhewitt.com.

- 2nd Story Software—www.taxact.com.

- UDS ELECtroTAX—www.usdtax.com.

- Universal Tax Systems—www.securetax.com.

E-file Internet sites take you through the entire tax-filing process by asking you simple questions. Just answer a few questions and the Web sites will do the rest. Once you are done, you can print your tax forms and snail-mail them or e-file them directly to the IRS. If you owe money, you can either pay with a credit card or have the money deducted directly from your checking account. If you are eligible for a refund, you can have the money automatically transferred into your bank account, all from your computer. And once you choose and use a particular service, your personal information is stored for following years to make the tax process faster.

Of course, if you are uncomfortable completing your taxes on your own, we strongly suggest you consult a tax professional. Taxes are one area where you should exercise extreme caution. The last thing you want is the dreaded audit.

According to the IRS, the average e-file tax submission will have 18 percent fewer errors than a paper return, and refund checks will show up in your bank account five times faster—anywhere between eight days and three weeks. Now, that is an interesting statistic!

● MORE JUNK FOOD

Here is Sage's list of the Top Ten Tax-Efficient Funds as of March 1999. While this list may or may not still hold true, it should give you some food for thought.

Sage's Top Ten Tax-Efficient Funds (Number one is the best.)

10: Vanguard Tax-Managed Growth and Income (VTGIX).

The Tax-Managed Growth and Income Fund has no load, with a low expense ratio of 0.17 percent, but it does have a two-tiered redemption fee structure in which you are charged 2 percent if you redeem within twelve months and 1 percent if you redeem within five years. Unlike the majority of Vanguard funds that have a minimum initial investment of $3,000, this fund has a minimum initial investment of $10,000.

9: Schwab 1000 Investor (SNXFX).

Traditionally, most fund managers use the first-in, first-out accounting method, where the shares first sold of a given stock are compared to those first purchased to calculate the amount of capital gain. With this fund, the managers take a more active approach to manage tax liabilities. The portfolio is realigned once a year based on the brokerage's own Schwab 1000 Index, which consists of one thousand of the largest publicly traded companies, excluding investment and brokerage firms. The fund is a no-load with an expense ratio of only 0.46 percent.

8: Nationwide (MUIFX).

The fund has a rather hefty front-end load of 4.5 percent and an expense ratio of 0.6 percent. The performance, however, has been outstanding.

7: Domini Social Equity Fund (DSEFX).

This fund invests in an index of four hundred companies that meet a number of social criteria, which is referred to as the Domini Social Index. The fund is a no-load, with an expense ratio of 1.17 percent.

6: Wilshire Target Large Growth Investors (DTLGX).

After listing 750 of the largest cap companies in the Wilshire 5000 Index, the fund managers then seek the growth companies.

Again, this indexing type of strategy leads to a tax-friendly fund. The fund has no load, with an expense ratio of 0.73 percent.

5:    Rydex Nova (RYNVX).

Seeking to match returns that are 150 percent times those of the S&P 500, this fund invests in index futures contracts and options on equity indices. The fund is no-load, with an expense ratio of 1.11 percent. It does have a high minimum of $25,000, but is available for lower minimums at a number of mutual fund supermarkets. At Waterhouse the minimum is $5,000, and it is even lower at Charles Schwab with a $2,500 minimum, but you can get in most economically at both DLJdirect and Ameritrade for a minimum initial investment of $1,000.

4:    Vanguard Growth Index (VIGRX).

Vanguard Index Growth invests in the S&P/BARRA Growth Index. BARRA divides the S&P 500 into two groups: those with high price-to-book values, which make up the S&P/BARRA Growth Index, and those with low price-to-book values, which make up the S&P/BARRA Value Index. In the ten-year period from 1975 to 1984, value investing dominated, but since then growth stocks have been outperforming value. The fund is no-load and follows Vanguard's philosophy of low expense ratios with 0.22 percent. Fund manager George Sauter has the ability to employ futures contracts on the indexes to simulate a fully invested position and manage cash flows efficiently.

3:    Legg Mason Value Prime (LMVTX).

Manager William Miller III runs his portfolio in a very tax-friendly manner. The fund does not have a front- or back-end load, but does have an expense ratio of 1.73 percent. Taxes or no taxes, this is a great fund!

2:    Flag Investors Communications (TISHX).

The majority of technology-oriented funds tend to be highly tax-efficient, but with a low 26 percent turnover rate, this telecommunications fund has a history of being tax-friendly. It does have a front-end load of 4.5 percent with an expense ratio of 1.11 percent. Load or no load, flag this fund down.

1:   Rydex OTC (RYOCX).

This fund seeks the same returns as the Nasdaq 100 Index by investing in a sample of the equities in that index, as well as using index futures and options on equity indices. The fund is no-load, with an expense ratio of 1.13 percent. Not for the meek, this fund can be incredibly volatile. Like Rydex Nova, it also has a high minimum of $25,000, but is available for lower minimums at a number of mutual fund supermarkets. Again, Waterhouse has a minimum of $5,000, Charles Schwab can get you in for $2,500, and both DLJdirect and Ameritrade are the lowest, with minimum initial investments of $1,000.

CHAPTER WRAP

Everything else being equal, Sage advocates investing in tax-advantaged funds when available, if the investment would otherwise be subject to taxes.

There are two general ways to reduce your taxes with mutual funds: investing in tax-efficient mutual funds and investing in qualified retirement plans.

- Types of tax-efficient funds include low-turnover funds, index funds, municipal bond funds, and tax-managed funds. In addition, there are funds within variable annuities and variable life plans that may be attractive depending upon your financial planning situation.

- Tax-qualified investment plans allow investors to reduce their adjusted gross income—thereby reducing the yearly tax bite. More important, however, is the fact that these plans allow money to compound unhindered by the IRS. Popular types of tax-qualified retirement plans include IRA, 401(k), and 403(b) plans. Any kind of mutual fund can be held within a tax-qualified retirement plan.

- 401(k) or 403(b) plans are generally more attractive than alternative investment vehicles.

- Put money in your pocket by controlling your taxes, not having them control you. One way is by managing your redemptions.

Another way is by managing your distributions. Keep track of your cost basis and avoid the five deadly tax sins.

- Managing your fund's taxes is going to take some time. Online investing helps facilitate this task, and online communities can point out tax-savings tips that you never knew existed!

● IN THE TRENCHES WITH SAGE

PTSeraphMary: I just had a baby and I am looking for a way to save money for my son's college education. Should I open an Education IRA or are they only for retirement?

Stephen Cohn: "Despite the name, Education IRAs have absolutely nothing to do with retirement. They are, however, a new tax-deferred way of helping families save for college tuition.

This type of IRA is a simple investment that provides tax-free earnings and withdrawals for a child's qualified higher education expenses. The maximum annual contribution allowed is $500, which is nondeductible. That may sound small, but if you start when little Johnny is born, then you will be a happy camper by the time those tuition bills start rolling in.

Individuals qualify who have modified adjusted gross income (MAGI) levels below $160,000 for joint filers, or $110,000 for single filers. Any child under the age of eighteen may be named as a beneficiary on an Education IRA account as long as a parent or legal guardian is named as the responsible individual.

A child may be the beneficiary on more than one account, but the Education IRA contributions must be limited to a total of $500 per year per child. Any kind soul is allowed to contribute to an Education IRA, not just parents and relatives, but the maximum annual amount is still $500 per child. For example, a parent and a grandparent could each give $250, thereby contributing a total of $500 for one child, but each person could not make an individual $500 contribution for the same child. A contribution to an Education IRA does not affect what you may contribute to your retirement IRA.

Contributions to the account are allowed until the child reaches the age of eighteen, and although no additional contributions are allowed after that point, the account may remain open until the beneficiary turns thirty years old.

The costs associated with post-secondary education, such as tuition, books, fees, supplies, and housing expenses, are eligible for tax-free withdrawals. That also goes for students enrolled part-time.

With an Education IRA, if your son decides not to go to college, you have several options. The account is transferable to another member of the beneficiary's family, or as previously mentioned, the account can remain open until the beneficiary reaches age thirty. If he has not used the funds by that time, the account balance must be withdrawn within thirty days. Applicable taxes, plus a possible 10 percent penalty for not using the account for education, would apply to earnings. The responsible individual would retain control of the Education IRA until all of the assets are distributed.

Sage's Top Ten Fund Tips

A JOURNEY OF A THOUSAND MILES STARTS WITH ONE STEP.

Lao Tzu, Chinese philosopher

The most difficult aspect of investing, like so many other things in life, is getting started. Where do you start? How do you invest? Which investments do you choose? Yes, starting from scratch is daunting. There seems to be so much information to absorb, just so much to digest. But now you have tools to get yourself financially fit.

Do not waste another minute. Take time now, while you are still motivated, to make a plan and a commitment. Set aside a few hours a month to plan and monitor your investments. That is really all it takes. In fact, a study described in *The Millionaire Next Door* by Thomas Stanley found that the average millionaire spends about five hours a month on his or her investments. The average nonmillionaire spends about half that amount. Make some time to amass your fortune.

One of the most common excuses we hear at Sage is that one lacks the money needed to become an investor. It does not take much to get started. Set aside 10 percent out of each paycheck to fund your investments. If your company offers the option, have the money automatically deducted from your paycheck to eliminate the temptation of skipping investment cycles. We have some great tips (with number one being the best) for how you can do this effortlessly and inexpensively.

● TIP TEN: TAKE FIVE HOURS AND MAKE TEN PERCENT

"Begin with the end in mind."

Stephen Covey, author of The Seven Habits of
Highly Effective People

By following this simple "five-and-ten" rule, you virtually eliminate the chances of retiring a pauper. Suppose you make $40,000 year and invest 10 percent, or $4,000, in a tax-friendly plan such as a 401(k) or 403(b). After thirty years your portfolio will be worth slightly more than $1 million. If you do this for forty years, you will have almost $3.5 million.

Now, let's put that in context: Sixty hours a year (five hours month) for forty years is a total of three hundred hours of a time commitment over your entire investment life. If three hundred hours results in a portfolio of $3.5 million, you are in effect making $11,500 each hour you commit to investing.

Take the time, make the money.

● TIP NINE: FUND YOUR TAX-QUALIFIED RETIREMENT PLANS

"You can be young without money but you can not be old without it."

Tennessee Williams, playwright

Facing the reality that the future of Social Security is bleak at best, the government has made a mad dash to encourage taxpayers to save for retirement. As an incentive, the government has given you the option of deducting the amount you invest in a tax-qualified retirement plan up front and paying taxes when you withdraw the money, as with a 401(k), 403(b), or Traditional IRA, or paying taxes on your investments initially and then withdrawing your money tax-free, as with a Roth IRA, SEP-IRA, or Keogh.

Your income level and age will dictate which type of plan is best for you, but no matter how much or little you make, one of these plans is right for you. You should take advantage of them before you make any other long-term investments.

These plans either lower your yearly income tax bite by adjusting your taxable income down by the amount you invest, or reduce your tax burden during retirement. These reasons alone make them compelling investments. But there is one more kicker that makes them just too good to pass up.

Normally when you buy and sell investments, you pay a short- or long-term capital gains tax. In addition, when a fund makes a capital gains or dividend distribution, as most do at least once a year, these are taxed. But in a qualified tax plan, all distributions and capital gains are sheltered from taxes. You can buy and sell as much as you like without the tax bite.

All long-term money belongs in a qualified tax-friendly plan. Even if your investment options are limited, as they often are in a 401(k) or 403(b) plan, the added tax benefit of these plans makes them appealing even if the offerings are less then stellar. An average fund in a 401(k) or 403(b) is better than a great fund outside of a qualified tax plan. However, be careful: Uncle Sam does put limits on the amount you can invest in these plans.

TIP EIGHT: THINK THROUGH YOUR DECISIONS

"Not doing more than average is what keeps the average down."

William Winans, author of Reminiscences and Experiences in the Life of an Editor

Unfortunately, most investors buy and sell based not on sound financial planning principles, but on hunches and fear. A stock is down after being downgraded, the market is falling due to the latest economic numbers, a stock is soaring on a takeover rumor—these are the reasons people usually sell.

This type of herd-mentality fast lane leads to mediocre returns. The market insanity reflects the current perception of the general investment public. Because we as humans tend to overreact to good and bad news, the market—and individual securities in general—can fluctuate wildly in terms of price. Generally, everyone wants to buy or sell at the same time, moving the stock, or the market, up or down. The absolute worst time to make an investment decision is when emotions are involved. When you act on emotions and follow the herd, you invariably lose out.

Every investor, especially when starting out, makes at least some investment decisions based on split-second thinking. Accept the fact that you too will commit herd-like errors in the beginning. Just realize that each trade you make based on an emotional state will result in some type of loss, based either on taxes or on a poor investment decision. It is just an unfortunate part of investing that you must willingly work to overcome.

Sage community leader WWilliams947: "When my mother sold her house and moved into an apartment, she gave me a portion of the money she made to invest. Initially I bought just two stocks—Dell and America Online. I was making decent gains in each stock and then the market took a dive. I needed to do something. I just needed to act. I sold America Online and doubled my Dell position. I am not really sure why I did that but at the time it made a lot of sense. America Online popped back up strongly over the next few weeks, as did Dell, just not as strongly. I calculated that I lost over $10,000 on that transaction and was kicking myself for making such a foolish mistake. I sold half of my Dell position and bought back America Online, now at a higher price. Both did well, though America Online did a little better. Though the initial mistake cost me 'only' $10,000, after splits and gains (America Online has since split a few times) the move has lessened my portfolio by over $50,000. That is a lot of money and a very expensive mistake. In addition, I wish I had invested in funds instead of stocks. It would have lessened my anxiety, delegated my buy and sell decisions to a pro, and allowed me to sleep much better at night."

There are a few day traders and active investors who do well flipping in and out of stocks, but they are more of an anomaly than the norm. Make a willful commitment—write it down if you must—to limit the number of trades you make, and you will make investment decisions based only on financial planning needs, not on hunches or emotions. Do this from the onset, before you become an active investor and certainly before you take to online investing.

● TIP SEVEN: DRAW UP A PLAN—DEFINE YOUR GOALS

"Unless commitment is made, there are only promises and hopes . . . but no plans."

Peter Ferdinand Drucker, management guru

Without a clear investment direction, your investment decisions and the performance of your portfolio will be lackluster. Far too many investors buy stocks and funds because they hear about them from a friend or family member. Add a fund here, buy a stock there. The result is a portfolio—if you can call it that—consisting of investment oddities. A few biotech stocks, maybe an Internet fund or two, and a number of hoped-for next Microsofts.

Many investors will take the course for years on end, playing the market instead of creating a sound investment plan. The sooner you decide what you want out of your investments, the sooner you can get down to making real money.

It does not take much. Take the self-test in Chapter Two to determine what type of investor you are, where your goals lie, and what type of risk tolerance you have. Once you do that, sit down, choose some funds, and follow the Sage investment strategy outlined in this book. Generally funds will stick to their investment style and managers will make good investment decisions. If not, your online community will surely let you know that it's time for a change.

All that is needed beyond this is a little monitoring—say, maybe once a quarter—to see if allocation is in check and that your funds are performing up to snuff. Stick with your plan, do not deviate, and make changes only when your goals change.

Follow this course of action, resisting the urge to invest in areas that fall outside of your plan, and you will vastly increase the returns of your portfolio and reach your goals. Guaranteed.

TIP SIX: JUMP ON THE NET—GET WIRED

"Information about money has become more valuable than money itself."

> Walter Wriston, former chairman and CEO,
> Citicorp/Citibank

The Web is an enormous investment research resource, more so than any book could ever reveal or hope to be. To make your investment career more profitable and enjoyable, get connected to the Internet. Use sites such as Sage, TheStreet.com, Motley Fool, Multex, Morningstar.com, and many others as investment tools and community outlets.

You can research investments using scores of free fund and stock screening tools, talk with fund managers and corporate CEOs, chat with other investors, and get expert assistance and community opinions. What you used to pay thousands of dollars for, you can now get on the Internet for free, in a manner that is faster and more comprehensive. The Web is a liberating investment tool, unarguably the best tool that has ever been created.

You can now buy a high-quality computer (including a monitor, software, and a modem) for a fraction of what it cost several years ago, and often this includes free access to the Internet. Given that most investment sites and research tools are available free of charge, the initial setup is relatively cheap. In fact, given the range of information you will be exposed to and the cost-saving investment steps you will take by conducting your investments over the Web, your computer will more than pay for itself in less than a year.

TCaitlin 90: "Before I became an Internet junkie I conducted all of my financial transactions via a fund company and a bank. Once I signed on, I immediately transferred my funds to an online brokerage account. Right off the bat, I lopped off $180 in commissions from each trade. When I was looking for a house, I was initially set on using a mortgage lender that was recommended to me by an office-mate. After meeting with the lender, I got the feeling I was being taken for a ride. I did a little research and found a lender online that could give me a much better rate. Obviously, my initial lender was irate. But the bottom line was this: by going with an online lender I will save over $10,000 in interest payments over thirty years. And with my online brokerage account, I can check my fund investments with a click of the mouse. I bought my computer a few years ago and it turned out to be one of the very best investments I have ever made. The Web has already saved me thousands of dollars."

TIP FIVE: TRUST THE NUMBERS

"Numbers serve to discipline rhetoric. Without them it is too easy to follow flights of fancy, to ignore the world as it is and to remold it nearer the heart's desire."

Ralph Waldo Emerson, poet

Numerical investing is a little scary. Simply following the numbers is a hard thing to do. We humans like a little hand-holding and schmoozing. We are inclined to act on our emotion. While this may be a good course of action to take with respect to most of life's endeavors, it is a terrible thing to do when investing.

Jonathan Hoenig, editor of *The Capitalist Pig,* chats with Sage Online: "There's not a man, woman, or child alive in the world who knows what Microsoft or Dell Computer or whatever is going to do over the next two weeks. . . . Over the short term, price is influenced by psychology and herds. I think once market sentiment changes, lots of quality names will get the tar beaten out of them. *That's* when I want to buy."

Follow the disciplined process outlined in this book and you will take the emotions out of your investments. Numerically screen your mutual funds. Subjectively evaluate if they pass your litmus test. Find out what your online community thinks of your selections. Access the fund managers via message boards and chats. This process has worked for us in our financial planning practice, and thousands of individual online investors follow our advice. Why mess with success?

GORounds33: "How blind am I? How dumb am I? I fancy myself as a savvy guy who can see through marketing garb and useless drivel. For years now I have held a fund. I thought it was a lean fund with an awesome manager. I considered selling when performance tailed off, but each time I got the urge, I would receive one of the fund manager's metaphorical musings on long-term commitments. I remained faithful, holding the fund through thick and now thinner and thinner times. Then it dawned on me, this guy I love so much has stepped away from the fund and has handed down the reins to some flunky. Supposedly he spends his time on the ski slopes and his only relationship with the fund is the quarterly writings.

   "Here this character is talking about sticking with an investment, remaining true, dancing with the date that brung you, while he is off on my dime yucking it up with the rich and famous. I am the only loser here and the only one to blame. Long ago the fund was a sell, as it still is. Yet I have held, losing out on huge gains in more suitable investments. Why am I such a lemming? For starters, I paid more attention to the manager's writings than the fund's steady performance decline compared to its peers. If I would have only invested with the numbers instead of through blind loyalty, I'd be a much richer man today."

● TIP FOUR: OPEN A MUTUAL FUND SUPERMARKET ACCOUNT WITH AN ONLINE BROKER

"Everything should be made as simple as possible, but not simpler."
Albert Einstein

Investing is a game of economics. You go where the gains are plentiful and the fees are nominal. The mutual fund supermarket offered by online brokers is basically a marriage of both.

With a supermarket you have the choice of thousands of different mutual funds, as compared to a fund family where you are limited to just a few funds. Economy of scale allows Internet supermarkets such as E*TRADE, DLJdirect, and Charles Schwab to offer a myriad of mutual fund choices at no additional cost to you.

As an added benefit, supermarkets allow you to consolidate all of your investments, making the investment process and tax preparation incredibly easy.

The downside associated with Internet supermarkets lies with the ease of trading. For an undisciplined investor, subject to trading at a whim, the Web supermarket is a dangerous tool. If you are not careful, investing can turn into gambling all too easily.

● TIP THREE: DECREASE VOLATILITY—INVEST IN VOLATILE MARKETS

"Fortune favors the bold."
Virgil, Roman poet

A successful portfolio holds dissimilar investments that complement each other well. A growth fund by itself can be very volatile, as can an international fund. But when you put them side by side in a portfolio, their sharp ups and downs work to offset each other.

Diversification is basically the act of putting opposite-style funds together to create a portfolio with a sum that is greater than its parts. To successfully assemble a portfolio, you must invest in all types of investments. Growth needs value; small needs large; and domestic needs foreign.

In theory and on paper, it is easy to assemble a well-diversified portfolio of funds. But in practice, it takes a great deal of fortitude and strength. The cyclical nature of the market results in very small segments of stocks doing well at one time. In the late nineties, large caps were hot. Before that, small caps were on fire. Before that, international holdings performed well. When you create your portfolio you will be buying into, and holding on to, areas of the market that are out of favor.

Do not worry about this. All areas come in and out of favor. By making a commitment in areas of the market that are not the current toast of the town you will, in the short term, hamper the returns of your portfolio. But when the cycle moves to another area of the market, your laggards will turn into leaders (and vice versa) and you will benefit from your holdings in that area.

Concentrating all of your assets in just one segment of the market will result in average long-term returns and above-average volatility. By holding various segments of the market within your portfolio, your gains over the long run will be market-like, but the volatility of your portfolio will be reduced greatly.

Risk is not volatility, as it is often considered to be. Volatility is a short-term phenomenon that has no lasting effects. Risk, however, is a lasting factor in the returns of your portfolio because it dictates what actions you take and what type of investments you make.

The fear of taking an investment risk will lead you into overly conservative funds. The result will be a portfolio that has not reached its full potential. It will not be able to adequately fund your retirement and it will force you to stay in the workforce longer than you desire. Now, that is risk.

Social Security is a prime example. Today, as we have all heard countless times, Social Security is in dire straits. Yet by traditional measures, there is no less risky an investment than Social Security. Social Security is basically a large mutual fund. The caveat is, of course, that it can only invest in Treasury bonds—a pathetic long-term investment. As a result, the huge portfolio of money that has been placed in the Social Security system over the years has not grown at a rapid enough rate to fund future retirees. If Social Security funds had been invested in a diversified mutual fund portfolio, they would be worth hundreds of times what they are today. While there are other complexities specific to Social Security, this lesson can nevertheless be applied to one's own portfolio.

Overly cautious investors will face the same fate. By playing it safe, buying conservative investments, investors are placing themselves at a disadvantage. The greatest risk you will encounter over your investment lifetime is not a crash, it is inflation. Inflation eats away at your returns. The only proven method to outpace inflation is through stock-based investments.

Of course, this does not mean you should invest exclusively in high-volatility investments. You should keep a well-diversified portfolio and stick to a predetermined plan. Just realize, the farther you fall down the conservative ladder, the greater the chances are that you will lose to inflation and your portfolio will simulate the returns of Social Security.

● TIP TWO: DO NOT INVEST IN HOT TIPS

"With enough inside information and a million dollars, you can go broke in a year."

Warren Buffett, renowned investor

Let's be honest here. Online mutual fund information is less subject to abuse than online stock information. Individuals cannot tout the price of a fund like they can a stock. In addition, people can chat directly with a fund manager online. It is difficult to have the same kind of opportunity to talk to the CEO of a company. Let's look at some examples of some online stock touting. These types of rumormongering just cannot happen in a fund community.

Case Study One: The PairGain Files

In the beginning of the first quarter of 1999, the U.S. Attorney's office in Los Angeles arrested PairGain Technologies employee Gary Hoke for fraud, alleging that he posted a fake Bloomberg News story on the Internet that boosted PairGain's shares. Bloomberg filed a suit in the U.S. District Court in Manhattan. It alleged that five "John Does" infringed on Bloomberg's trademarks and unfairly competed with the New York–based company. Two of the five allegedly spread the fake announcement on the Yahoo! message board, while two others allegedly posted messages on the techstocks.com Web site. Their news story sent PairGain's stock up by over 30 percent.

This was a situation in which individual Net investors knowingly duped other investors by spreading false information. While there are undoubtedly a fair number of Net-goers who willingly traverse the Internet spreading misinformation, this was a highly unusual case. In addition, a moderated community would have negated the risk of the false dissemination of the rumors by exposing the perpetrators.

Case Study Two: The Iomega Files

This case has to do with the Motley Fool's message board coverage of Iomega. Iomega manufactures storage solutions based on removable-media technology for personal computers and consumer electronics devices. Iomega's data storage hardware includes disk drives and disks marketed under the names "Zip," "Jazz," and "Clik!." But to read messages posted by "Iomegian's," as staunch followers of the company were called, you would have thought the company was the next Microsoft. In fact, many suggested it would be.

The offline financial media took note of Iomega's rapid rise in price, attributing it to online "hypesters." While there was a fair amount of hype on the Motley Fool's message board, there was also a wealth of in-depth analysis. Eventually the excitement over Iomega proved to be too much and the company failed to deliver. The stock tumbled sharply, and many first-time online investors lost a great deal of money. An active moderated community might have avoided this carnage by responding to every tout and exaggeration.

Case Study Three: Rick's Cabaret Files

Because the financial media are seen as objective and authoritative, they can have a powerful influence over the movement of stocks. In April of 1999 two journalists appeared on CNBC to talk about stocks that were moving that day. They made mention of a very tiny company called Rick's Cabaret International. The company had announced its intention to enter the adult Internet business, changed its ticker symbol to RICK from RICKD, and reported that its new president and chief executive officer had taken a voluntary pay reduction of 20 percent, or $34,320. The news was not really news at all, but since Rick's Cabaret operates an adult nightclub offering topless entertainment, a restaurant, a bar, a discotheque, and billiard club, it was considered, at least by these two reporters, to be noteworthy.

The stock immediately shot almost 100 percent higher before falling late in the trading session. Had a movement such as this occurred as a result of online message board or chat speculation, you can be sure the offline financial press would have had a field day. Yet the irony is that a moderated community would have blown that information out of the water by putting the report in proper perspective.

Case Study Four: The Compaq Files

On a warm spring day in 1999, Compaq chief executive officer Eckhard Pfeiffer met with Ted David, anchor of CNBC's "Market Watch." Pfeiffer appeared on the show to alleviate investors' concerns over a recent announcement that the company would not meet analysts' earnings estimates. Because of the shortfall, Compaq's stock had taken a sharp hit. Pfeiffer steadfastly argued that the company was on track and would return to solid growth.

After the interview on CNBC, Sage Online was deluged with investors' questions about Compaq. Sage Live Event commentator SageMath told Sage chatters that Compaq had been in a steady corporate decline for some time, that the earnings warning should come as no surprise, and that a sell-off was long overdue. Math warned investors that the worst was not over for the company and they would do well to stay clear away from the company. The following Sunday Compaq's CEO resigned, and Compaq stock tanked. SageMath had saved Sage chatters millions of dollars. Ahhh, the power of moderated communities.

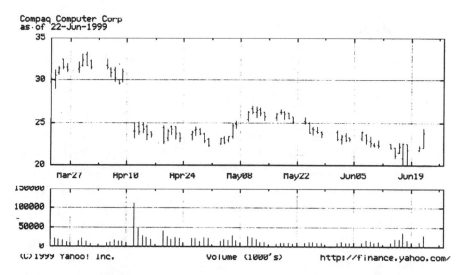

Figure 13.1. A graph showing the poor performance of Compaq stock after its CEO resigned.

TIP ONE: ALLOCATE YOUR ASSETS

"Eighty percent of success is showing up."
Woody Allen, comedian

Allocation is and always will be the driving force behind the gains of your portfolio. Study after study has determined that very few of your gains are due to actual fund selection. Rather, the push behind your portfolio will be determined by how you break up your investments between small caps, large caps, internationals, and bonds.

Work hard, but do not drive yourself crazy when picking strong funds. After you select your initial investments, spend the majority of your time keeping your allocation in check. Monitor your portfolio's composition once a quarter and make changes no more than once a year (unless the funds are housed in a tax-qualified plan) to reduce the tax bite associated with buying and selling.

Develop an allocation model, buy solid funds, make changes to keep allocation in check, and let the portfolio make you money. It is really that simple!

CHAPTER WRAP: SAGE'S TOP TEN FUND TIPS

Follow these tips and you'll be set for life.

- Take five hours and make ten percent.

- Fund your tax-qualified retirement plans.

- Think through your decisions.

- Draw up a plan—define your goals.

- Jump on the Net—get wired.

- Trust the numbers.

- Open a mutual fund supermarket account with an online broker.

- Decrease volatility—invest in volatile markets.

- Do not invest in hot tips.

- Allocate your assets.

Here is a quick list on how to follow these Sage tips:

- Set aside time to go over your investments on a regular basis.

- Maximize all of your tax-sheltered/deferred investments.

- Invest based on research; not on hot tips.

- Stay broadly diversified and never let the market scare you into selling an investment.

- Simplify the way you invest: Open a mutual fund supermarket account.

● IN THE TRENCHES WITH SAGE

MDPitts76: I want to double my money in six years. What do I buy?

Alan Cohn: If you want to double your investment in six years, you would need approximately a 12 percent rate of return. In the right market, that is not unreasonable. In order to get those returns, you need to invest in high-quality growth-oriented mutual funds—funds that buy large cap stocks, mid cap stocks, small cap stocks, and international stocks. In addition, you have to consider that you will probably need to take your money out one to two years before you actually need it, so that you do not risk having to take it out when the market is down. Although you think you are investing for six years, it is actually a three- to four-year period.

Wrapping Up

PEOPLE OF MEDIOCRE ABILITY SOMETIMES ACHIEVE OUTSTANDING SUCCESS BECAUSE THEY DON'T KNOW WHEN TO QUIT. MOST MEN SUCCEED BECAUSE THEY ARE DETERMINED TO.

George Allen, Washington Redskins football coach 1971–1981

You know it all. You are now fit to be a Sage. But before you go, take a few moments to read over this final chapter, which summarizes all that you have learned throughout the book.

🔵 DEVELOPING AN INVESTMENT PROFILE

Before you commit a red cent to the market, you need an investment profile—a concise biographical sketch of who you are, why you are investing, what your goals are, and what your comfort level with respect to risk is. To get this picture we employed a test in Chapter Two, which gauged your:

1: Market Comfort Level: How you feel about investing.

2: Personal Investment Confidence: How you feel about making investment decisions.

3: Time Horizon: How long you plan to invest.

4: Life Stage: What stage of your life you are in.

5: Risk Tolerance: How you can handle market turbulence.

6: Investment Goal: Why you are investing.

Based on your answers to this investment profile test you were given a score, which placed you into one of three categories:

- A conservative investor who feels uncomfortable taking risks. You probably realize that you will have to take some calculated risks to attain your financial goals, but this does not mean you will be comfortable doing so.

- A moderate investor who feels comfortable taking moderate risks. You are probably willing to take reasonable risks without a great deal of discomfort.

- An aggressive investor who is willing to take high risks in search of high returns. You are not greatly stressed by taking significant risks.

You developed your investment profile in Chapter Two so that you could concentrate in the rest of the book on fulfilling your specific investment needs.

Before you chose your specific fund investments, we talked about the pros and cons of the mutual fund industry.

ADVANTAGES OF MUTUAL FUNDS

- Diversification: Funds offer investors the ability to achieve instant diversification. When you purchase one fund you indirectly buy a hundred or more stocks or bonds in different industries and of different sizes. By investing across a broad range of stocks or bonds you eliminate the risk that one specific holding can bring your entire portfolio down.

- Economy of Scale: Funds are essentially vessels where hundreds, thousands, or even millions of individual investors pool their money to increase purchasing power. This pool of money allows fund management to buy stocks or bonds "in bulk," which entitles them to special high-volume discounts.

- Liquidity: Funds are obligated to surrender your money to you in the form of cash anytime you desire. It does not matter what the market is doing or how your fund is faring. If you want your money—for any reason whatsoever—you get it. Many mutual funds have established lines of credit to meet a mass exodus, should one, in a rare event, occur.

- Professional Management: Funds are run by men and women who do nothing but follow the market and study stocks or bonds each and every day. They know when to buy, when to sell, what looks good, and what does not.

But, as we have told you, mutual funds do have their problems.

DISADVANTAGES OF FUNDS

- High Fees: Although there is some evidence that fund expenses are dropping, they are not doing so fast enough—and in many cases they are not doing it at all. A study conducted by Sage Online found that the largest fifty funds (in terms of assets under management) will take in an average of $162.9 million in expenses in 1999. (This assumes the largest funds will be flat for the year; should the average fund post a gain, the amount taken in will be higher.) The mutual fund industry still has a long way to go before it reaches the point where the majority of funds are pure bargains.

- Too Many Choices: In 1990 there were fewer than two thousand different funds; today there are well over ten thousand. As the number of funds has steadily risen, finding the good ones has become increasingly difficult. Fortunately, online screening tools have dramatically improved the selection process, but finding gems is still a formidable task for unfortunate offliners.

- Poor Performance: Before the rapid Internet-fueled exchange of information, the performance of mutual funds relative to their respective indexes was difficult to measure. As investors have become savvier, the performance or lack thereof of some mutual funds has come under criticism. Just as online screening tools can help solve the problem of too many choices, weeding out laggards can be done with a click of a mouse.

We then outlined the different fees associated with funds. After establishing a firm understanding of mutual fund expenses, we turned to different measures of risk.

- Interest Rate Risk: As interest rates increase (in tandem with rising inflation) stocks tend to fall. Stocks are, loosely speaking, inversely correlated with interest rates. Therefore market watchers and economists spend a great deal of time watching for each piece of economic news to be released. Because the economic data foretell the future strength of the economy and the state of interest rates and inflation, the stock market can experience wild gyrations based on data that indicate a rise in interest rates.

- Market Risk: The market is in a constant state of flux. It is way up one day and way down the next. At times the market will enter a prolonged period of decline—called a bear market—which poses a risk to the investors who sell. However, this risk is *perceived*, meaning that it is a risk only if you react to it. If you sell while the market is down, before it enters its inevitable rebound, you may suffer a loss. Remember, the long-term trend of the market is up, so if you can handle the short-term ups and downs, and don't react to the movements with hasty selling, you are essentially immune to market risk.

- Company Risk: There are no guaranteed returns in the stock or bond markets. Companies prosper and companies fail. Company risk is merely the risk that you will make an investment in a company that ultimately fails. Fortunately, because mutual funds hold so many stocks and bonds, company risk is not a concern for fund investors.

- Currency Risk: International funds take your money and convert it into local currency, whether it is the Italian lira or the Uzbekistan sum. That local currency is then invested in local stocks or bonds. The dollar will fluctuate in relation to foreign currencies. If the dollar strengthens against foreign currencies, the mutual fund will lose value when it is converted back into dollars, as it must every day for share price reporting.

To understand how funds compare to other funds, how successful management is, and how volatile they are—we looked at standard deviation, beta, and alpha.

- Standard Deviation: Some funds bounce around a lot, while others are somewhat sedentary. Standard deviation measures how much a fund moves up and down. The higher the standard deviation, the more volatile the fund is.

- Beta: The market, by definition, has a beta of one. The beta of a fund shows how sensitive a fund is to the market. For example, a fund with a beta of 1.2 would move 20 percent higher than the market during market upswings and 20 percent lower than the market during down days.

- Alpha: The fund manager's success is easily quantified with alpha. Alpha is a somewhat complex measurement that looks at beta and standard deviation. Fortunately, online databases will do the calculation for you. An alpha of zero or greater indicates that management is adding value. A negative alpha may indicate that management is diminishing value.

Though it is important to have at least a cursory understanding of all of these measures, in the fund screening process we look only at alpha. Since we take an overall approach to creating a portfolio, we are concerned more with how funds complement one another within a portfolio, than with how they perform by themselves. We do use alpha, however, because we feel that all funds within a portfolio should have a management team in charge that actually adds value.

At this point, we introduced the Sage investment philosophy—a two-tiered approach to investing that is built on the sturdy footing of diversification and asset allocation.

- Diversification: Spreading your assets over a number of different stocks and bonds eliminates company risk, or the danger that any single holding will sink your portfolio. Beyond the movements in individual stocks and bonds, different sectors of the market, different styles of stocks, and different-sized companies tend to fall in and out of favor. Some years small cap value stocks do well, other years large cap growth stocks are strong performers. There is never a point in time when all segments of the market perform in line with each other. Because the market fluctuates in this way and it is impossible to predict which segment of the market will do well at any given time, Sage investors diversify across many different types of funds.

By spreading your investments over a range of different stocks and bonds, you shield your portfolio from dramatic ups and downs. The result is stable returns, as represented by the graph in Figure 14.1.

- Asset Allocation: The returns of a portfolio are determined not as much by the specific funds you hold as by the types of funds you hold. How that portfolio is broken down over small cap, large cap, and international stocks, as well as bonds, dictates over 90 percent of the returns of the portfolio. Because of this well-documented fact, we have devoted most of our research to developing the best portfolio asset allocations.

Based on your investment profile of conservative, moderate, or aggressive, we apply the following portfolio allocation formulas (see Chart 14.1).

Class	Conservative	Moderate	Aggressive
Bonds	30%	20%	0%
Large cap	50%	40%	40%
Small cap	10%	20%	30%
International	10%	20%	30%
Total	100%	100%	100%

Chart 14.1. Sage model portfolios.

At this point, you have a profile and a portfolio model, but no funds. We select funds in a two-step process. First we numerically screen for candidates using a database such as Morningstar.com, then we dig beneath the numbers to subjectively weed through the remaining funds to find the best ones to purchase.

NUMERICAL ANALYSIS

- Screen for Returns: We employ a screen that selects top performing funds over the past three years. Despite what is often said in the fund industry, past performance is to some extent indicative of future performance. We have found that three years of strong returns usually results in solid future performance.

- Screen for Expenses: Expenses, as any investment academic will tell you, have a direct bearing on fund performance. As expense ratios increase, fund returns decrease. Of course, there are examples of funds that have done well with high fee structures, but on average, high fees kill returns.

Once you have broken down the mass of available funds into a handful of potentials, you now apply a subjective screen. The subjective screen requires a little more digging, since the information is not easily screenable using the current online databases.

Subjective Analysis

- Screen for Management Continuity: Before you buy a fund, you want to make sure that the current manager is responsible for the strong three-year track record. If the current management is not responsible for the returns, the fund's past performance is no longer an indicator of returns to come, since each manager has a different style and stock- and bond-picking methodology.

- Screen for Expense Ratio: Remember, an important advantage of funds is economy of scale. Ideally, a fund's expense ratio should decrease as its assets increase. If it has not decreased, the fund's management is not conducting business in a manner that is beneficial to you. Move on.

- Screen for Year-by-Year Performance: Aggregate or annualized returns, such as the ones you screened for during your numerical analysis, can be misleading. Funds that experience one incredibly strong year of performance will almost always have strong three-year returns, since that one year will compensate for performance degradation over the other two years. For a fund to meet your standards, it must have consistent year-by-year performance.

- Screen Through an Online Community: Mutual fund communities, such as Sage Online, offer investors many free investment services, such as the chance to chat with fund management. Communities also have experts in different investment areas that can answer your personal questions and streamline the investment process for you.

Once you have internalized the Sage investment philosophy of diversification and asset allocation and the two-step fund selection process of numerical and subjective analysis, you are ready to assemble your portfolio. But because most investors do not have the money to create a full-blown portfolio off the bat—we sure didn't when we were starting out—there are different investment methods (see Chart 14.2) that you can use to assemble a portfolio. The method you choose most likely will be dictated by your available investment dollars.

Method	What it Is	Notes
Lump Sum	Creating an entire portfolio with one large investment.	If you have a large sum of money and can meet the minimum initial investments for all funds, you could create your portfolio instantly.
Partial Average	Making monthly dollar commitments to a group of funds.	Initial investments are typically $2,000 per fund, with a range from $0 to over $10,000. However, many funds will allow investors into the fund for a lesser amount if the investor agrees to make consistent fund purchases.
Cycle Average	Cycling investments into different funds at different times to cut down the number of transactions you make.	Many banks charge for automatic drafts, it can be costly to have five withdrawals deducted from a checking or savings account on a monthly basis.
Asset Build	You concentrate on one fund at a time, investing small amounts until the minimum investment is reached. Once the minimum is reached, you move on to another fund.	This is a good method for investors with limited means. The downside is that you will not have a full portfolio; rather, you will build a portfolio with one fund at a time.

Chart 14.2. Summary of regular investment plans.

Once you decide which method is most appropriate, you have to choose the way in which you are most comfortable buying funds.

- Dial the Digits: All fund families have toll-free numbers that you can call to have information sent to you. The drawback with this method is that it takes time, often a great deal of time, to get the information that you have requested.

- Surf the Web: Not surprisingly, an increasing number of fund families are offering their investment materials and applications over the Web. Simply log on to the fund family's Web site, download a mutual fund prospectus, and mail off your check. Bear in mind, there are still many funds that do not yet have the technology to offer investment material on their Web sites.

- Shop Till You Drop: Firms such as Charles Schwab, DLJdirect, E*TRADE, and many others have created one-stop clearinghouses where you can purchase among thousands of different funds and hold them in one consolidated account. However, these funds still have minimum initial investments, and adding additional money to a fund holding is sometimes restrictive.

- Go for Broke: If after reading this entire book you are still uncomfortable making your own investment decisions, or you have special circumstances that need to be addressed, you should consult a broker or a financial planner. You will get tailor-made, one-on-one financial assistance and expert advice.

If you choose to open an online brokerage or supermarket account, you should consult www.Gomez.com. Gomez's site is dedicated to making online transactions painless. The size makes it easy to find the online broker that will best suit your needs.

Once you have begun to assemble your portfolio, you should begin tracking your holdings online. America Online, Excite, Yahoo!, and scores of other sites allow you to track multiple portfolios for free. You will not have to wait for the following day to track the value of your portfolio or get breaking news via a newspaper. The online portfolio tracking tools enable you to keep tabs on your money from anywhere around the globe at any time of day—assuming you have access to the Internet.

The online portfolios easily let you monitor how your funds are faring relative to their peers and the major market indexes. Poor performance is the most obvious reason to sell a fund. While you can monitor a fund's performance easily by using an online portfolio, you will have to be vigilant in looking for telltale signs that you and your fund should part ways.

The following points typically lead to poor performance. Keep an eye out for them so that you can cut loose a soon-to-be laggard before it brings your online portfolio down.

- A Failure of Expenses to Decline as Assets Increase: If economy of scale does not take hold, a fund should be eliminated.

- A Rapid Rise in Assets: Assets typically take off after a bout of super-strong short-term performance. Once the offline publications take note of a fund and label it a "Must Buy Now!" you can be sure assets will increase rapidly. A rise in assets is not necessarily a bad thing in and of itself; it is how the fund reacts to the influx that matters. If a fund you hold experiences a rapid increase in money, be on the lookout for changes in management style and portfolio composition. If the fund starts holding cash or investing outside of its stated area, it should be considered a sell candidate.

- Selective Advertising: Funds are notoriously adept at painting the best of all possible pictures for shareholders and prospective investors. If a fund you hold is playing games in the way it advertises, chances are this is not the only place it is acting in a devious manner. It is best to do business with honest fund families.

- A Management Shakedown: Occasionally, though not often, you will come across a fund family where there is a proxy battle or a public struggle for control of the family. A situation such as this never ends in a way that is beneficial to fund investors. There are simply too many distractions within the family for management to successfully run the fund. Furthermore, it adds an element of uncertainty over the future state of the fund. You have far too many funds to choose from for you to be wasting time with one that is bogged down in troubles.

- A Change in Management: Once the fund manager leaves, the fund that you knew and bought no longer exists. No two investors are alike. Likewise, no two fund managers have exactly the same stock- or bond-picking prowess and investment style. When the manager leaves, consider doing the same.

Investment buy and sell decisions can be stressful and frustrating. Online communities, such as Sage Online, offer investors the ability to chat with fund managers, other investors, and industry sages via message boards and chat rooms. On the message boards, you will receive personal attention from investors who specialize in specific areas like large cap funds or tax planning. On Sage, all of your questions will be answered within forty-eight hours. In the chat rooms, you can get real-time answers to your questions, as well as opinions from like-minded investors who have walked in your newbie shoes.

The community also acts as a support group to get you through difficult market times. It will provide you with an endless supply of investment education and offer investment ideas from leading market minds. Best of all, it will keep you in tune with the pulse of the market, so that you know why the market is doing what it is doing and why your portfolio is acting the way it is acting.

The final investment step you must take is to maximize your tax sheltered/deferred retirement plans such as your 401(k), 403(b), Traditional IRA, or Roth IRA. When you maximize these plans you enhance your portfolio in a few different ways:

- Transactions inside of these plans are not subject to capital gains or income taxes. You can buy and sell as often as you like, or as often as your plan allows you to, without paying taxes.

- Traditional IRAs and 401(k) and 403(b) plans can lower your adjusted gross income (AGI), which may lessen the amount of income tax you pay.

- When you take money out of your Roth IRA upon retirement, you do not have to pay taxes on any gains.

- According to a study conducted by Strong Funds, many employers match employee 401(k) contributions. Essentially, companies are paying their employees to save for retirement.

Now that your mind is bursting with investment information, you are ready to turn dreams into reality. If you have not yet started investing, time's a'wasting! Get moving, and we will see you online. Oh yeah—if you have any comments, questions, or interjections, feel free to post a message on the Sage boards or visit us in the Sage chat room. We will be waiting!

Appendix A

Reading a Mutual Fund Prospectus

To fully understand a prospectus it is best to have an accountant, financial planner, and lawyer handy while you read it. Few things in life will be more abstract and dull as a prospectus. You will not find the meaning of investing located in the prospectus and you certainly will not uncover any revelations. Fortunately, most of the prospectus is so general that if you have seen one, you have seen them all.

RISK AND OBJECTIVE

The function of the prospectus first and foremost is to protect the fund family from any legal recourse. Consequently, the prospectus spends a great deal of time and paper talking about risk, and the guidelines which the fund must operate under. Risk is usually talked about in broad terms (the following is paraphrased from multiple fund prospectuses):

> "As with all equity funds, the share price of the fund will fluctuate in response to market conditions. The share price may fluctuate due to a broad market decline, a downturn in a specific industry. . . . The market may decline for many reasons such as political instability, a change in investor psychology . . . "

This discussion on risk usually continues for a page or so, but it all boils down to one very important statement:

- The fund's share price may decline, so when you sell your shares you may lose money.

The objective of the fund and the guidelines it must operate under is talked about in equally broad terms (the following is paraphrased from multiple fund prospectuses):

> "The fund must invest at least 65 percent of its assets in large cap companies with established earnings growth and solid dividends. . . . While most of the fund's assets will be invested in domestic equities, we reserve the right to invest in foreign securities, bonds, options and futures . . . "

For some unknown reason, the mutual fund industry has a strange fixation with 65 percent. Virtually all funds invest at least 65 percent of their assets in large cap stocks, small cap stocks, foreign stocks, and so on. If the fund strays outside of this 65 percent boundary, internal fund auditors force the fund to liquidate, so you can be certain that a fund will stick with its stated objective.

Prospectuses also contain an "Is this fund right for me" section, which borders on useless. What is important is that you understand the risks involved in the different types of funds, which we reviewed earlier in the book.

PERFORMANCE AND FEES

Each prospectus must highlight a fund's performance relative to its respective market index, and many families choose to include performance relative to its peers. Since prospectuses are updated only yearly, this information is usually dated.

The fee portion of the prospectus is the most important. Management fees, 12b-1 fees, loads, and other miscellaneous fees are itemized in a tabular format. In addition, each prospectus breaks down how expense ratios may translate into dollars paid by you over different periods. This helps you compare the cost of investing in different funds.

TAXES, DISTRIBUTIONS, BUYING AND SELLING SHARES

Each prospectus has a generic section that discuss how you can buy and sell shares—which methods are acceptable, what time trades must be placed by—and any dollar limits that exist in the fund. There is also a rather dry discussion on taxes (yes, you must pay them if the fund is held out of a tax-qualified account) and when distributions (capital gains and dividend income) are paid out.

MANAGEMENT, CORPORATE ORGANIZATION, AND STOCK SELECTION

This is the only section where the fund family will go out of its way to pitch the fund to you. Aside from information on which Ivy League school the manager graduated from or how long the fund family has been in existence, you will find some interesting fund-specific information on stock selection criteria, which will give you insight into how the fund is run.

FINANCIAL HIGHLIGHTS

Towards the back of the prospectus, there is a balance sheet of the fund's assets, performance, turnover, distributions, and expense ratio.

APPLICATION

An account application is located at the end of the prospectus. If the fund is to your liking, simply fill out and sign the application, enclose a check made out to the fund, fund family, or transfer agent (this will be noted in the application), and mail it off. You can also set up an automatic bank account transfer, if you desire. In a week or so, you will receive a confirmation. If you are completing the application online via a brokerage account, the information will be processed immediately and shares can be bought that day if the order is placed by a certain time.

Appendix B

Chatting Online

When you first log on to an online chat room, you may feel lost. People will be "shouting" at each other, asking multiple questions, and offering differing opinions. At first glance, it may appear to be quite chaotic. To get the most out of your online chatting experience, follow these simple rules:

BE DIRECT

Frequently the chat rooms you enter will be filled with hundreds of other investors. Within this large pool, there may be ten different conversations taking place simultaneously. To avoid confusion and to make sure you get all of your questions answered, or comments heard, always precede your entry with the person's name to whom it is directed.

For example, if your screen name is "Austin959" and you want to ask "SageCFP" a question, you would type something like this:

"SageCFP, do you know what that fund's largest holding is?"

And his answer would look like this:

"Austin959, yeah, its largest stock holding is Level 3 Communications."

While this may seem trivial, it makes the chat process run smoothly.

DO NOT BE SHY

In the beginning, more than likely, you will feel a little timid. But remember, you are essentially hidden by your screen name. So, folks can only get as close to you, or know as much about you, as you choose to let them. The chat room is a great opportunity for the shy among us to stand up and ask all the questions we want answered, without fear of embarrassment or intimidation.

KNOW THE LINGO

Shorthand jargon that borders on a foreign language flows from many participants in a chat room. Onliners—and we are as guilty as the next keyboard—tend to fall into a lull of laziness where standard grammatical rules no longer apply. Rarely will you see a sentence typed free of typos, let alone proper punctuation. But after a short time, you will come to easily understand the world of online chatting.

Although most onliners may not be familiar with the term, seasoned chatters are armed with an extensive mental dictionary of emoticons. Emoticons (emotional icons) are used to compensate for the inability in written communication to convey voice inflections, facial expressions, and bodily gestures, or just to shorten the amount that needs to be typed.

The following list of common, and not so common, emoticons should help you translate online speak into offline English.

Emoticon	Translation
:-)	Smiley face
:-(	Frowning face
<G>	Grinning
<J>	Joking
<L>	Laughing
<S>	Smiling
<Y>	Yawning
AAMOF	As a matter of fact
ADR	American Depository Receipts
BBFN	Bye, bye for now

Emoticon	Translation
BFN	Bye for now
BOL	Burst out laughing
BRB	Be right back
BTW	By the way
BYKT	But you knew that
CMIIW	Correct me if I'm wrong
CMRS	Back real soon
DCA	Dollar cost averaging
EOL	End of lecture
FAQ	Frequently asked question(s)
FITB	Fill in the blank
FWIW	For what it's worth
FYI	For your information
HTH	Hope this helps
IAC	In any case
IAE	In any event
IMCO	In my considered opinion
IMHO	In my humble opinion
IMNSHO	In my not so humble opinion
IMO	In my opinion
IOW	In other words
LOL	Lots of luck, or laughing out loud
M*	Morningstar
MF	Mutual funds
MHOTY	My hat's off to you
NRN	No reply necessary
OIC	Oh, I see
OTOH	On the other hand
ROF	Rolling on the floor
ROFL	Rolling on floor laughing
ROTFL	Rolling on the floor laughing
RSN	Real soon now
SITD	Still in the dark
SOL	Sage Online
SPDRs	Standards & Poor's Depository Receipts
TIA	Thanks in advance
TIC	Tongue in cheek
TTYL	Talk to you later
TYVM	Thank you very much
WYSIWYG	What you see is what you get

BE HONEST

When you are positive or negative on a stock or fund, always disclose if you have a position in this investment. Of course, there are no rules that require you to do this, but it is a courtesy gesture that will lend credibility to the stance you take and the statements you make.

BE SKEPTICAL

Just like the offline world, the online world has its fair share of scam artists and tipsters. Always research whatever information you glean from a chat before you take any investment action. In addition, never give out personal information, such as your address or phone number in a chat room. Though instances of investors being duped are rare, it is just good old common sense to keep your guard up and take any and all protective measures.

Approach online chatting much the way you would offline chatting. Ask direct questions, be polite, and take a stranger's advice with a grain of salt. Remember, as with anything else, you get what you pay for.

Index